Praise for *Falling...in Love with San Miguel:*
Retiring to Mexico on Social Security

"*....you're getting nothing but the honest truth, an unvarnished guided tour through the minds of a retired couple in a Guanajuato town who do batik and write and participate in a reading discussion group. A thousand New Yorker short story writers try to get at what these two tell us directly. The authors don't shy away from discussing the controversies.*"
—Kelly Arthur Garrett/The Herald Mexico/El Universal

"Falling... in Love with San Miguel: Retiring to Mexico on Social Security *is a simple testimony to the joys of retiring in San Miguel de Allende, an art and cultural center 165 miles northwest of Mexico City, named one of the top ten cities in the world to retire by "Money Magazine." Written by Carol Schmidt and Norma Hair, two women who came to escape the sweltering Phoenix summer and stayed when they became captivated by the joy of daily life,* Falling... in Love with San Miguel *is part memoir, part practical guide, as it details the first year of the authors' retirement life in San Miguel including their expenses on the costs of average Social Security, the problems they encountered and the adjustments they had to make, language issues in a Spanish-speaking country, the excitement of celebrating the fiestas of the Mexican calendar, and much more. Enthusiastically recommended for anyone considering vacationing in or moving to San Miguel, as well as for armchair travelers.*" — Midwest Book Review, Oregon, WI

"*As a newsletter that reports on Mexican destinations appropriate for budget travelers and would-be retirees, we had all but written San Miguel off years ago. These women have helped us reconsider and so should anyone else who thinks San Miguel is just for the wealthy.*"
— AIM Adventures in Mexico Newsletter

"*Full of light and love and insight and delight. Carol writes with an artist's eye for detail, and I can see Norma's vision filling in the canvas. We aren't always given the privilege of finding our own piece of heaven, let alone living in it—but these two women have done it, and this book is a testament to their achievement. It's a joy to read, and a joy to share their lives in this amazing place called San Miguel de Allende.*"
— Alma Alexander, Bellingham, WA, author of *The Secrets of Jin-Shei*

The Best How-To Book on
Moving to Mexico

The Best How-To Book on
Moving to Mexico

Carol Schmidt
Norma Hair
Rolly Brook

SalsaVerde Press
Laredo, Texas

Some material appeared previously in different forms in Carol Schmidt's and Norma Hair's website, *www.fallinginlovewithsanmiguel.com*, and in Rolly Brook's website, *www.rollybrook.com* and his columns in *www.mexconnect.com*. Refer to these websites for updates to information contained in this book and for supplemental information pertaining to all aspects of moving to Mexico and expat living.

ISBN 978-0-9787286-7-0

SalsaVerde Press
Laredo, TX
www.SalsaVerdePress.com

Printed in the United States of America

Contents

Part One: Your Deal-Breaker Questions: Costs, Health Care, Personal Safety

health care programs. Keeping Medicare Part B. Varying quality of care. The two government hospital systems and private hospitals. Applying for IMSS. Private insurance plans. Medical evacuation companies. Different attitudes toward prescription drugs, hospices, living wills, medical power of attorneys, prepaid funeral plans. Living in Mexico with disabilities and with HIV/AIDS. Allergies, amoebas and food poisoning. Dentistry. Vision care. Alternative and holistic medicine. Rolly's experience in a Hospital Angeles ER. Carol's report on having two knee replacement surgeries in Querétaro.

Part Two: Where in Mexico Is Best For You?

Part Three: Making the Move

Passport requirements today. What is a visa and which one is right for me? Everything about FMTs, FM3s, FM2s, *inmigrado* status and Mexican citizenship. What if I know from the start that I intend to become a dual citizen? Should I get the most common residency visa, the FM3, while in the US or Canada, or when I arrive in Mexico? What is this about having *apostilles* for some documents and how do I get them? What paperwork do I need for my pets to cross the border? Finding a pet-friendly hotel on the road.

To use a *menaje de casa* or not. Bringing all your household versus having a garage sale and buying new in Mexico. Dealing with a moving company. What you can't include in your packing for a moving company. Duty-free items. Prohibited items. Which lane to choose at the border if you're driving. Customs brokers if needed. Should you take a chance and drive through the Nothing to Declare lane? Shipping by sea.

Only one vehicle is allowed in your name. 10-year permits for RV motor homes. What you need for the Temporary Vehicle Importation Permit of a foreign-plated vehicle. Getting the permit online. Article 106, in English and Spanish, to carry with you in your car. Emissions testing. Crazy not to get liability insurance. Getting Mexican plates (nationalizing) your car. Should you buy a Mexican-plated car when you arrive instead? What should you consider for a car to use in Mexico? Do you really need a car? Different rules for Baja.

Part Four: Living in Mexico

Part One

Your Deal-Breaker Questions:
Costs, Health Care, Personal Safety

Chapter 1

Why We Say This Is the Best How-To Book on Moving to Mexico

In this chapter: The attraction of a new lifestyle and culture. The decisions you'll face. Our experience helping others make the move. A predictor for your happiness in Mexico. Why this is The Best How-To Book on Moving to Mexico—we tell you both the laws and what we and many expats have experienced with the laws.

US and Canadian citizens have always been drawn to their neighbor to the south, enjoying vacations to the beaches, historic colonial towns, world class cities, pyramids, and, more recently, ecotourism resorts.

And now the news is all about 76 million US baby boomers facing retirement who may want to rediscover themselves and explore new ways of living with their newfound freedom—and probably reduced income. More than a few will choose Mexico, especially as the global economic crisis may have slashed their retirement savings.

Some people say a million US and Canadian citizens have already moved to Mexico, while others look around and can't figure out where that many could be, since the few cities with the most expats have maybe 12,000 to 15,000 each. We can't give any exact figures on how many expats live in Mexico or in each state or city. All population figures in this book are inexact, often guesstimates or hearsay. Not even the US State Department, the Canadian government, or Mexican immigration knows for sure how many foreigners live in any one area of Mexico, either full-time or for a few months a year.

Not everybody registers with the nearest Consulate; not everybody has residency visas; not everybody wants to be found.

To confuse the issue, many US citizens (including many thousands of children) living in Mexico have one or more Mexican parents and were born in the US during temporary or long-term residency across the border. Whether they have dual citizenship or not, they identify and live primarily as Mexicans. And many foreigners live primarily as citizens of their home countries and don't consider themselves expatriates, even though they may have returned to the same area of Mexico each winter or summer for many years.

(The term *expatriate* is defined as someone who lives in another country, not to be confused with someone who is an *ex-patriot*, one who no longer loves his or her country. It is very possible to love two or more countries at the same time the way that you can love two or more children no matter how different they are.)

Usually the oldest immigrants who have relocated either direction have the hardest time learning the language of their new homes. They may hold on the tightest to old ways, while the second generation becomes fully bilingual and bicultural, and the third generation may not even know their grandparents' tongue or much about their heritage. This is mostly true all over the world and all through history. (Carol's great grandparents from Germany spoke very little English, her grandparents were bilingual, her father knew not a word, and she did equally badly in German classes in college as she does in Spanish classes in Mexico.)

Those *norteamericanos* who criticize Mexican immigrants who have difficulty learning Spanish should listen to some older gringos trying to learn Spanish in Mexico, some even giving up or never trying. Of course to fully understand your new home you will probably want to at least try to become as fluent as possible, but that is part of the *Living in Mexico* section.

It's Not Only Retirees

It's not simply retirees and those whose employment with an

international industry requires them to move to Mexico. More and more young people and families are choosing Mexico, freed by the internet to work anywhere, or willing and able to take the risks of starting a business in a new country with different regulations and requirements.

Like this book's authors, once many experience the magic of Mexico on a visit, they begin to ask themselves, why not move here? It took Carol three days in San Miguel de Allende before she asked Norma that question. If they'd had the money they might have bought a house that very day. Some people do. But of course it is better to do your research first, which is why you are reading this book.

Mexico is far more different from the US and Canada and even Europe than those countries are from each other. In **Part One** we'll first give you an overview of the geography and history that have shaped the culture. You'll see that changing countries is not like changing suburbs.

Then, moving to Mexico is a huge decision, involving hundreds of questions, not the least of which is whether you can afford it. Is it really cheaper? What will you do about health care? Are the stories true about banditos and kidnappers? We'll talk about these issues that are deal-breakers for many in **Part One**.

Perhaps then you will be ready to consider becoming an expatriate. Once you begin to seriously think about moving to Mexico you have some major decisions to make about where to live. Will you be happier living at the beach, colonial town, big city, or even a village where there are no other foreigners? What are some of the major expat settlements that might be a good place to start? Will you want to live in an area with many other English-speaking expats with all of the conveniences that go along with a large US and Canadian presence, or do you dream of finding a town where you may be the only foreigner? Do you need to be close to the border, or to an international airport, for frequent visits to family and friends from your previous home? Do you have medical requirements such as the need for a low altitude? **Part Two** will help you figure out areas of Mexico that may meet your needs.

Once you have an idea of where you want to live, how do you make the move? How do you apply for a visa and what kinds are there? What will it be like crossing the border? What should you bring and what should you sell at a garage sale? Can you bring your pets? How do you get your car across? Should you bring your car or buy a Mexican-plated vehicle? Will you really need a car? What is a customs broker, and a *menaje de casa*, and will you need either one to bring your "stuff" across? These are the questions we'll answer in **Part Three**.

Should you rent or buy, and how do you find an inexpensive apartment or deal with the realities of buying, building or remodeling a house in Mexico? What are the labor laws governing employees? What is involved in getting work papers if you decide to work in Mexico? Will you be able to learn Spanish, and how necessary is it to become fluent? If you have kids, what kind of education will they receive in Mexico and how do you pick the best school?

Will it be possible to get involved in some kind of charity or social group? What cultural differences will you encounter? Will you be able to make friends, with other foreigners and with Mexicans? Do you hope to become a part of Mexico and experience the culture and friendships fully, or are you like most first-generation older immigrants to a new country who largely keep within their foreign community?

And here's the question that bothers especially those busy folks who are nearing retirement and can't imagine letting go of their work: what will you do all day? In **Part Four** you'll find out. (The standard answer many retirees who are now living in Mexico give to that question is, "I don't know, but at the end of the day I'm only half done.")

This book will help you find the best answers for your situation, and raise many more questions for your consideration than you have even begun to think about.

One thing about Mexico—many decisions, many processes, are not easy or simple. That fact alone can rule out Mexico for you, or it can make you fall in love with a country where you never know what to expect. The constant changes will keep you flexible and young as well as sometimes drive you nuts.

The underlying philosophy of Mexican culture is different, more centered on self-respect, family, friends, church and country. Time is viewed as more of a circle, so don't worry about deadlines, things will come around again, priorities change—while those from European backgrounds tend to see time as a direct arrow, so you'd better hurry.

Some business consultants who help executives make the move to foreign countries say that Mexico is more like Japan than Europe in such aspects as the importance of saving face and the use of psychological masks. (Mexicans also love the freeing experience of wearing real masks for the frequent fiestas.) This book will help save you frustration and wasted effort as you learn to go with the flow, and not impose US and Canadian expectations on your new neighbors.

Of course these generalizations don't apply to all of Mexico, or to everyone in Mexico, or to every Mexican all the time. With workers and students frequently crossing the borders and sharing viewpoints and expectations, and the internet, mass media, movies and music all crossing those borders constantly, all three countries are learning from each other and influencing long-standing traditions.

A Caveat

This entire book requires a caveat: things change fast in Mexico. What is true today may not be true tomorrow, or true to the border agent in the next lane, or even to the same agent before and after lunch. Though the authors provide the latest information current as of mid 2009, individual states, towns, offices and officials can vary on their interpretations of the rules. The authors can provide no guarantees that what we publish today won't change tomorrow, and we can't accept responsibility for problems that occur due to these kinds of changes and different interpretations. Always check on current conditions and laws as best you can—and be prepared to hang loose!

The three authors have helped hundreds of American and Canadian citizens make the move to Mexico during their combined 22 years living here. They present the variables and share many cases of how you need to be flexible, and they'll help you keep your cool through the process.

Who Are the Authors?

Rolly developed much of this information for his popular authoritative website, *www.rollybrook.com,* the source many expats go to first when they have a question. Carol and Norma have been answering questions from potential expats on their website, *www.fallinginlovewithsanmiguel.com,* which has had nearly a quarter million hits in three years and has 800+ registered forum members.

Rolly is a forum moderator and frequent contributor on *Mexconnect.com,* and Carol has been both a Mexconnect columnist and forum moderator and participant on many other forums, on which she is often called the "voice of reason." Norma gathers Carol's writings from all over the internet and can bring 300,000 words down to a book-sized 100,000 and make that book happen. (Our book designer Jon Sievert makes that book look good and read easily.)

In September, 2006, Carol and Norma published *Falling...in Love with San Miguel: Retiring to Mexico on Social Security,* sharing their first years of joy and enthusiasm experiencing all of the fiestas packing the Mexican calendar year, the problems they ran into, the adjustments they learned to make, and their resulting new outlook on life. Readers wanted more of the how-to details, which is when the idea for this book was born.

All of this experience from three people who have been helping others make the move to Mexico comes together under one cover in this book, with many new insights and examples.

This book is not a public relations puff piece on how wonderful it is to live in Mexico—though all three of us agree it is and have no plans to ever move back NoB (North of the Border). We've found our individual spots in paradise and want to help others make the discovery, too.

Your Biggest Adjustment May Be the Noise

But we don't sugarcoat the problems. What is the biggest surprise and adjustment for many expats? The noise level of much of Mexico. Fireworks announce a birth, a death, a farewell to someone going on a trip, a birthday, an anniversary, a religious or civic celebration, or almost any other reason to wake you up at 4 or 6 am.

Church chimes ring out for many of the same reasons as the fireworks, plus they announce a religious service is coming in half an hour, in ten minutes, and you're late. (Sometimes they even tell the time. On the hour, the number of hours rings out; at 15 after the same number of chimes for the hour rings out followed by a pause and a single chime; at the half hour the same number of chimes for the hour rings out followed by a pause and two chimes; and at the 45-minute point the same number of chimes for the hour rings out followed by a pause and three chimes. On the next hour the number of chimes goes up to reflect that hour. Not to say each bell ringer keeps good time or remembers the pattern).

If the church near you has a 6 am Mass, expect a 5:30 bell ringing, a 5:45 bell ringing, and a last minute crescendo at 5:55. Or not.

Neighbors may have barking dogs, squawking parrots, roosters who don't know when it is dawn, or even bleating goats. Parties traditionally start late, possibly after your bedtime, and run even later, accompanied by loud music and talk. Garbage trucks, knife sharpeners and milk deliverers will have their own special whistles or horns to announce their coming. Nothing is going to change on your protests. If you want peace and quiet, you'll consider these factors when choosing whether Mexico is for you or where in Mexico or in your selected city you can find the least noise.

You can set your attitude to finding these sounds charming, or you can live with perpetually gritted teeth, hating it. Mexican living is not always peaceful and quiet. Mexicans have two sayings that summarize the kind of attitude that will help you enjoy Mexico: *ojalá*, if God wills it, if only it is to be, and *ni modo*, never mind, it's not a big deal. If these concepts seem perverse to you, Mexico may not be for you.

And then you may not be prepared for the generosity, the openness, the giving from many Mexicans, whose warm family life you may come to envy. You will probably hear more laughter, more good times, more joyful music, than you ever expected. You will experience a whole new and freeing way of viewing life. You will be surrounded by brilliant colors and rich flavors and open emotional expression that will expand your own way of living.

The biggest predictor of your happiness in Mexico is whether you want to recreate your familiar North of the Border lifestyle, expecting Mexico and Mexicans to be the same as your home town, or whether you are open to learning and appreciating a new way of life in a totally different culture. Do you think everything in the US or Canada is superior, or are you open to a culture that goes back thousands of years, already flourishing when European cities were still in the Dark Ages? Can you appreciate a slower way of life, or must everything run on time for you?

We deliberately chose the title, *The Best How-To Book on Moving to Mexico*, because this book is exactly that. You'll find the rules and the practical advice you expect, plus our personal experiences of what it is like to fall in love with Mexico and make the big move to a happier, healthier, less stress-filled, more fulfilling, fun and creative way of life. Welcome to your journey. And hang loose.

You Really Are Considering Moving to a Different Country

In this chapter: a brief geological and historical look at Mexico to give you some perspectives on the forces that have made Mexico what it is today. You are joining 10,000 years of history and evolution, not a static postcard Mexico.

exico is more than Cancún and Tijuana, resort and border. For starters, Mexico is the 13th largest country in the world and the fifth richest in biological diversity. It has 6,000 miles of coastline, 18 million acres of ecological preserves, and 44 national parks.

From deserts in the north, mountains down both sides of the country often capped with snow, tropical jungles along southern beaches, volcanic ranges taller than any in the US, Copper Canyon that includes four canyons bigger and deeper than the Grand Canyon, and a temperate central desert plateau more than a mile high, its landscapes are endlessly varied.

Expand your thinking if you think Mexico is nothing but beaches, borders, and desert towns. Not all of Mexico is pleasantly warm and sunny all year—southern beaches can be scorching and humid in the summer (and April and May are the hottest months in much of the country). Mountain towns can experience winter freezes in December and January. In much of the country the rainy season can turn a sunny morning and afternoon into a downpour for an hour or so later in the day, most days from June to October. You can drive from miles of desert to miles of jungle in a few hours.

Within this diversity is a climate for everyone. And many a Mexican city claims it has the most perfect weather on earth, with good reason. Most favorite expat destinations allow short sleeves and sandals most days of the year, with a sweater or jacket required most nights. You can't get much more perfect than that. Your occasional glimpse of "that white stuff" will usually be on mountain peaks on some horizons—you can even ski in parts of Mexico. Overall the good weather is one of the major draws for US and Canadian citizens looking at Mexico to live.

You Are Joining a 10,000-Year History

Adjust your thinking, too, when you consider the history that shaped today's Mexico long before the Spaniards arrived. Archaeologists trace Mexico's civilization to at least 8,000 BC when indigenous groups began to cultivate plants, an early sign of any civilization. The Olmecs, famous for their gigantic stone statues of heads with Negroid features, started to become a major force in southern Mexico around the time of Moses and the Hammurabi Code. By 1,500 BC the Olmecs were growing corn, beans, chiles and cotton, and making pottery, fine art, and hieroglyphic symbols for historical record-keeping. They developed a conduit drainage system at the city of San Lorenzo, and discovered the mathematical concept of zero and an early calendar, later perfected by the Mayans.

By 600 BC Mayan, Zapotec and Totonac civilizations were developing, around the time Buddha was born, and before the Great Wall of China was built. Mayan civilization in the Yucatan Peninsula peaked around 500 AD, long before Mohammed started Islam and Moors defeated the Visigoths in Spain (and ruled much of Spain for the next 700 years until 1492).

The city of Teotihuacan near Mexico City was settled centuries before the birth of Christ and at its peak around 500 AD was one of the largest cities on earth, certainly larger than Rome (though nowhere near the million or more people living in Xi'an in China around 500 AD).

Teotihuacan's Pyramid of the Sun and the pyramid at Cholula near Puebla are two of the three largest pyramids on earth. Depending on whether archaeologists measure by height, base size, or volume, Cholula's pyramid can even be considered larger than the Pyramid of Giza in Egypt.

(That mighty Cholula pyramid was recently discovered and partially excavated. It was hidden for centuries as a grassy hill with the Iglesia de Nuestra Señora de los Remedios built on top of the site in 1594. Out of respect for that church, not much digging has happened above ground, but more than five miles of maze-like tunnels underneath Cholula have been discovered so far.)

The warlike Toltecs began to subjugate their neighboring societies around 600 AD, during the Dark Ages in Europe, and their reign was still extending during the period in Europe of the first Crusade (1096), and the Magna Carta (1215).

By 1325 AD nomadic Chichimecas of the tribe of Mexica, later called the Aztecs, followed a prophecy of the god Huitzilopochtili to found what is now Mexico City, first called Tlateloco. (They stopped searching when they saw the sign they were looking for: an eagle on a cactus with a snake in its mouth. That symbol is on the Mexican flag today.) Its sister city was Tenochtitlan, which later absorbed it.

By 1428 the Aztecs were the dominant force in Mexico, and their commercial marketplace Tlatelolco was visited by 50,000 people on major market days. The Tlatelolco and Tenochtitlan population of the time has been estimated as between 100,000 and 350,000. For comparison, London's total population was about 60,000 at that time.

The Aztecs excelled in tapestries, gold, silver and copper work, jade and turquoise gems, and magnificent temples. They were hated because they developed to the extreme the practices of human sacrifice started in earlier cultures. They subjugated other tribes for taxation and human sacrifice. Warriors of that time didn't attempt to kill other warriors, the goal was to injure, not kill, so that they could be captured and later sacrificed. Cannibalism was also widely practiced.

And then in 1517 Córdoba landed in the Yucatan from Cuba and sent word back to the Spanish governor of Cuba. Cortés followed in 1519, marking the end of the pre-Conquistador glory of Mexico. The Spaniards didn't care about the artistry and craftsmanship of Atzec treasures, they wanted the base gold and silver and melted away the artwork, ignoring the jade which was valued even more highly than gold in Aztec culture. Their weapons were designed to kill. They played tribal hatreds against each other to conquer the Aztecs easily. A factor that played in his favor: the blond Cortés happened to arrive at a time in history when the blond Feathered Serpent god Quetzalcoatl was expected to return.

It was the beginning of the extermination of 90% of the native Mexican population from smallpox and other diseases (some local plagues) within a few years. Consider the changes that would happen in the US or Canada if 90% of their populations dropped dead within a few years. What would be the ramifications to the US or Canada if invading men from another country raped and impregnated every woman they could? What would this conquest do to the nation's and individual's psyches? Also consider how the Spanish built 12,000 Roman Catholic churches in their 300-year reign, often on top of existing pyramids and temples to wipe out all evidence of Aztec and Mayan culture.

But the Indians hid symbols of their gods in the foundations and walls of these churches and continued to worship their original gods, while appearing to be worshipping Christ. Mexico has been called the most Catholic country in the world, and also the least, with Aztec conchero dancers surrounding the exhibition of the Blessed Sacrament in many a religious procession.

The mass extermination of the population and the civilization is the catastrophe that reshaped Mexico. But the decimated yet indomitable indigenous civilizations survived, and today there is a triumphant rebirth and celebration of all of these assimilated complex cultures and histories. There is nothing simplistic about Mexico, on the surface or in its depths.

From Independence to the Present: 300 Years in 300 Words

Many books tell the history of Mexico under Spain up to the present. From the war for independence from Spain launched in 1810; to the 1846-48 war with the "Manifest Destiny"-bound United States that ended with Mexico losing half its territory (which became the US states of Texas, California, Nevada, Utah, and parts of New Mexico, Arizona, Colorado and Wyoming); to France sending Maximilian and Carlotta to rule Mexico from 1864 to 1867; to Santa Anna's eleven presidencies from 1833 to 1855; to the five terms of Mexico's first full-blooded Indian president, Benito Juárez, from 1858 to 1872; to the dictatorship period of Perfidio Dias from 1876 to 1911; to the Revolutionary War of 1910 and the vast migration of Mexicans to the US fleeing the violence in the tumultuous years that followed (and during which Pancho Villa and Zapata became legendary heroes); to the Cristeros Wars of rebellion in 1926-27 against the 1917 Constitution's rules severely limiting the power of the Catholic Church; to Mexico's fight alongside the Allies during World War II; to the 71-year one-party reign of the PRI; to the student uprising against repressive police practices that led to the government's massacre of hundreds in the Tlatelolco section of Mexico City before the 1968 Mexico City summer Olympics; to the election of President Vicente Fox from the PAN party in 2000 ending those 71 years of PRI rule; to today's fight to stop the drug cartels, Mexico has a remarkable history of (not always successful) struggles against oppression from within and without.

Throughout it all, Mexico's artists, writers and musicians have portrayed their country's sorrows and victories for the world to acknowledge and appreciate, though few outside of Mexico have done so. Too many stereotypes ignore this complex history and the tenacious Mexican spirit.

This early history is given to show that there is far more to Mexico than colonial cities and resort beaches. Moving to Mexico means joining this 10,000-year parade of change. Mexico has never stood still, it will not remain "quaint" and undeveloped, it is simultaneously a third-world country with nearly half its population living in poverty, a second-world country that is trying to grow its own economic base, and a first-world country the equal of any place on earth. Even if you find your own little paradise, it is not likely to stay the same as you found it and fell in love with it, the same way that gentrification, civic decay, internal migrations and other factors keep changing the interior of the US and Canada. Those who complain about the influx of expats changing parts of Mexico might keep in mind the vast changes in US culture from Mexican influences.

Is It Really 25-33% Cheaper to Live in Mexico?

In this chapter: It's true, you can live 25-33% cheaper in Mexico, depending on how you choose to live. What costs higher and lower? Property taxes of a few hundred dollars a year are your biggest potential savings, followed by cheaper and tastier local fruits and veggies. Very little heating, A/C is rare. The minimum monthly income the Mexican government says you need for an FM3 residential visa. INAPAM senior discount cards. Living like a middle class Mexican family versus importing an upper class US or Canadian lifestyle. Sample budget for a single person on $1,350 USD/month income. Housing costs in Lerdo, Durango, compared to those in the more expensive expat haven San Miguel de Allende.

People are generally as happy as they let themselves be, and people are generally as content with the way they live and the possessions they have as they allow themselves to be. The Mexican government determines the minimum monthly income from outside sources (like Social Security) you will need, in their estimation, to live comfortably without becoming a burden on Mexico's overstretched safety net. The law states that the minimum monthly income to obtain an FM3 *rentista* visa, the most common visa used by expats who live fulltime in Mexico and need to renew it once a year, is 250 times the Mexico City minimum daily wage.

In 2009 the Mexico City minimum daily wage was 54.8 pesos, and 250 times that is 13,700 pesos. Most years the Mexico City minimum daily wage goes up a few percent, so the FM3 requirement goes up a few pesos.

What that means in terms of the US dollar depends on the conversion rate for pesos to dollars.

At an exchange rate of 10 pesos to the dollar, about what it was for much of early 2008, and for several years before that, 13,700 pesos equals $1,370 US dollars.

In early 2009, the exchange rate lingered around 14.3 pesos to the dollar, which meant that the 13,700 pesos monthly minimum income required for an FM3 by federal law was equal to $958 USD.

Each Mexican consulate in the US and each immigration office Mexico can set its own rates, no matter that federal requirement. Many immigration offices stay close to the 10:1 ratio, though sometimes if they are challenged to convert 13,700 pesos to a more accurate peso:dollar rate they will relent. The immigration office in San Miguel de Allende, for example, kept $1,200 as the minimum monthly income requirement to qualify for an FM3 for 2009, but a director told a meeting called by the US Consular Agent in SMA that if you ask for the supervisor, you can get that rate reduced to the current peso:dollar rate. It all depends on which supervisor, where, and maybe whether it is before or after lunch.

The average US Social Security check in 2009 was $1,153. The Mexican government apparently still believes it is possible to live in Mexico on about that amount of income on an FM3 *rentista* visa, without any danger you will ever need Mexico's meager safety net. Many thousands of expats are doing exactly that. You can live well in Mexico on average US Social Security, despite protests by those who have never lived on as low as $1,153 in the US, either, and claim it is impossible. Of course the more income you have, the more comfortable you will be anywhere you live.

Throughout this book we are going to convert prices from pesos to US dollars at a rate of 13 to 1, which at least some financial experts believe is where the peso and dollar will stabilize in the near future. Of course we all learned recently that national and global economies can shift rapidly.

If at the time you read this book, the exchange rate is higher than 13 pesos to the dollar, you can know that prices quoted in the book are lower in terms of the US dollar. Conversely, if the exchange rate falls lower, prices will be higher in terms of the US dollar.

Here is a very brief history of the last 30 years of the peso to dollar exchange rate so that you can see the importance of exchange rates to your own budgeting. By the way, the Mexican peso was considered the world's most stable currency from 1572 to 1918 during which time the amount of pure silver in each peso was a set 24.44 grams. And then in the tumultuous aftermath of the 1910 revolution, less and less silver was used and other forces disrupted the Mexican economy. In the early 1980's the peso devalued sharply because the Mexican economy destabilized and inflation was 100% a year. There were two exchange rates from 1982 to 1991: the official controlled rate, used for government accounting, and the free rate. President Salinas in 1993 established the *nuevo peso*, the new peso, worth exactly one thousandth of the previous peso, and the exchange rate with the US was 3:1. Such influences as negative international press on the Chiapas political fighting, fears about NAFTA, and every presidential election caused shifts in the exchange rate. Expats in Mexico in the early 1990's sometimes could make 100% interest on their US dollar savings in Mexican investments. That time is long gone.

By the late '90s the Mexican government worked hard to stabilize the economy again and by the time of the July, 2000 presidential election the rate was stable at about 9.2 to 1. For the election month itself the peso went to 10:1 over fears what the first election of the first non-PRI president in 71 years might mean, but it was back at 9.3 to 1 shortly afterward. For the last ten years until October of 2008, it fluctuated between 8.46 to 11.69 to the dollar.

The conversion rate was around 9.6 to one when Carol and Norma arrived in Mexico in 2002, and it rose very slowly the next six years, during which time they became accustomed to thinking of the peso at 10:1, which made mental conversions of prices in pesos back to their US mindset of US dollars very easy. With the tumultuous global economic crisis of late 2008, the peso fell to as low as 15.42 to the US dollar on March 9, 2009, and today it is fighting back to stay around 13:1.

Consequences of the changing peso on a loan repayment

For those considering long-term investments it is important to know that changes in the peso exchange rate can have huge consequences depending on whether the contracts are set in US dollars or Mexican pesos. A $100,000 USD loan made when the rate was 10:1 required a payback in pesos of 1,000,000 pesos. That same loan, if it were to be repaid when the peso is at 13:1, requires a payback in pesos of 1,300,000 pesos. Those 300,000 pesos are equal to $23,076 more dollars.

Despite well-publicized, sensationalized charges that Mexico is in danger of becoming a "failed state," few knowledgeable experts believe that is possible. Mexican government runs smoothly, the cities function, crime is low in most of the country outside of the drug cartel battlegrounds. Improved relationships between the United States and Mexico and a growing realization that the US is at least partially responsible for the drug wars and must step in to help President Calderón tackle his country's biggest problem make Mexico's future even brighter and more secure.

The peso is likely to stay very near its present exchange rates, but even small fluctuations can have some effects on your budget. Carol and Norma were originally asked by their landlord to pay their rent in pesos when the exchange rate was below 10:1. Now they pay with a US check in US dollars since the exchange rate has gone up. Mexican landlords and business people are well aware of the changes in the exchange rate.

The official way to write a $111 US dollar amount is $111 USD. The official way to write a Mexican peso amount is $111 MXN. (You used to be able to tell whether the dollar sign applied to pesos or dollars because one had two bars down the S, the other had one, but today most keyboards have only the dollar sign with the single bar on the $.) Solely for the sake of easier understanding by those unfamiliar with the two currencies, we are writing the Mexican peso amount as 111 pesos and dropping the dollar sign and the MXN. And we are not giving the amounts in Canadian dollars, since Canadians are used to quickly converting a US dollar figure into Canadian dollars already, and to add yet another variable conversion rate into the mix would really be confusing. (We also use "he" rather than "he or she" in sections where it will be a male you will be encountering in that position in Mexico. We wouldn't say "he or she" about Catholic popes, either. Employment ads here can still specify male or female, ages 18-35, and attractive.)

Each immigration office can set its own requirements and may require a slightly different minimum monthly income. Generally the offices stick with one figure for the entire year rather than trying to adjust the requirements for an FM3 on a daily or hourly basis as the conversion rate may change.

Some might feel strapped on $100,000 USD a year

You can live well in Mexico on that FM3 minimum monthly requirement. Or, you can live on $100,000 USD a year in Mexico and feel strapped financially. You can feel trapped in Mexico because your million-dollar home would cost five million in the US and you don't want to give up having low-salaried full-time Mexican housekeepers, cooks and gardeners. It is a matter of your own personal expectations.

Carol and Norma wrote about their first four years living in Mexico on mid-range Social Security in *Falling...in Love in San Miguel: Retiring to Mexico on Social Security*. They continually were challenged—"It's impossible to do what you say you're doing," they were told repeatedly.

"But we're doing it," they responded.

"Yeah, but it's impossible..."

It isn't impossible. Some expats live happily in various parts of Mexico on even less than the FM3 requirement, though that means they must run to the border every six months to get a new FMT tourist visa instead of renewing a residential FM3 visa near where they live in Mexico once a year. (After five years on a slightly different visa, an FM2, you can apply for *inmigrado* status or Mexican citizenship and never have to reapply for anything again. But at this stage you're probably not concerned about that.)

A few brag they're living on $600 USD a month, though that does seem unrealistic to the authors. At that income level they're probably relying on house sitting or other underground income, or they own a small, paid-for house. If they rent, their apartment may have dirt floors and no utilities, and their menus are heavy on tortillas, rice and beans. Just like half the Mexican population.

Once housing is set, your costs are pretty much up to you

Your primary expense is housing, and if you put some effort into finding an inexpensive apartment or house that you can be happy with, the rest of your expenditures are pretty much up to you.

It is still very possible to buy a nice home for well under $200,000 or to find a two-bedroom rental with all the expected conveniences for under $500 a month, if not right in the center of the most popular areas. Outside of the popular cities you may even find a fixer-upper for $50,000, and remodeling labor is inexpensive compared to the States and Canada. Or you can find plenty of million-dollar homes and $5,000 a week rentals in popular areas as well.

Rolly's Story

Rolly reports on housing costs in Lerdo, Durango, where he is the only gringo in the city, compared to Carol's and Norma's figures from the more expensive expat haven of San Miguel de Allende.

Apartments are not common in this area. I have a friend who rents a fairly new, quite nice, unfurnished, air-conditioned three-bedroom with a wood burning fireplace for $100 USD per month plus utilities. Across the river in Torreón, there are a few high-rise buildings with more expensive apartments. I am not aware of any studio apartments; most are two or three bedrooms—Mexicans tend to have large families.

Rental houses are far more common than apartments. In a nice neighborhood, an unfurnished two- or three-bedroom house can be found in the range of $100 to $500 USD a month, with most being about $200/$250. High-end houses may rent for as much as $1,000 USD.

Existing houses are available for purchase for around $40,000 USD and up, depending on size, age, quality and location.

Custom built houses start at about $40,000 USD plus the cost of the land. For one of my building projects, the land cost $20,000 USD. There are properties for less than $1,000 USD on the edge of town with no paved streets or utility connections.

A very nice house in a good part of town can be built for $100,000 USD or less including the land. It is not uncommon to see old houses on desirable land purchased and torn down to be replaced by new construction.

There are plenty of fixer uppers. One of my projects was to remodel an old, run down place into a modern home. The cost of converting the two-bedroom, single-story house into one with five bedrooms, two stories and air conditioning was about $38,000 USD. This was an owner upgrade, but if the house had been purchased as a fixer upper, it probably would have sold for around $35,000 USD. So for less than $75,000, one could have had a nice modern home in a nice part of town.

My own house is the only single bedroom house I have seen here. I designed it as a simple bachelor's retirement cottage. The building cost was about $7,500 in 2000. It could not be duplicated for that price today. I had no land cost because my friend allowed me to build on a corner of his large lot. This low cost was also partly the result of much donated labor by me and my friends. So it's clear that housing costs vary considerably between an area like San Miguel de Allende and one like Durango.

Your choices

Do you have to eat out in the best restaurants every day? Must you have air conditioning even though housing walls are often of thick concrete and stay cool most of the year? (In the hotter south,

A/C is more of a necessity for most expats, but it is not common in much of the country.) Must you have a pool? Do you need imported ingredients to be able to cook, and the best wines and liquors to entertain? Do you require a big car and the latest clothes and the most advanced electronics and and and?

The more closely you live like middle-class Mexicans (average yearly income around $8,000 USD a year) rather than requiring an imported luxury lifestyle, the more likely you will be able to live happily on less.

The oft-repeated statement is that you can live a quarter to a third cheaper in Mexico than in the US, and this tends to be true.

It is also true that you can live more cheaply in some Midwest and southern US towns than in some areas of Mexico and have the US safety net besides.

Of course a Mexican will usually be part of an extended family that can provide backup in a financial crisis, and often owns a house that has been handed down for generations, and is part of the underground and bartering economy, and has insider information from family members on the best deals and ways to survive on little money. An expat usually won't have those kinds of financial and emotional resources.

For those living close to the financial edge, taking into consideration the US and Canadian safety nets that don't reach all the way to Mexico, especially for medical expenses, it may make more sense to stay home.

This chapter and the ones on health care and on finding a place to live may help you decide whether Mexico makes more sense for you financially—not taking into account any of the myriad other factors that should influence your decision to choose Mexico.

Don't move for the sole reason to save money

If you move to Mexico specifically to save money and have no intentions of embracing the culture and the people, you may always feel like a fish out of water, even with money left in your wallet at the end of the month.

Once your housing is set, the rest of your expenses are pretty much up to you. And even if you choose to buy a house and find initial purchasing costs in many parts of Mexico are higher than you expected, your savings each year on property taxes alone will be huge.

More on the particulars of purchasing and maintaining a home, or building or remodeling one, or finding an inexpensive rental, will follow in later chapters. The biggest financial surprise to those from north of the border is that Mexico is largely a cash society, and most homes are bought for cash, once another house has been sold for cash. Mortgages are becoming available to expats in Mexico but usually at higher interest rates than in the US and Canada. Many NoB homeowners who desire to move to Mexico are putting their plans on hold until their US or Canadian home sells, and with the crash of the housing market, they have no idea how long they may have to wait. More on these questions will be in Part Four.

Keep in mind that for those who do buy a home in Mexico, your property taxes on your home in Mexico will probably be a few hundred dollars a year, compared to many thousands in the US or Canada. A $4,800 USD savings in property taxes a year equals $400 USD a month freed to spend on other needs, a de facto $400 USD a month income increase.

If you pay taxes in the US your IRS obligation to file continues no matter where you live. Here is the US IRS Publication 54 on tax information for Americans living abroad: *www.irs.gov/pub/irs-pdf/p54.pdf* (especially page 32).

Switching to more fresh fruits and veggies

Your next biggest area of potential savings is groceries. Food, particularly if you eat more of the inexpensive and tasty fresh fruits and vegetables that are abundant in Mexico, will be cheaper overall, not to mention healthier.

Norma never bought a pineapple in her life in the States, and now she buys a large ripe beauty every week for about $2 USD, compared to hard green ones in the US currently selling for at least $5. A heaping basketful of oranges, limes, grapefruit, tomatoes, onions, chiles, green peppers, cucumbers, lettuces, spinach, pineapple, melons, green beans, grapes and other produce for the week usually runs under $15 USD.

Eating out at the most inexpensive Mexican restaurants can be cheaper than even fast food chains in the US. Many restaurants serve *"comida corrida,"* similar in concept if not price to a *"prix fixe"* meal in Europe—a low price for a complete meal that includes a soup and/or salad, main course, and sometimes a simple dessert. It is not unusual to pay $3-5 USD for a *comida corrida* in Mexico. A taco or tamale at a street stand may cost 40 cents USD. A very nice family restaurant meal for two may be half what it would be at a comparable US chain.

Or, expats can find in most cities extremely expensive gourmet restaurants. Back home, do you eat out every day, and, if so, do you choose McDonald's or La Gourmet? If you cook at home are your skills limited to broiling a fancy steak or using the microwave, or do you have a dozen favorite recipes using chicken, beans, rice or tortillas, supplemented by plenty of fresh veggies, salads and fruits? Are you willing to learn to cook using tasty and fresh Mexican ingredients? Or are you always going to be searching for Major Grey's Chutney and jumbo prawns?

Clothing costs will probably be less because of the more temperate climate. You may need a few jackets and sweaters for winter, but you won't need four different wardrobes for four distinct seasons. Winter clothes are usually far more expensive than summer outfits. Sometimes you can find even top-line but off-season brands sent to Mexico and priced at deep discounts in the open-air markets. Sears and other department stores sell similar kinds of clothes as you will find at their northern outlets. Soon you may find yourself preferring Mexican styles made locally.

Or you can always pick up your favorite styles on occasional shopping trips up north or on the internet. Carol and Norma like to plan an occasional bus trip to the Texas border town of McAllen, which has all the US stores and outlet malls, in the fall when the summer clothes are on sale there but they're still appropriate for warmer Mexican climes.

Big and tall sizes are less available in Mexico

Larger sizes, though, are not as easily available in Mexico, and you will probably need to buy from catalogues or go north for women's shoes larger than size 8 1/2, for example, unless you can adjust to men's tennis shoes and sandals. A tall or large man or woman may still need to shop at US and Canadian big and tall shops and catalogs.

Rolly is a large man. The availability of big men's sizes is very limited and very expensive, so he orders online. His orders are sent to his sister's address in Texas where he picks them up on his annual visits. His sister also has used the post office to send clothing to him. Mexican law prohibits the shipment of used clothing, so it is important to mail new purchases in their original packaging and with an invoice or receipt so there will be no question that the items are new.

If you buy from the open-air markets your clothing expenses will be almost nothing. But if you still want brand names your clothing budget may be even higher than it was in the States or Canada.

Electricity is more expensive

One expense that can be more than double in Mexico is electricity. Unlike in the US, the more you use, the higher your rate. It is often unreliable, requiring the purchase of a UPS (Uninterrupted Power Supply) for each electronics station, a special voltage regulator designed for refrigerators, more frequent computer backups, and replacement of electronics damaged in brownouts and blackouts. You probably will have to pay to have an electrician ground your electrical system so that these voltage regulators and UPS systems really protect you. Surge protectors protect against spikes, not the far more frequent and troublesome drops and brownouts.

In much of the country, air conditioning is rarely used. The higher altitudes and lower temperatures in summer supplemented by the use of thick concrete construction keep inside temps down. In general Mexico's milder climate means lower costs overall, including for clothes. But those who live in the most southern areas may think of air conditioning as a necessity, as much as Carol and Norma did in Phoenix, and have to budget accordingly.

Few Mexican homes have central heating, though many homes will have at least one wood or gas fireplace. (Because of the cost of electricity, electrical heating is impractical, plus it will often cause more brownouts.) Wood is scarce in many areas of Mexico where the trees have been felled for centuries for agriculture and cooking, and in northern desert areas such as where Rolly lives, so it may not be a bargain to use wood in home furnaces. Convert those fireplaces to propane log inserts.

Propane gas is far more widely available than natural gas, and it must be delivered to your home every few weeks or months. Carol and Norma estimate that their propane costs for both cooking, hot water, and a small portable furnace for occasional winter use average $50 a month on a year-round basis (more in winter for heating, less in summer).

In comparison, in rural Michigan their winter heating costs were more than $400 USD a month, and in Phoenix where it can be over 100 degrees Fahrenheit half the year, their summer air conditioning expenses were equally outrageous.

More and more expats are installing solar panels and some even manage to live pretty much off the grid. The initial expense will be high, however, and there can be hassles dealing with local electricity companies in making the transition.

With all of the conversions from liters to gallons and pesos to dollars, in mid-2008 when the peso was equal to about 10 to one US dollar, gasoline was about $2.70 USD a gallon in Mexico, compared to $4-5 USD in many parts of the US and Canada.

By year's end, at 14 pesos to the dollar, Mexican gasoline was around $2.25 USD a gallon, while prices had plummeted back down to below $2 USD a gallon in much of the US. Oil prices continue to fluctuate wildly throughout the world depending on political as well as economic factors.

Pemex gasoline subsidies mean fewer rapid fluctuations

But since Mexico controls its nationalized Pemex gas stations, and has subsidized gas prices for the sake of its poorer citizens, gas prices may fluctuate less rapidly in Mexico. There is political pressure to end gas subsidies but the Mexican government is unlikely to let gasoline prices soar the way they have in gas wars in the US.

The rate of inflation is another factor that is out of the control of the individual buyer. In Mexico as in the US, the annual rate of inflation for 2008 was around 6%. In mid 2009 the worry was deflation. Friends living in California report that their home that may have been worth a half million dollars a few years ago is now worth maybe $200,000. How long will this last? No one knows.

Because most homes in Mexico are paid for in total with cash, there is less pressure on the part of many homeowners to sell rapidly to pay a mortgage, so Mexican housing prices can remain high. All these factors are in flux. The best anyone can do is to make an educated guess as to how the future economy will impact you.

Car repairs are much cheaper for labor, but if you have an unusual car model where parts must be sought and shipped from across the border, those costs can add up, not to mention the inconvenience of not having the use of your car while waiting for parts. Mexican mechanics often say: buy Chevy or Ford. (Honda, Toyota, Volkswagen, Nissan, Suzuki and other foreign manufacturers also are readily available in Mexico.)

Water is cheaper delivered to your tap, but in many places you'll have to either pay for bottled water delivery for drinking —Carol and Norma spend about $16 USD a month for eight 20 liter (about five gallon) plastic jugs called *garrafons* delivered to their apartment— or you'll need to pay for an in-house water purification system.

Where Rolly lives, the water is safe to drink right out of the tap. This is true in some cities, but certainly not much of Mexico. The government is working to improve both the quality of the water and its consistent availability. In some areas you may experience water cutoffs on certain hours or days. Having a large cistern and holding tank can ameliorate these shortages.

Much of Mexico is high desert, facing the same problems as much of the world as water shortages are expected to become more serious in coming years. And while research is ongoing into ways to solve this global fresh water shortage, there are no guarantees that these cutoffs won't become more frequent and water rationing may be necessary. (Carol and Norma remember the stiff fines threatened on those who did not reduce their water usage considerably in Los Angeles in the late '70s.)

Phones and Internet

Basic telephone service, under 100 calls a month on a landline, is about $18 USD, cheaper than most US cities, but the US phone companies supply far more bells and whistles for the price, and competition keeps their prices down.

Mexican phones are under a monopoly, Telmex, owned by Carlos Slim Helú, one of the richest men in the world. Many expats have turned to VOIP and other internet-based phone services for their long distance calls. Because of the high cost of land lines many Mexicans purchase inexpensive cell phones and rely on replaceable phone cards instead.

Internet service will be 100-400% higher than in the US, and probably somewhat slower, though high speed internet is now available almost everywhere. Many cities have public free wi-fi areas. Internet cafes are far more abundant in Mexico and the cost per hour may be $1-1.50. For comparison, Carol and Norma paid $30 an hour several years ago in Provincetown, MA to use the internet at a mail service, and $11 in LA.

Carol and Norma estimate that all their utilities, a housekeeper three days a week for three hours a day, high speed internet, and satellite TV each month cost about $350 USD above their rent. Add that figure on top of your rental, and consider your personal choices for food, entertainment, transportation and usual medical expenses. Use this amount as a rough guideline.

Another genuinely expensive category in Mexico is electronics. The cost of electronics and computer supplies purchased in Mexico may be double that in the US and Canada, though some individual items may be similar in price. Many expats make their electronics purchases NoB, or have visiting friends bring down items like printer cartridges.

If you purchase over the internet and have a product mailed to you, duty will likely be charged at the border, adding another 17% or so to the cost of shipping and handling. That could bring the overall cost of something shipped from the US or Canada in line with the costs charged in Mexico. And you'll be able to utilize a warranty on a product purchased locally.

For each major purchase you'll probably be going through a cost analysis rather than simply driving down to your favorite store in the US or Canada for a quick buy. But with the peso:dollar conversion rate fluctuating, it is important to take into consideration the exchange rate at the time of any purchase. Carol and Norma had long wanted a stacking washer/dryer that cost more than $1,000 USD at Costco. They spotted a floor model on sale when the peso was at 14:3 and saved hundreds of dollars on the same model.

Household appliances and furniture may cost more, in the quality and styles expats may prefer (expect most Mexican-made living room sets to feel hard), although there are certainly inexpensive Mexican brands and styles. Comparable top of the line imported big name appliances cost more in Mexico. You may come to appreciate Mexican brands you never heard of before. And there's always Costco, and they deliver.

The US and Canadian "big box" discount stores like Costco, Wal-Mart and Sam's Club are in every large Mexican city, carrying most of the same products with similar prices, though some will be specific to Mexico and a few of your "necessities" won't be on the shelves. Carol and Norma are always on the hunt for corned beef and pastrami. One Costco will carry the Tillamook extra-sharp cheddar they have become addicted to, another won't, same as the US. If you choose a city with a sizeable expat population, you will probably also find gourmet import shops to satisfy US and Canadian desires.

Expats learn substitutes for most items they can't find in Mexico, or buy them north of the border on occasional shopping excursions, and are prepared to pay the approximate 17% duty, or rely on friends and relatives to be "mules" to bring them the longed-for goodies.

English language books and magazines will be more expensive in Mexico, as will most imported goods. Leather goods usually will be cheaper. (Like in the US and Canada, Asian markets are affecting the economy. Even in Leon, one of the leather centers of the world, Chinese imported shoes are undercutting Mexican producers.)

Services and employees will be cheaper

Almost all services will be considerably cheaper in Mexico— few people in the US will work for $3-5 an hour as a domestic or gardener, and starting salary for a physician in a Mexican general hospital may be $20,000 USD a year. A doctor's visit can be as low as a few dollars (more likely $15-25), and top specialists usually charge $30-60 for an hour-long attentive consultation. A private hospital bed may be $75-150 USD a night compared to more than a thousand dollars in the US. A colonoscopy or MRI might cost $400 USD in Mexico compared to $4,000 in the US.

(Since Medicare usually pays 80% of medical charges, a procedure might cost you less in Mexico paying for the entire cost out of your pocket than it would in the US on Medicare, not to mention the cost of traveling NoB and associated living expenses. Each elective medical cost needs to be evaluated using many factors.)

You may be able to get a live-in aide for an elderly parent for perhaps $150-200 USD a week, compared to thousands of dollars a month for assisted living residences in the US and Canada. A new assisted living complex near Carol and Norma charges $1,400 base monthly rate, with additional assisted living services added as needed bringing the total to as much as $2,400 USD a month, while a similar facility near Detroit was $4,900 a month for the same services. A very basic home for frail elderly in San Miguel charges $700 USD a month, and the few expat residents who pay that full amount subsidize the Mexican citizens who can't.

Most prescription drugs will be cheaper in Mexico—many are over the counter—but a few, especially the newer, highly advertised medicines, can be even more expensive in Mexico. If you qualify for US Medicare, you need to evaluate whether Part D, the prescription drug benefit, will work for you in Mexico, since your prescriptions will have to be purchased in the US and either mailed to you (sometimes this can be problematic) or you will have to go to the border frequently.

It has always been the law, if not always enforced, that you need permission from the Mexican Ministry of Health to have your prescriptions shipped by FedEx, UPS, DHL or the post office into Mexico. The form to file is SSA-03-025-B, "Solicitud de Permiso Sanitario de Importación o Exportación de Insumos para la Salud y para el Programa Cerificado de Exportación" ("Request for Medical Approval to Import or Export Healthcare Consumables and for the Export Certification Program").

There is no way of knowing what lies ahead for the health care system in the United States, with growing political pressure for a national one-payer system similar to Canada's—and what the final outcome might mean for those attempting to figure out a budget for their health care long-range in Mexico.

Fewer lawsuits in Mexico

Car and medical insurance can be cheaper in Mexico because there is less likelihood of punitive lawsuits. Mexicans don't sue as often, and there are fewer options for pursuing lawsuits. (The chapter on health care will have far more prices and details on medical costs.)

You can take advantage of the many free fiestas and parades in most cities to cut your entertainment costs way down, and you may find that you enjoy no-cost afternoons people-watching in the town square, alongside Mexican families utilizing these public spaces as their living rooms since their homes are usually small. Even the most expensive concerts and plays will usually be cheaper than similar top-notch entertainment NoB, though you might still pay $100 a ticket for internationally renowned entertainment in a Mexico City venue.

Luxury buses throughout Mexico make travel between beaches and tourist areas cheaper than in the US and Canada. (If you're over 60 and have a residency visa, you can get a Mexican senior citizen discount INAPAM card and qualify for 50% savings on bus travel and many other items.) You can spend $500 USD a night for a fine resort anywhere on the continent, but you can find very nice $60 a night and under hotels near Mexico's attractions. In some nice towns your hotel may be under $30 USD a night. Hostels are located in most cities for $8-12 USD a night.

A haircut in a Mexican neighborhood barber or beauty shop may be $2 USD while the same cut in an expat-oriented boutique may be $40 or more. If you want, you'll probably be able to afford an occasional massage when you couldn't before. Movies at a Mexican multiplex are much cheaper—Carol and Norma pay 35 pesos, around $2.70 USD at 13:1, on Wednesdays at their local eight-screen theater, or 40 pesos other nights with their INAPAM senior discount cards. The most expensive evening movie price is 45 pesos, compared to more than $10 US at many US cities.

A sample budget for someone on $1,350 USD a month

Let's get down to the nitty gritty: how does a single expat live on, let's say, $1,350 USD a month in Mexico, a little over average Social Security?

First consider how well do you make it in the US on $1,350 a month? Where would you live, what would you eat, how would you entertain yourself, what would you miss? You'd probably live in a small town or a poor area of a city in a small apartment and have an old car, if any, and you wouldn't be eating out much. Keep that image in mind as a comparison.

In Mexico you can do better than that, but you'll still be aware that you can't have all you'd like—depending on your expectations and how you were raised, whether you are used to making do, or whether you always had "enough" money and unexpectedly now you don't. Making do with less can be more a matter of mental attitude than wallet thickness.

In Mexico you'll probably want a city where there is enough free entertainment going on that you won't be bored silly and feel deprived. You will be able to find an apartment for $500 a month or under, but it may be smaller than you'd prefer and it won't be right in Centro. You should try to learn some Spanish before the move so that you can live in a Mexican neighborhood and take advantage of Mexican services rather than paying top dollar for everything geared to foreigners.

You will have to fix up the apartment to make it bright and cheerful, with a few niceties that make you feel good and at home. It will take some effort to find a great low-rent apartment that meets your needs; there aren't as many of them out there. Oh, there are many very inexpensive rentals that lower-income Mexicans think are perfectly adequate, but you might not. Expats pretty much insist on indoor plumbing and floors.

You will look for one near a bus line, and you will shop as much as possible at local mercados with occasional trips to a big box store like Costco or Wal-Mart. These could be your monthly expenses.

$500	Rent, including electricity, tap water, and garbage pickup
$40	Propane gas for hot water and cooking
$50	Cable TV and high-speed internet
$20	Local telephone
$25	Vonage or other internet long-distance phone service
$25	IMSS Mexican health insurance
$20	Mail service with U.S. address
$40	Housekeeper for three hours a week
$20	Four loads of laundry by a laundry service
$10	Five 5-gallon bottles of purified water delivered
$50	Local transportation (buses and taxis)
$10	Round-trip bus fare to big-box store

$260	Food
$40	Medical-intermittent expenses
$20	Cleaning supplies, household, personal items
$20	Four cheap restaurant meals
$12	Two visits to the movies with popcorn on discount days

These common expenses total $1,162 a month with $188 a month left for emergencies, charitable donations, and occasional purchases of clothes at the local *mercados* or the big box stores. You'll be learning Spanish via free sites on the internet, Spanish language publications and movies, used textbooks, and conversations with Mexicans unless you can find inexpensive classes that fit into your few remaining dollars.

Your family in the US or Canada will either be coming down to visit you or paying for your visits north if they won't come down. There isn't much room for vet bills and dog grooming, or expensive haircuts for yourself. You'd better hope that you don't need an expensive prescription of a heavily advertised US drug that doesn't have a generic.

If there are two of you on Social Security or similar fixed incomes, your life is much easier. Two can't live as cheaply as one, but it helps. Taking in a roommate, renting a small studio for as low as $300 a month, and doing your own housecleaning are other ways to cut corners. You're cutting it tight, but it can be done. And you're living in an exciting new culture with all sorts of challenges to keep you stimulated and alive. Remember, $1,350 USD a month is far more than most Mexican families live on who maintain a middle-class lifestyle.

In summary, it is cheaper to live in Mexico than in the US or Canada for a comparable lifestyle—even a quarter to a third cheaper But it is also possible to spend even more in Mexico than at home if you choose an imported luxury lifestyle. What makes YOU feel poor and deprived is the variable. Depending on your attitude and temperament, you can live on what would be poverty income in the US or Canada and feel very rich indeed in Mexico.

Chapter 4

Health Care—Probably Your Biggest Worry

Cost of doctors. ERs and hospital care. Differences in health care in Mexico. Medical tourism. Medicare and Canadian health care programs. Keeping Medicare Part B. Varying quality of care. The two government hospital systems and private hospitals. Applying for IMSS. Private insurance plans. Medical evacuation companies. Different attitudes toward prescription drugs, hospices, living wills, medical power of attorneys, prepaid funeral plans. Living in Mexico with disabilities and with HIV/AIDS. Allergies, amoebas and food poisoning. Dentistry. Visioncare. Alternative and holistic medicine. Rolly's experience in a Hospital Angeles ER. Carol's detailed report on having two knee replacement surgeries in Querétaro.

Probably the number one question people ask who are considering moving to Mexico is, "What about health care?"

The stereotype refuses to fade that everyone who goes anyplace in Mexico is kidnapped by banditos, and so do the medical misconceptions.

The truth is that health care in Mexico varies all over the place same as in the US, but you can get excellent medical treatment at lower cost and often with more caring attention paid to you. Mexico has some world-class hospitals with doctors equal to the best in the US and Canada. Or you can get terrible care at a hospital, same as north of the border.

Some doctors are located next to pharmacies and will sign off on almost any prescription you want for $2 USD, after a cursory "exam." But you'll find excellent doctors who make house calls for as low as $15 USD. (If a doctor makes a house call to a tourist with the flu in a luxury hotel, the price might be $85 USD.) You'll be able to call a specialist for an appointment and get in probably that afternoon or the next day for $40-60. The specialist will spend an entire attentive hour with you. You'll be able to buy most prescriptions over the counter at many times less the cost.

If you have to go to an emergency room, you may be treated in one of the government's general hospitals for a basic fee of around $6 USD. A private room in a private hospital may run under $100 a day, and a family member will be able to spend nights with you on a cot or sofa in the room.

(Family members are encouraged to stay with patients—they get to do many of the caretaking tasks a nurse's aide might do in the US such as feeding and assisting you in walks to the bathroom. Yes, that means the hospital has fewer nurses and less costs.)

You will also probably be healthier in Mexico because you are eating more and tastier lower-cost fruits and vegetables, you will be walking more and dealing with less stress, and probably sleeping better (other than being awakened by fireworks, church bells and roosters).

At the same time, medical expenses can quickly add up for those who hope to rely on self-insuring—paying for all their own medical care. A heart attack might cost you $10,000 USD for life-saving treatment and stabilization before you can return to the US for additional care, and Mexican hospitals want to be paid before a patient is discharged. Some private hospitals may require a thousand-dollar deposit upon admission. They usually do take credit cards.

Private health insurance

If you can't get private health insurance in the US, you probably can't get it in Mexico. But you may be able to get into the Mexican government's IMSS health insurance plan.

Those who have sufficient income to pay for a good international or Mexican health insurance plan will sleep better at night knowing they are covered financially. Those who were among the 45 million US citizens without health insurance because they couldn't afford it there, or couldn't get it because of pre-existing conditions, probably won't be able to afford it or qualify for it in Mexico, though they may be able to use IMSS. That's Instituto Mexicano del Seguro Social, the Mexican social security system.

Expats on lower incomes put together many kinds of approaches to affordable health care, often using the government's very low-cost IMSS medical insurance plan as their backup plan for catastrophic medical expenses that they can't afford to pay for themselves, or for which they can't get to the US or Canada to utilize their coverage there. Later we will examine more closely these various approaches.

An entire medical tourism industry, arranging "vacations" to India and other countries as well as to Mexico, has developed in the US to supplement often inadequate and too-costly health care in the US. Thousands cross the border each year for plastic surgery, medications, dental care, glasses and other medical treatments.

Carlos Slim Helú, one of the richest men in the world, is partially funding seven Mexican medical centers to cater to US medical tourists through Grupo Star Medica. Donald Trump is also investing in medical tourism to Mexican border hospitals. (In early 2009 Trump was being sued for pulling back on his investments to a luxury hotel and resort area in Baja because of the economic downturn.) Christus Hospital, a nonprofit based in Irving, TX, owns six hospitals in Mexico. Rough estimates from that chain's website are that a hip replacement that would cost $43,000 to $63,000 in the US may cost as little as $12,000 USD at one of their hospitals. An angioplasty in the US may cost $57,000 to $82,000, while at a Christus hospital it may be $10,000 USD.

International Hospital Corp. in Dallas owns four hospitals in Mexico and plans to have US patients make up 20% of its admissions overall; already US patients are 40% of their Tijuana hospital admissions. The largest private hospital chain in Mexico (20 hospitals) is Hospital Angeles, part of Grupo Angeles Corp. that is in many other businesses and industries, including entertainment, education and tourism. Their two border hospitals in up-scale areas of Tijuana and Ciudad Juaréz attract 50-75% of their patients from the US.

Blue Shield's Access Baja HMO Health Plan allows San Diego County and Imperial County clients living within 50 miles of the Mexican border to use approved medical providers in Tijuana, Tecate, and Mexicali. The one out-of-country HMO licensed to sell group insurance in California is SIMNSA, which owns its own hospitals and employs 200 doctors in 50 specialties, has its own dental, vision and lab services, and contracts with other area hospitals when necessary. It also can offer its insurance solely to Californians living within 50 miles of the border. Aetna and Health Net have arrangements with SIMNSA to offer group medical insurance to US companies with many Latino employees within that 50-mile range. SIMNSA charges about $400 USD a month for a family of four with no deductible and usually no co-pays, while many US group plans charge $1,000 USD a month. Delta Dental is another group insurance plan for the US border strip, with 50-50 coverage and co-pay. A crown that costs an average of $800 in California may cost the insured $400 total. With these advances in cross-border coverage we can hope that more insurance plans in the future will expand their Mexico coverage, once they realize their own savings as well as their patients' savings.

Medicare doesn't apply in Mexico

If you are over 65 or disabled, Medicare will pay for most of your hospitalization in the US, while it does not apply to your health care in Mexico except in certain emergency situations where a tourist can later be reimbursed. You can buy a Medicare supplemental policy that may even have easier restrictions on emergency coverage if you are out of the US—every policy differs.

Many expats living in Mexico with no health insurance gamble that they will be able to get back to the US for expensive medical care under Medicare once stabilized in Mexico. And Canadians need to consult with a Canadian legal advisor on how to retain their coverage under the Canadian health care system if they want to live outside Canada for more than six months a year.

Many Mexican doctors have been trained in the US, and the UNAM medical schools are comparable to those in the US. Some of the best hospitals in the world are in Mexico—the acclaimed ABC Hospital (American British Cowdray Hospital) in Mexico City is a university hospital that opened in 1886 and has a closed staff of Board certified specialists. Its address is Calle Sur 136 at the corner of Av. Observatorio, near the West Bus Station, phone 01 (55) 5230-8000. Like the top private hospitals in the US, it is expensive.

At the same time, many smaller Mexican towns have inadequate medical care and patients may die from a delay in getting blood from the nearest big city, for example. Small towns in the US also suffer the same kinds of shortages and inadequacies. Health care can be a crap shoot, depending on where you are when you get sick and who happens to be on staff at the time you're brought into the hospital, etc., same as in the US.

Rolly had a terrible health care experience while living in the US. Acquiescing to Rolly's insistence on a PSA test (a test for prostate cancer), his HMO doctor ordered the test which came back positive. He then ordered a confirming test and a biopsy; all were positive for cancer. Additional tests, consultations and unexplained delays pushed back radiation treatments nine months after the original positive test. In Mexico there would never have been that kind of delay, Rolly is sure.

In Phoenix during the winter, where Carol and Norma last lived before moving to Mexico, so many elderly snowbirds were crowding the hospitals that ambulances sometimes had to drive for hours trying to find an ER with an opening. And in Los Angeles Norma once spent 16 hours in a county hospital's ER waiting to be seen—she finally forced herself to throw up all over the floor in the waiting room and nurses came running.

Lousy health care in the US, too

Norma also lost three close relatives to death caused by California hospital misdiagnoses. Her brother was discharged three times from an ER that claimed he had a kidney stone but his aortic aneurism ruptured in the cab outside the ER at the last discharge. If he had been diagnosed correctly hours earlier, surgery might have saved him. But in the US you can then sue and probably win. In Mexico few people sue over anything, including medical malpractice. The attitude is often *ojalá*, God willed it.

Another big difference in health care is that the patient is responsible for maintaining personal records—you'll get your own mammograms, other x-rays and lab reports to keep for your own records rather than expecting a doctor or hospital to keep your files.

Each time you go to a doctor, it may be as if you are there for your first visit, and you will be responsible for bringing the doctor any background records that may be important. This may seem disconcerting at first, but then in the US Carol had a stack of medical records at one clinic that was a foot high, and no one ever looked back through all those papers. A doctor had 10-15 minutes per patient allotted by insurance program requirements and could go no deeper than the top page or two of those medical records.

(When Carol and Norma found a very good cardiologist-internist who spoke English and kept patient records on his laptop and understood the concepts of living wills and hospice care, they breathed a sigh of relief. It had been a long search. He charges $45 USD a visit and will follow the ambulance to the nearest Angeles hospital to oversee one of his patients who needs critical care. That's better than any doctor they had found in the US.)

In Mexico you can go to any medical lab and order your own tests for cholesterol, etc., so that you are truly in charge of your own health care. The illusion that some family doctor is overseeing your care and has the greater picture in mind does not exist in Mexico. You are in charge of your own life.

Four hospital systems

Mexico's health care system is based on three government systems—the IMSS and Hospital General systems and one for government employees—and on private health care facilities. An estimated three percent of the Mexican population has private medical insurance, though more than half of Mexico's total medical expenditures are for private health care. Even Mexicans with IMSS who can afford to often prefer to go to private hospitals and doctors for most of their care. Many Mexicans in general are distrustful of their government and all government services. Mexico has a long way to go to rid its government of corruption and bureaucracy so that its people will totally trust government officials, even those running health care systems.

The basic government system which covers more than half of the population through their employers is IMSS, which expats can also join for several hundred dollars a year (how to join and the pros and cons of IMSS will be discussed in detail).

For the 40% or so of the population which does not have IMSS coverage through an employer, there are the Hospital General facilities. Insurance at Hospital General is through Seguro Publico, not available to non-Mexican citizens. Expats can still utilize the Hospital General system and will be charged on a sliding scale, determined by an interview.

Carol has gone through the ER at the San Miguel Hospital General twice for heart arrhythmias and tachycardia, and the fee for both four-hour ER stays was in the $40-50 USD range, to give you a feeling for the costs. The fee was based on a ten-minute financial interview with a social worker on household income, home ownership, education, pensions, other income, etc. Expats have had broken limbs set at a Hospital General and have been charged under $200 USD total costs.

How do you make your own decisions, including whether you can realistically move to Mexico based on your own health care issues? Following is more detailed information on all of these questions.

Should you keep Medicare Part B?

At age 65 in the US, you qualify for Medicare Part A, which is free, and which covers primarily hospital stays. You can also sign up for Part B, for about $100 USD a month, deducted from your Social Security check, to pay for doctor visits and many of your deductibles and co-pays. Part D is the drug benefit, but it can be difficult to get medicines from the US into Mexico under the plan. Whether to join Part D needs careful consideration if you need many prescription drugs and have a way to get your medicines to you in Mexico. For many expats, it doesn't make sense.

Many expats also decide to opt out of Part B since they expect they will never be able to use Medicare as long as they live in Mexico, and they can use that monthly payment for their out-of-pocket medical expenses in Mexico. But once you have opted out, it can be very difficult and expensive to ever get back in. You will pay heavy fines depending on how many premiums you missed paying while you were out of the system.

If you plan to live full-time in Mexico for the rest of your life, and you don't have any pre-existing medical conditions or advanced age that would make it impossible to change to a private insurance plan, and you have enough money to be able to pay for such coverage if you can get it, and you are absolutely sure you will never develop a medical condition for which you would be more comfortable being treated in the US, and there is absolutely no way you will ever have to move back to the US, you may choose to drop Part B. Rolly did—more on that decision later.

You will also have to evaluate whether Part D, the prescription drug benefit program for Medicare, works for you—Carol and Norma decided against it and so far have not regretted their decision.

Though Medicare will not cover you in Mexico there are always rumors that will change, and political expat organizations are working toward that day. If you have a private health insurance plan now, it may or may not cover you if you move to Mexico. You may have to change to an international policy. If you don't, you may or may not be able to get away with saying you are on a lengthy vacation in Mexico. You may have to come up with a very large amount of money up front and hope you will be reimbursed later by your insurance company after you file the necessary paperwork. (Some international policies work with some Mexican hospitals in a way similar to US insurance.)

Alternatives, none of them perfect

How do expats integrate their health care costs into their overall planning for their lives in Mexico? There are many alternatives that can be used singly or in combination.

1. Self-insure. Office visits and routine tests are so inexpensive that paying these fees out of pocket is practical. Major medical/hospitalization can also be covered by self-insurance, although most people choose to have insurance for that. (Personally, Rolly has chosen to self-insure. In seven years his health care costs, including one major hospitalization, have amounted to less than he would have paid for insurance.)

2. Buy a private insurance plan for Mexico. Major medical/hospitalization insurance is much cheaper in Mexico—sometimes as little as 20% of the cost in the US. But some international health insurance plans with extensive coverage can cost many thousands of dollars a year, especially after age 65 or 70.

3. Buy IMSS insurance. If you live in an area with a good IMSS facility, you may wish to consider this very inexpensive option.

4. Drop Medicare Part B. If you are committed to health care in Mexico, you can save several hundred dollars per year by dropping Part B. Rolly dropped Part B. Thus far the money saved has paid for almost all his self-insurance and drugs. Carol and Norma have opted to keep their enrollment in case a future costly illness could require expensive care in the US.

5. Legitimately claim an address in the US if you can. It some cases it may be possible for those on Medicare to join a PPO or HMO in that state that will cover their health care expenses if they can get to the US. These kinds of programs do not cost any more than Medicare Part B—Medicare premiums are turned over to the companies, which then agree to accept Medicare payments for all charges, in return for their managing your health care. They often emphasize prevention such as weight loss, exercise and smoking programs. Carol

and Norma turned their Medicare over to a PPO based in Texas and evaluate each time they have a major medical decision whether it will be cheaper to take a bus to McAllen for treatment there, or pay for the treatment out of pocket in San Miguel or Querétaro (a nearby city of a million with good hospitals). So far, it has always been cheaper to have the treatment locally, but they know that for expensive treatment in the future they have that option open.

It must be taken into consideration that the US may be changing its health care system in the future, as promised in the last presidential campaign, and these kinds of Medicare supplement plans could go on the chopping block. All aspects of health care in the US might be changing in the future. Or not.

Getting to the border with a medical emergency

McAllen in the Brownsville region of Southeast Texas is a city with many major hospitals catering to US retirees who are snow-birds, who RV fulltime, or who travel to the area for their health care. Houston, Austin, Dallas and San Antonio are other Texas cities which have many medical facilities that appeal to senior citizens, and it may be possible to find an insurance option that would allow an expat to get complete medical care there if you can get to the border. For those living in other parts of Mexico, Arizona, New Mexico or California may offer options for someone who can get to the border for treatment of a major illness.

Some expats carry IMSS for the kinds of catastrophic medical emergencies like a heart attack or traffic accident trauma where you can't get to the border and you need immediate and expensive care as close to home as possible. They rely on Medicare or a PPO/HMO or Medicare supplement for any kind of care that they can get in the US, for expensive conditions like cancer where you can still go back and forth to the US for chemo, etc. And they self-insure—pay out-of-pocket—for as much as possible.

Similarly, many wealthier Mexicans also pay for private care as much as possible and rely on their IMSS insurance for the most expensive kinds of treatment. The IMSS system is overloaded and underfunded already by its Mexican patients, not to mention the increasing number of expat members. You will often experience long waits and the prescription drugs you need may not be available.

Health insurance is probably your biggest expat decision

Each person has to evaluate what kinds of insurance may be available and in what combinations, considering where they choose to live and their own health needs. This is probably the biggest decision expats must make when moving to Mexico.

It is widely known that prescription and over the counter drugs cost less in Mexico than NoB. For most drugs, this is true. But not always—there are some medicines that cost the same or more. Also, not all drugs available NoB are sold in Mexico; and, sometimes, drugs are not available in the same strengths. For example, in the US Rolly took one 10 mg tab per day of a medicine, but in Mexico he could find that drug in 1 and 2 mg tabs. Now to get 10 mg, he spends more in Mexico than in the US.

A bright side of buying drugs in Mexico is that most are available without a prescription. Medical supplies (such as needles) and equipment are also available over the counter. Heavy-duty pain meds and mood-altering drugs such as Valium and anti-depression drugs will require prescriptions, however.

Pharmacists as physicians

Pharmacists will often serve as physicians, for good or bad, and many Mexicans rely on a pharmacist for most of their health care. Pharmacists may decide you could use a series of corticosteroid shots for pain, for example, or a series of Vitamin B shots to pep you up, and you show up each morning at the pharmacy for your injection.

Pharmacists do not have the advanced education and licensing that they do in the US and Canada, however. The chemist required to be on the application papers for a new pharmacy may move on and you may be trusting your medical decisions to someone with a second-grade education. But for routine ailments someone familiar with common local medical problems may be sufficient. Sometimes your mother did know best, sometimes she didn't. You make the decision whether to rely on a pharmacist or to go to a physician who *will* have a broader understanding of the interactions of various medications and disease conditions and know when a condition that looks to be routine may not be.

When deciding whether to find a Mexican equivalent for your US prescription, be careful at "*similares*," stores that specialize in finding generic or similar medicines. "*Equivalentes*" are drugs with the same chemical composition of your original prescription, and you need to check the ingredient lists on your medicines to be sure they are really identical. A *similare* may not work for your condition. These pharmacies can provide great savings if you can get the exact medications you need. The same pharmaceutical companies that make the drugs for US and Canadian markets make them in and for Mexico. Vague warnings that Mexican drugs are somehow inferior have been proven groundless. Make sure the package indicates the exact generic chemical name and dosage that you have been prescribed.

Insurance Companies

Many companies write medical insurance for Mexico. The following have been recommended though we have no personal experience with any of them.

Allianz Mexico, *www.allianzworldwidecare.com/*, an affiliate of Allianz International, is a very large company with several options.

Blue Cross/Blue Shield, *www.blueexpat.bcbs.com*, lists affiliated companies that offer plans for Mexico. You can download a short PDF booklet detailing the plans.

BUPA International, *www.bupa-intl.com/*, is the world's largest international medical insurance company, with 8 million members in 190 countries.

Global Insurance, *www.globalinsureall.com/CitizenSecureBrochure.pdf*

Grupo Inbursa, *www.inbursa.com*, offers a PPN (Preferred Provider Network) insurance program as well as a wide range of non-

PPN plans, ranging from the very basic PPN plan to a traditional plan to a "go to the Mayo Clinic for elective medical care" plan (which is expensive). The prices for the plans vary with coverage.

IMG, International Medical Group, *www.imglobal.com*, offers world-wide medical coverage. You may include or exclude coverage in the US and Canada with corresponding changes in cost.

ING Commercial America, now AXA, has offices all over Mexico. Call them without cost in Mexico at 01-800-001-8700 or from the United States or Canada at 1-888-293-7221. These numbers are for their *Centros de Atenciones* where you can be forwarded to a local agent. Local agents are also listed in local phone books. (Do not confuse ING with IMG, above.)

MultiNational Underwriters, *www.totaltravelinsurance.com/tti/ product/international-medical/insurance-plans.asp?v=699382*, has a number of policies you can apply for online. They have options for Worldwide or Mexico policies. They are licensed in the state of Indiana. An obvious advantage to purchasing coverage from a company based in the US is that the policy is written in English. If you apply before age 64, you may qualify for lifetime coverage. If you apply between the ages of 65 and 74, your coverage may end at age 75.

International Health Insurance Danmark Mexico, S.A., *www. ihi.com*, part of the British United Provident Association, allows people to apply up to the age of 74.

Seguros Monterrey New York Life works with Olympus Medsave (*www.omhc.com*) and United Health Care (*www.myuhc.com*) for international coverage.

There may be more companies which offer health insurance in Mexico, and check with any current insurance you have to see what may be available to you already. Based on the comments Rolly has received, from the above companies, ING/AXA and Grupo Inbursa seem to be the most popular. Carol and Norma have friends who are happy with their IMG and BUPA plans. With the corporate consolidations underway globally, any of these companies may merge or leave an insurance area; you will need to verify current availabilities and prices at the time you are comparing companies.

When a group of people in San Miguel decided to try to put together a new private medical insurance group plan through Lloyd's of London, the costs ended up being so prohibitive that few could afford it. Though those in good health under age 65 would have had premiums of a few hundred dollars a month, as they increased in age their premiums would have been $500, $700 and more, not feasible for many people. Read the fine print in any policy you are considering on rate increases as you get older, as well as the sections on deductibles and pre-existing conditions. That is probably the most important piece of advice regarding any health insurance company: read every word of the contract.

It is also important to make sure that whatever agent you choose is authorized by the *Comision Nacional de Seguros Y Fianzas* (The National Insurance and Bonds Commission). Verify at *www.cnsf.gob.mx* if you have any doubts.

IMSS

Instituto Mexicano del Seguro Social, IMSS, is the Mexican social security system. Among other programs, it includes an extensive, country-wide HMO-type health care system offering free out-patient clinics, hospitals, and drugs. Membership is automatic and free for employees of covered businesses (which includes most companies). You may have to pay IMSS membership fees for your employees—see Part Four on employee law to learn more about when it will be required. It is available for very low annual fees to everybody else including foreigners holding an FM2 or FM3 visa. The cost depends on age—for example, at age 60+ the yearly premium was 3,211 pesos in 2009, or under $300 USD a year.

The out-patient clinics are notorious for overcrowding and long waits to see a doctor—not unlike many general hospitals in the US. The IMSS system, like Medicaid in the US, is overloaded and always in financial trouble. For this reason, people who can afford to see a private doctor do so rather than going to an IMSS clinic. Often it is the same doctor who could be seen in either place. Many doctors split their days between IMSS and their own offices. This provides the doctor with a steady income and, importantly, a good retirement benefit.

(Doctors in Mexico rarely make anywhere near as much money as doctors NoB. Starting salary for a staff physician at a Hospital General may be under $20,000 USD a year. Even medical school graduates have been known in the past to go north illegally to make more in construction jobs.)

The free drug program is often rather hollow due to the lack of funds to stock the pharmacies. The IMSS free drug coverage applies to drugs from their pharmacies; there is no reimbursement for drugs purchased outside the system. The drug program also covers immunizations (flu, etc.), and those always seem to be available. Flu shots are generally available free to anyone over 55 whether a member of IMSS or not. In Rolly's home town, each fall and winter health care workers go from door to door giving free flu shots.

The IMSS hospitals vary from pretty plain in smaller communities to outstanding in the larger cities. Most expats who join IMSS do so for the hospitalization benefit, not for the out-patient clinics or the drug program. As with the clinics, the hospitals are staffed with both full-time doctors and with private physicians who share their time with IMSS.

IMSS medical insurance is available to foreigners holding an FM3 or FM2 visa. The cost is quite low. To apply you will need two copies of your passport and of your FM2 or FM3, two copies of proof of residency (such as a utility bill in your name or a lease), two copies of your birth certificate and of your marriage license if applicable, and two smaller than passport-type pictures, called *infantil* size if you have a local photographer take them. (The photographer's cost may be around $2-5 USD.) The birth certificate and marriage license may have to have an *apostille* (to be explained in the chapter on visas) and to be translated into Spanish by an approved translator. Some offices accept applications only during certain months of the year.

A physical exam is sometimes required, depending on the answers to the questionnaire. Coverage of pre-existing conditions is complicated. Some may be covered after two years, others are never covered, and some will disallow your enrollment. Pre-existing conditions may include cancer, chronic degenerative disease including heart attacks and strokes, emphysema, diabetes, hepatitis, renal failure, or vascular or neurological diseases.

As always, check with your local IMSS office to verify requirements and costs.

Rates for 2009	
Age	Pesos
0-19	$1,222
20-39	$1,428
40-59	$2,134
60+	$3,211

Benefits are phased in over a three-year period. In the first year minor illnesses such as colds, turista, etc. are covered. These are basically out-patient services for which you will probably want to see a private doctor rather than wasting half a day or more waiting in the IMSS out-patient clinic. The first year will cover automobile and other accidents and emergencies such as heart attacks. You will not receive coverage for benign breast tumors the first six months, or births within ten months after coverage starts. Other conditions which may not be covered the first year include kidney stones, gynecological conditions other than cancer, vein surgery, hemorrhoids, tonsils, most hernias, sinus and nasal surgeries, and anything considered elective.

The second year adds everything except broken bones and orthopedics. The third year offers full coverage including medications, so long as you get them from IMSS, though your IMSS coverage will never include plastic surgery, glasses or contact lenses, hearing aids, corrective vision surgery, dental care other than extractions, fertility treatments, and anything considered psychiatric or behavioral including self-inflicted injuries.

You will not be reimbursed for drugs bought from other pharmacies. This drug benefit is often meaningless as IMSS is chronically short of medications.

Following are a few of the questions on the IMSS application. You'll want to give your name as it appears on your migratory document (always use your full name as it is on your visa and passport). Be prepared to give your height in centimeters (multiply your height in inches by 2.54). For your weight in kilograms, divide your weight in pounds by 2.2.

You'll be asked your education level, sports participation, occupation, alcohol use, smoking history, drugs taken including over the counter, allergies, cancer, tumors, diabetes, problems with your kidneys, eyes, nerves, blood circulatory system, heart disease, liver disease, psychiatric history, blood pressure, arthritis or rheumatism, TB, ulcers, AIDS/HIV+, genetic diseases, bronchitis, embolisms, movement problems from accidents or illnesses, addictions, and so on.

In areas where there are many expats, you can hire an assistant or a lawyer to help you navigate the IMSS application process.

Medical Air Evacuation

Many companies offer emergency medical evacuation. Check to see if they are accredited by the Commission on Accreditation of Mexican Transport Services. Before choosing a company, read the details of coverage very carefully. There are considerable differences among policies, and it is easy to buy less than you think you are getting. For all of the companies, be sure to read their exclusions and conditions.

Global Underwriters, *www.globalunderwriters.com*, has a variety of policies for various parts of the world. **Air Ambulance Specialists**, at *www.airaasi.com*; **Air Medical** at *www.air-med.cal.com*; and **Sky Service Air Ambulance** at *www.skyservice.com* are others to consider.

This question was posed to *www.SkyMed.Com*: "I am a US citizen living full time in Mexico. Can I purchase an annual SkyMed family or individual policy that would provide an evacuation for me to my former US home/hospital?"

SkyMed's response in mid 2008 was: "We have a separate product for ex-pats that provides dual coverage. We would air evacuate you from your home (hospital) in Mexico to the States for medical care. Or, if you were traveling within our covered areas and you were hospitalized, we would return you to Mexico upon discharge. This is vastly different from our basic product, that stipulates you must be traveling and 100 air miles or more from your home. The cost for an individual is $480 USD a year, and for a family, $780 a year, plus a one-time application fee." —Sandy Jones, Director, Member Services, 1-800-475-9633, *sandy@skymed.com*

Hospices, living wills, medical power of attorney

Hospices are relatively new to Mexico, and the idea of a living will, where you choose the level of medical care you want when you have been diagnosed as having a terminal illness, is contrary to traditional Catholic belief that suffering is God's will. By law Mexican hospitals and doctors are expected to do everything possible to keep someone alive. But recently a federal law was passed that eases the restrictions on morphine and other heavy-duty pain relief drugs for those who are in the last stages of a terminal disease.

In San Miguel de Allende a hospice recently began that works with sympathetic local doctors, paid employees, and volunteers to help those who are diagnosed as being in their last six months of life, to help ease their pain and provide needed services. One important benefit is providing relief to the primary caretaker, such as a spouse, who needs to have time off from care-giving.

Living wills and medical powers of attorney may not be followed in Mexico; it is important to find a local doctor who will do his or her best to see that your desires are followed as much as is possible. Having the legal papers drawn up ahead of time is a key factor in at least attempting to make this happen.

Assisted living homes are a relatively new development in Mexico, and there are a few pioneering facilities in Ajijíc, San Miguel de Allende, and elsewhere that are meeting this growing need. More often someone who needs assisted living hires a Mexican employee to live in and provide daily care.

A friend of Carol and Norma lived independently to age 92 with the assistance of a mother-daughter care-giving team who lived in and did whatever was necessary to help the woman live as complete of a life as possible, such as helping her walk outside and take a cab to various events. They charged under $200 USD a week, plus their room and board.

Planning for death is a part of taking charge of your own health care. Many cities have some sort of prepaid funeral service that will take over completely once notified, and will follow your instructions on getting your will followed, your burial or cremation handled, and appropriate family or friends notified. Other prepaid funeral services should be questioned on whether it is likely they will still be in business when you need them. San Miguel de Allende is one city that offers a 24-Hour Association that will handle your burial or cremation according to your wishes and prepayment, and make all the contacts of family members, obtain the death certificate and mail copies to your executor, etc. Investigate these kinds of companies and associations in your own area.

Wills drawn up in the United States are recognized in Mexico according to international law. If you have Mexican property, it can be important to have a Mexican will as well, to make the transition process for the property quicker. It is important that the lawyers in both countries know of the existence of each will and make sure that the wills do not contradict each other in any way. Make sure someone who is likely to be informed of your death knows where your will is physically located.

If you die without a will, often it is the US Consular Agent or Consul who is the first to be notified. That person may oversee the police locking your apartment and assuming control over your property to ensure that there is no thievery. Often it is your housekeeper who will find you if you die alone at home. Make sure the housekeeper knows to call the Consulate first. Often when the police are the first to be called, there can be petty thievery even by the police— Mexico is constantly battling police corruption on all levels.

You may choose to register with the local Consulate to make sure your will is readily found. Another option is to have your important papers in a manila envelope right by your computer or some other obvious spot where they will be found immediately. Consular agents do not particularly like having to dig through all the personal papers in a house trying to find a will, family members to contact, cremation or burial wishes, etc.

One option recommended by the San Miguel hospice is that those who live alone may form support groups of perhaps half a dozen friends, each of whom has an envelope for each other member with house and car keys, a copy of the will, family members to notify, and any other important papers. Having some plan for your pets in case you die suddenly would also be a good idea, and make sure someone knows of that plan.

Taking charge of your own life and health

Taking charge of all aspects of your own life, from your health care to your death, is part of rediscovering yourself in Mexico. Your move to Mexico can be an opportunity to reevaluate your entire life, including your health and lifestyle.

For Carol and Norma, they found they were healthier in Mexico and came off of many of their prescriptions as they ate better, walked more, and got rid of US stress. Others who develop major medical conditions may find that they have to move back to the US for specialized care. Some with conditions like emphysema may find they must move to lower altitudes of Mexico, such as the beach or border areas, rather than the central plateau.

Those with disabilities need to consider the particular area of Mexico to which they are moving in relation to available health care services and their particular handicap. People who use wheelchairs for mobility may find that many Mexican cities make no provisions for curb cuts and ramps, and cobblestones, irregular streets and sidewalks can make mobility extremely hard.

Steps are everywhere, including at the entrances to many stores, and many houses and apartments have stairs throughout the floor plan. To keep out the rain, an otherwise one-story house or shop may add a step at each door. Many public and private bathrooms have steps at the entrance or at the stalls.

As the Mexican population ages and as more expats with mobility problems move to Mexico, there will be more one-story homes without stairs, and more businesses and government buildings will have curb cuts and ramps. But not yet.

Those who are living with disabilities may wish to contact the Society for Accessible Travel and Hospitality, *www.sath.org*, for information on accessibility in various cities and areas of Mexico. Other valuable organizations and websites include Accessible Journey at *www.disabilitytravel.com*, and Mobility International USA, *www.miusa.org.*

People living with HIV/AIDS/SIDA (SIDA is the Spanish abbreviation for AIDS) or other conditions requiring a strict prescription regimen need to make absolutely sure they will be able to get their life-saving medications on a regular basis, by mail or through a local physician or by frequent trips to the border. Long after the US had finally come around to recognizing HIV/AIDS, many parts of Mexico remained in denial about the existence of gays, drug users, and straight people with the disease. Many patients had to move to Mexico City or stay at home in the closet and die basically alone.

Now more and more cities have doctors aware of these specialized treatment needs, though not every town will be suitable for those with HIV/AIDS/SIDA. Mexico City hosted its first International AIDS conference in September, 2008.

If you are prone to external allergies, it may take a couple of years for you to develop allergies to Mexican plants and dust. Norma has noticed it takes her several years in a new environment before new allergies develop. In Mexico she and many others experience sinus congestion and eye irritation every March when the beautiful purple jacaranda trees start to bloom. She uses OTC allergy medications each spring. Allergy specialists in larger cities can provide more intensive care for those with more severe or lasting allergies. Construction dust, and dust during the driest parts of the year, particularly before the rains start around mid-June, can be hard on those with breathing problems. Some Mexicans and expats wear disposable paper face masks to filter the air, like many in Japan.

Common food poisoning

One condition which Mexican doctors may know more about than US doctors is amoebic and bacterial infection from food poisoning and unsanitary conditions.

Norma had many cases of food poisoning before Mexico, including in Paris on her birthday after eating at a very expensive restaurant. For weeks she'd felt she needed to go to an internist in SMA for intestinal upset but symptoms would come and go and she put it off. On a trip to Pátzcuaro and Morelia in late 2007, both Carol and Norma came down with severe food poisoning. Carol got better on her own, Norma didn't, and so she visited an internist connected with Hospital de la Fe when she got back to San Miguel. He took one look at her and ordered, "Hospital—now."

He walked her over to the hospital that is connected with a physicians' office building and made sure she was put onto IV antibiotics and rehydration immediately. Her potassium levels were so low that she could have gone into cardiac arrest at any point. The hospital required a 5,000-peso deposit, which Carol put onto a credit card, and she asked how much a private room was: about $85 USD a night. But the final bill for the 48-hour hospitalization and doctor bills was about $1,300 USD, mostly for the cost of the IV antibiotics.

The doctor didn't wait for the final tests to determine which kind of food poisoning she had, he wanted her on the antibiotics immediately, and Cipro was the drug of choice for all of the common ones, anyway. He said she probably had had Shigella.

A few weeks later Norma started to have some of the original symptoms of intestinal distress and this time went to an infectious disease specialist from Hospital Angeles in Queretaro. He said she probably also had the parasitic disease Giardia, and she was placed on a much stronger antibiotic that is more commonly used on AIDS patients with infections. Total cost for that episode was under $100 USD for both the doctor bills and the pills.

You generally know in a few hours if you get food poisoning from bacteria. But the amoebas and other parasites that can be spread by a lack of hand washing and other unsanitary conditions can often cause minor symptoms for weeks and months before the patient decides to see a doctor, the delay possibly leading to severe damage of internal organs. Many Mexicans self-diagnose and take strong antibiotics like over the counter Cipro and Flagyl without knowing for sure they need it. (The problem of overuse of antibiotics is contributing to the growth of "superbugs," immune to existing antibiotics, in the same way that many US parents have demanded that a doctor give their child antibiotics even for a cold that can't be helped by antibiotics. The problem is global.)

A friend who had a heart attack

A friend of Carol and Norma had a heart attack related to diabetes and he is sure Hospital de la Fe saved his life, for a charge of about $3,000 USD for three days of intensive cardiac care. He then had an angiogram at Hospital Angeles in Querétaro for another $3,000, and if he had needed a stent at the same time it would have been about $10,000 USD. If the angiogram had indicated a heart bypass, he would have gone back to the US for Medicare coverage.

Another man who had a heart attack in San Miguel was rushed to Hospital Angeles in Querétaro as soon as he was stable, and his cardiologist in SMA went with him, an hour's drive, to make sure he got the best care at that hospital.

Another friend was admitted to the SMA IMSS hospital for intestinal distress of unknown cause, and they sent her to the larger IMSS hospital in Celaya. Her friends and family were not happy with her extended care there and transferred her to Hospital Angeles in Querétaro, where she was finally cured after many weeks hospitalization. Cost there: more than $20,000 USD, not covered by her IMSS policy.

These are the kinds of emergency situations in which expats may find themselves, and the kinds of cases that you should consider as possibilities in your health care planning. You cannot always get to the US for a medical emergency.

Dentistry

The quality of dental care in Mexico is as varied as the quality of other types of health care, with top-of-the-line dentists available in most areas who can perform every kind of implant, root canal, bridge, whitening or other procedure that you can get in the States, usually for far less money. Dentists who have studied abroad and who advertise that they speak English and do advanced procedures such as implants are likely to charge more than Spanish-speaking dentists who perform basic dentistry.

You can choose whatever level of dentistry you want, depending on what is available in the area you choose to live. Remember that thousands of US citizens decide to come down to Mexico each year for their dental work to save money on the same quality of dentistry they are used to receiving in the US. Carol and Norma spend $40 USD for teeth cleaning, $40 USD for a basic filling, and $5 USD for an oral x-ray with a Mexican dentist in San Miguel de Allende.

Vision Care

Similarly, there are small eyeglass shops that may offer the basics in eyeglasses at very low prices, a package including exam and glasses for perhaps as low as $80 USD. And there are ophthalmologists (medical doctors specializing in eye diseases) who may charge similar rates as ophthalmologists in the US and Canada and who can perform the most advanced eye surgeries.

As an example of costs, Devlin is one of the largest chains of optometrists in Mexico and in some cities they will make new glasses in an hour. In 2008 Carol and Norma both chose to go to a highly recommended ophthalmologist in the million-population city of Querétaro to get base line professional exams on their over-65 eyes. Their exams cost 500 pesos each for complete workups and an hour each with the technicians and the doctor. Next year Carol required a repeat visit, and she was told to eat spinach daily rather than being prescribed a nutritional supplement with the same vitamins and minerals. How often in the US does a doctor of any kind recommend a healthy food rather than a pill?

They took their prescriptions to a local optometrist and had polycarbonate progressive lineless bifocals with Transitions automatic lens darkening in sunshine, for under $300 each pair. The prescription exam would have been included in that price, if they hadn't already had their prescriptions. Of course more expensive designer frames were available that could have made the price much higher. Many expats go to Costco and other discount stores for their eyeglasses.

Alternative and holistic medicine

People who move to Mexico tend to be more open-minded and willing to explore new ideas, and so it is not surprising that every kind of alternative and holistic medicine practitioner can be found in various regions. There are also traditional Mexican health practitioners who can lead you through different approaches to physical, mental and spiritual health. Because of the lower costs, you may be able to have stress-reducing massages, take yoga or Pilates classes, try acupuncture, or use other kinds of alternative medicine in addition to or instead of Western medicine.

There is no one simple answer to the question, "What do you do about health care in Mexico?" These complex and interrelated issues may be the most important factors in your evaluation of the possibilities of moving to Mexico.

Rolly's Pulmonary Embolism

Rolly's personal experience being hospitalized with a life-threatening pulmonary embolism. I was having serious breathing problems. It had been getting worse over the past five days, finally forcing me to call my doctor. After hearing my symptoms described over the phone, the doctor ordered me to go to Hospital Angeles across the river in Torreón, which he said was the finest private hospital in the area. He also gave me the name of a cardiologist affiliated with the hospital.

The hospital looked like a four-star hotel, complete with a drive-up patient arrival area. A uniformed attendant whisked me away in a wheelchair through a grand lobby and atrium to the urgent care area, where I was met by an English-speaking doctor, a male nurse and a couple of stout orderlies who helped me on to the gurney and hooked me up to oxygen.

The English-speaking cardiologist arrived shortly on a late Saturday afternoon. Then came the rounds of tests, x-rays, EKGs, various injections, and, of course, a damned IV in my bad hand. He confirmed what my local doctor are surmised: I had suffered a pulmonary embolism, which was life-threatening.

He ordered me admitted to the hospital. After presenting my US credit card to the admitting office, I was wheeled up to a very nice room which, in Mexican custom, had a pullout bed for a family member or friend. I wanted my friend Enrique to go home, but the nurse said no, he needed to stay because my condition was unstable and I should not be left alone. Gad, how Enrique snores!

The food was good and always more than I could eat. I was allowed to order each meal from a menu printed in both Spanish and English. The nursing staff did not speak English, and my Spanish is a bit meager, but we managed fine.

In my four days in the hospital there were more shots and pills than I can remember, two more EKGs, and a very interesting sonic scan of the heart. My doctor set the screen so I could watch the scan. Very interesting indeed. The left side of my heart looked like other pictures I had seen, but the right side was obviously not OK.

I am self-insured, so I was a bit worried about the costs of all the high-tech stuff in this palatial hospital and the fees of the high-powered cardiologist. The hospital bill was about $2,800 USD, and the doctor wanted $350 USD for his services, which included lengthy, unhurried visits twice each day.

My plan to self-insure still seems to be working. I have spent less on medical care in the past eight years than insurance would have cost. In fact, it has all been covered by the money saved from dropping Medicare Part B.

Carol, too, has been hospitalized in Mexico. Here is her account of her two knee replacement surgeries.

Carol's Knee Replacement Surgeries in Querétaro

Increasing arthritic knee pain in 2007 made me think about having replacement surgery, the right knee first. The main question was whether to have it locally or go back to the States. The cost per knee in 2007 and 2008 done by an internationally renowned surgeon in nearby Querétaro was 68,000 pesos, or $5,230 USD at 13:1. Websites for US hospitals and clinics offering knee replacement surgery averaged about $40,000 USD per knee, much of which would be covered by Medicare in my case.

But the deductibles and co-pays, the cost of transportation, a hotel, local transportation, and restaurant costs for Norma, plus maintaining our SMA apartment, having our pets cared for, and the likelihood that we'd have to go back and forth to the States several times for various tests added up. It would be cheaper and easier to have the surgery done in Mexico.

I came through the Saturday morning surgery fine, was kept in the hospital until Tuesday because the doctor knew I had 21 steps to maneuver to get into our apartment, and in a few weeks was walking around already as well as before the surgery. I needed three months of biweekly rehabilitation therapy ($30 USD a visit) to finish the straightening, since for years apparently I had been favoring my right leg.

I'd been processing this decision for months, the same as any expat who doesn't have the money for excellent full medical coverage does. Dr. Michael Schmidt does orthopedic surgeries out of Munich, the US, Hospital Angeles in Querétaro, and Clinica Querétaro, a small clinic above the offices of about ten medical specialists.

My research found that it is better to have something specialized done at a clinic concentrating on the procedure, since all the staff and facilities will be geared to the procedure and they will have handled hundreds of cases. I'd read that the chances of developing an infection also are less in a specialized clinic without the exposure to general hospital patients.

Dr. Schmidt's reputation is excellent, I know many people in San Miguel who have been operated on by him, and we could stay at home for the recovery and not board our pets and have all the travel hassles and expenses of a US trip. No brainer decision.

Clinica Querétaro has six patient rooms, plus two operating suites and recovery area. A lumbering elevator to the second floor requires a staff member with a key. Usually you take the stairs. The first room we were to be in for an Aug. 4 scheduled operation was fairly small and the sofa on which Norma would sleep for the duration was typical hard-as-rocks Mexican furniture.

But that room did get BBC on the TV set. When a larger room became available the nurses moved us. For some reason our next room a few doors away didn't get BBC. We watched some pretty sappy movies in English with Spanish subtitles on the Hallmark channel Sunday and Monday.

We checked in at 8 pm Friday night with a small suitcase mostly of clothes for Norma, our robes and slippers, and plush towels, our own pillows tucked under our arms. We also brought a cooler of Diet Pepsi and snacks on ice for Norma, and she walked to a nearby supermarket and restaurants to replenish her cooler.

The hospital food wasn't spectacular—yes, I have had pretty good meals in hospitals, mainly private ones in LA. These were boring even by most US hospital standards, though. Norma could have had the staff bring her a tray at each meal same as I was getting, but she preferred her own from the nearby super-market and restaurants.

For me, every meal after the surgery included a cup of fresh fruit such as a thinly sliced apple or pear, a cup of Jell-o or yogurt, a glass of juice, and either hot chocolate or a cup of hot water, usually minus a tea bag. Breakfast or late meal would include a cup of corn flakes and milk, and the other meals included plain quesadillas, a fried mystery meat with a tomato sauce, or an egg and veggie frittata.

I've had eight semesters of Spanish and am still barely at in-termediate level, which did hamper me somewhat in the hospital. A nurse would ask me something too quickly and I'd do the stan-dard, *Repete, por favor, mas despachio* (please repeat slowly) and she'd give up on me, ask if I were from nearby San Miguel (home to some 12,000 expats), use some sort of sign language to convey her message, and leave the room fast.

But other nurses hung in there with me and we did communicate. One saw me hobbling with my walker the first time after my surgery and called me Speedy Gonzales. I said no, more like *un caracol* (a snail). So I was nicknamed The Snail.

We'd brought a complete set of toiletries, not expecting to get a welcome packet of soap, shampoo, toothbrush, toothpaste and slippers in a Mexican hospital, but there it was. But it did not come with your very own take-home bedpan and washing tub. Those were in the room.

I never felt the nurses were less than attentive, they did check on me frequently, and certainly they were prompt with the shots and pills. I had to dial 111 on the phone to get a nurse between visits, and one always came much more quickly than when I pushed the help button in US hospitals.

I wasn't automatically given a sleeping pill at 9 pm the way US hospitals usually did, even if I had to be awakened to get that routine sleeping pill in the US. Dr. Schmidt checked in on me frequently all day long.

Another English-speaking doctor who was in the operating room helped with the tools and such. The rest of the six or eight people in the operating room didn't speak any English and I tried my best to understand word one. Probably good that I couldn't.

Though the doctors and nurses followed standard hand-washing and sterilization procedures same as a good US hospital, I did notice little things. One of the china cups in which my hot water arrived each meal had a chip out of the rim, right where you would drink from. One nurse trying to find a spot for my second IV gave up on the rubber gloves. (That's happened in the US, too—I have hard-to-find veins.)

And I doubt if the thick blankets were washed after every patient. The thin smooth blankets you get at a US hospital have definitely been washed and sterilized between patients, and often are even heated for you.

The patient's room had one of those stand-up cylindrical fans that we'd always ignored when we saw them advertised on TV or at Sharper Image shops. But this one was wonderful for moving the summer air and getting some circulation into the room. Of course there was no air conditioning, but the fan was sufficient. (The operating room was kept very cold, the same as in the US.)

The IV stand was the old manual kind, no hefty electronic marvel to beep and warn of almost-finished drips. So I was able to walk with it easily.

I think this account gives you the feeling of what it is like to be a surgery patient in a Mexican hospital, or at least one person's experience at one hospital. My second knee replacement six months later went even more smoothly since I knew what to expect.

Since I've been home I've seen two TV segments on US citizens coming to Mexico for health care, for example combining a beach vacation with intensive dental reconstruction so that the entire "vacation" plus dental work cost half what the dental work alone would have cost in the US.

Now if only the US government would realize how much they could save on Medicare costs alone if they allowed even a few select hospitals in Mexico to accept Medicare payments. Would we see an influx of expats into Mexico then! But that's not likely to happen in our lifetimes.

We hope that sharing these personal experiences in detail helps someone out there who has health care issues about moving to Mexico. Could we have had a medical disaster here? Certainly, and we have relatives who died from medical mistakes at US hospitals, too. Health care is the number one worry of many of those considering moving to Mexico, the same way that it is one of the major worries of those in much of the world.

Staying Healthy in Mexico

In this chapter: Careful walking. Turista. Water safety. Purifying produce. Street vendors. Immunizations. Mexico's response to the flu epidemic.

Though this chapter has more to do with living in Mexico after you've made the decision to move and you've gotten settled into your new home, it is a logical extension of the preceding health care chapter. Part of health care in Mexico is staying healthy, which in Mexico may require a few more safeguards, or at least different ones, than living in a US or Canadian modern suburb. Those contemplating a move to Mexico need to be aware ahead of the time of the changes they will incorporate into their daily lives.

Heads up, heads down while you walk

In much of Mexico you must watch carefully where you are walking. Modern cities may have good sidewalks, but colonial cities usually retain their cobblestones, at least in the historic section. Good news—walking on cobblestones has been compared to acupuncture for the feet.

If you step into a ditch dug for a utility repair, you aren't going to be able to sue anyone for your medical bills, even if the city worker marked the spot with a rock sprayed with a little red paint and someone kicked that rock aside.

Even windowsills and planter boxes jutting out onto the sidewalk area at forehead height can cause a spill or a cut—while you're watching your feet, you also need to watch for obstacles at head

77

height in your path. You will soon learn that you cannot sightsee or take photos while walking. You need to plant yourself every so often and take a good look around and snap that photo before resuming your walk. You will learn the sidewalk habits of Mexicans in your area—too busy to greet you, or eager for a *buenos dias*.

In areas with heavy rains, you may notice that curbs are surprisingly high. During a sudden intense thunderstorm you will learn why—in many areas the rushing water will be so deep you cannot even see where the curbs are. Flow-through sandals are great for rainy season wading, watching for those curbs as best you can. Each city is different—you may move to an area with kept-up sidewalks and smooth pavement. Or not.

Purified water

Staying healthy in Mexico largely revolves around drinking bottled or purified water (unless like Rolly you live in an area where the tap water is safe to drink); eating fresh fruits and vegetables soaked for 10 minutes in a Microdyn or similar purifying agent solution; being careful of food handling in general, and washing your hands.

You will probably be walking more, eating more fresh fruits and vegetables, and living a less stress-filled life with lots to do. It will be hard to be a bored or lethargic couch potato, the kind of person who is more susceptible to many kinds of diseases. These health benefits will probably outweigh any greater possibility that you may contract a serious form of bacterial or parasitic infection.

Yes, you're probably going to get a mild *turista* at least once while you're in Mexico. Mexicans get it when they visit the US or Canada. Norma got it in Paris. Any time your body experiences changes in internal flora and fauna you can get diarrhea. Usually it will cure itself in a few days, with or without Imodium D or Pepto Bismo. If you feel particularly weak, or develop a fever or chills, or see blood in your stool, it is time to get to a doctor.

Both Coca Cola (the brand name for its bottled water is Ciel) and Pepsi Cola (Santorini) deliver purified water to homes and businesses in large plastic jugs called *garrafons* that hold 20 liters, or approximately five gallons—40 pounds of water. The water trucks will pull up to your courtyard or block once or twice a week. Delivery men will collect your empty *garrafons* and about 18 pesos per new bottle and replace the empty with the new. There is a deposit of about $5 USD if you don't have a *garrafon* to exchange.

Other water companies may do the same in different areas, but a doctor who specializes in infectious diseases warned that, as in the US, some smaller bottling companies may simply fill up their bottles with tap water. At least Coca Cola and Pepsi Cola are known to have the major equipment and supplies for doing the purification, and they have reputations and financial stakes in providing high-quality purified water. If you choose a smaller company, do some checking to make sure that the company has the facilities and the history of consistently providing purified water.

If you are building or remodeling a home, you can install a purification system that will allow you to drink from the tap throughout your home. Generally it is recommended that you use at least two overlapping systems, since some are better at one aspect of water purification than others.

Microdyn, BacDyn and the similar over the counter products used to purify fresh fruits and vegetables are silver halide solutions, not iodine, despite the similarity of their names to iodine, and it is silver halide tablets that also make up one of the ways to purify your tap water for your entire home if you choose that route.

Since many cities and towns do not have running water to all neighborhoods every day, you might have your home water tank (a *tinaco*, usually installed on your roof next to your propane tank) filled automatically with tap water once or twice a week. The water may also be collected in larger cisterns, often underground. Many people are starting to collect rain water as well, which may be directed to the cisterns.

If one of the methods you use for in-house water purification includes silver halide tablets in your *tinacos* and cisterns, many companies will come out to your house, clean out your tanks, and return every six months or so to replace your silver halide tablets. Another system of house-wide water purification is reverse osmosis (R/O). That system involves a plasma-like filter that strains out all measurable impurities including common chemicals in water. When Carol and Norma lived near Phoenix, they had R/O on their kitchen and bathroom sinks to remove the harsh tastes of the chemicals found in local water there, not for purification.

Ultraviolet light is another common water purification system, to be used in conjunction with at least one other method. Check with local contractors and building suppliers to find which systems are available in your area and which are locally recommended if you want to have the water in your entire house purified. Newly built homes are more likely to have excellent pipes; older homes may have leaks within their plumbing systems and you will probably be advised to continue to use bottled water.

40-pound *garrafons*

Many kinds of devices have been invented to get water out of the *garrafons* without lifting 40 pounds each time. Various low-cost plastic pumps can fasten over the bottle opening, or some pieces of furniture allow the *garrafons* to be incorporated into kitchen storage units. You can buy decorative pottery pieces that allow the *garrafon* to be overturned into the piece quickly so that the water comes out of a faucet in the china bottom. Electrical heating and/ or cooling units will allow you to turn on a faucet and get cold or hot water out of the *garrafon* you've placed on top of the unit. Look in local shops to see what is available. Smaller pottery units may fit on your bathroom sink counter to make it easy to have bottled water for teeth cleaning and pill taking.

When you go out, most of the better restaurants in cities use bottled water for cooking and for ice cubes, and if you are in an area with many expats in a restaurant frequented by expats, you can be sure the produce is purified as well. If you are in a remote unfamiliar area, it is better to be safe and to order bottled water (with carbonation or not—*agua mineral* is carbonated, meaning with, or *con*, gas, and *sin* gas means not carbonated), no ice cubes, and cooked foods rather than salads and fresh fruit. Even in a dish that is otherwise cooked, sometimes fresh cilantro is chopped on top, or it is in a fresh salsa, and it may not have been purified. An infectious disease specialist told a San Miguel audience that, when in doubt, use lots of lime juice, which has a purifying effect. He wasn't completely joking.

Washing your hands before eating, or at least using a gel sanitizer, is the best way to avoid picking up many kinds of diseases. Don't accept a sample of freshly sliced produce from a street vendor no matter how good it looks. You don't know where the knife and his hands have been. Carol even got a minor case of food poisoning from a hamburger-based food sample handed out in a major Mexican supermarket; it probably sat too long or wasn't cooked to a high enough temperature.

Eating from street stands

Can you buy food from street vendors? Yes, if you are careful. One good sign is if the person who handles money uses a plastic glove, or even a plastic baggie instead of a glove, for the money, or if different people handle money and food. Do you know how long the food stand has been up? If there is not a steady source of heat or cold to keep prepared food at a safe temperature, you do not want food that has sat around.

Is there a crowd of customers? Mexicans get food poisoning, too—if the stand has many customers with high turnover of food it is probably safe. Examine the general cleanliness of the stand as well. What happens to the knives and spoons between uses? Are the same tongs used for raw and cooked meat? Can juices from meats not yet thoroughly cooked mix into the meat ready to serve? Some stands place plastic plates into plastic wrap so that the dishes don't have to be washed between customers; the wrapping is replaced.

When Carol first arrived in Mexico she longingly passed the street stands selling steamed corn on the cob slathered with mayonnaise, rolled in grated white cheese, and then sprinkled with chili and lime, but she didn't trust the stands. Finally she decided that the real culprit was the mayonnaise, and when a stand first opens a new jar of mayo, and the corn has been kept in water that is steaming, she will indulge. So far she's never been sick from street stand corn.

Paletas on the street? Those are the fruit bars on popsicle sticks that sometimes vendors will make at home and bring into town to sell at parades. They may or may not use bottled water when making their fruit mixtures. Carol and Norma will buy *paletas* from established shops but think twice before buying from someone walking around with an ice cooler.

The same safeguards should be taken on meats and other foods that you would follow in the US or Canada.

And still there can be problems, such as the particular strain of salmonella outbreak in most states of the US in mid-2008 that was at first blamed on certain kinds of tomatoes from either three states in Mexico or parts of Florida. In this case the salmonella was supposed to have entered the insides of the tomatoes from contamination of the plant in the flower stage.

Controversy over where and how the tomatoes got to consumers and whether the culprit was tomatoes at all continued for months in the summer of 2008. Finally tomatoes were allowed to be shipped into the US once more, the origins of the disease never discovered. The blame next shifted to jalapeños. Next it was the smaller, hotter serrano chile. Food poisoning is generally mild and few cases require doctor visits. Even then, the doctor may or may not report the case to health departments, especially in Mexico.

CDC: US has 76 million food poisoning cases each year.

A staggering statistic from the US is that the Communicable Diseases Center estimates there are 76 million cases of food-borne disease each year, and 325,000 require hospitalization. Some 5,000 die each year, mainly the very old, the very young, and those with immune system problems. Food poisoning is not unique to Mexico.

Immunizations

Many people take every possible vaccination and immunization for every possible disease they might encounter in Mexico. It's your decision, partly based on your own general health and on the area of Mexico where you are going. Some of the more common shots are for hepatitis, for tetanus if you have not had a booster shot in many years, and for the salmonella/typhoid varieties of food poisoning. Norma and Carol didn't get any before they came, though after a major bout with food poisoning Norma seriously considered the salmonella shot and may still get one in the future before starting a round of traveling through more remote parts of Mexico.

Flu shots are available in late fall for whatever current form of flu is expected that winter, same as in the US and Canada. One immunization shot is being developed for the H1N1 flu that hit Mexico in April and May of 2009 and eventually turned out to be much milder than feared, though it spread worldwide. Mexico reacted swiftly to the threat of the epidemic and closed down all schools and public gathering spots in the country, even though that decision wreaked havoc with the economy. Mexico gained international praise for its quick response. The Mexican government has shown itself capable of handling international health crises as well as most regions of the US and Canada do.

These are the main differences in how you may need to adjust your personal health routines if you move to Mexico.

Personal Safety and Crime

In this chapter: Will drug wars affect you? Putting crime in perspective. A few border cities versus the rest of Mexico. To pay or not to pay a traffic policeman a mordida (bribe) in the rare case you may be asked. Differences in the police and judicial hierarchy and in the underlying legal principles in Mexico. Taxis. Cultural differences for women, gays and lesbians, and African-Americans. Don't let stereotypes and fears prevent you from pursuing your dreams.

E veryone who moves to Mexico comes with some concern about safety. Most of these worries grow out of inflated crime stories in the media in the US and Canada, and old movies that portray a Mexico that never existed.

And some stereotypes about crime have their roots in prejudices against and ignorance of Mexicans. As you listen to the fears coming from your family and friends as you talk about moving to Mexico, you will see that those who have actual experience in Mexico or with a Mexican community north of the border have the fewest stereotypes and dire predictions of your fate.

It breaks the authors' hearts to hear the stereotypes and fears of those who have never spent any real time in Mexico who keep putting down Mexico for crime, telling us that we must be living in deathly fear of being murdered, beheaded, or at least kidnapped at any moment. We're not. Expats in general live our daily lives as we did in the US or Canada, many times feeling even safer here than we did when we lived in some big city areas to the north.

Once you come to know and love the Mexican people, you will find that they are as likely to be law-abiding, generous, caring people as the average citizen in the US and Canada, though there is a criminal element everywhere. You take the same kinds of common sense precautions when you cross the border that you learned to do anyplace you have lived.

These precautions are exactly the same kind of preparation you grew up learning to do, and you were not particularly aware or afraid as you learned of these safeguards. They are common sense practices in today's world. Mexico outside of its high crime areas is no more dangerous than the US and Canada outside of their high crime areas.

So, what about the drug cartel wars?

The media in the US and Canada frequently report horrifying stories about drug gang violence in Mexico. These stories are often overblown; nevertheless, the violence is real, and it is a major problem for law enforcement. These Mexican organized crime leaders use the most sensational techniques, particularly decapitations with messages on the bodies for rival drug lords, to scare people, the same way that Al Capone and the Purple Gang and all the Prohibition rum runners and the Mafia have done in US history. Remember all the serial murderers in the US who have used signature horrors.

A statement from the Mexican embassy in Canada noted that 93% of the deaths in the drug wars have been members of the drug cartels fighting for territory. More than 30% of the bodies are never claimed. Even when law enforcement officers are also killed, too often the officers were corrupt themselves and working for one of the rival cartels. President Calderón's massive campaign to stop the narcotraffickers includes major investigations of corrupt police and political figures, many hundreds of whom have been arrested and fired. Innocent bystanders are almost never involved in these battles, although a few incidents have happened.

Carol and Norma and all of Los Angeles really did live in fear every night of having their homes invaded and being brutally massacred by the Night Stalker, as one case. When they left LA largely to escape the crime, they unsuspectingly moved next door to a rural Michigan home that Timothy McVeigh visited, before he went on to organize the largest domestic terrorism bombing in US history in Oklahoma City, killing 167, many of them children in a preschool.

The Mexican drug wars are turf wars—gangs fighting each other over control of the drug trade, and sending warnings to law enforcement. They have almost nothing to do with the general population. You are as likely to run into street drug violence as you are to run into a violent crime happening in the US.

And of course your chances of being involved in a serious car accident anywhere are even more likely, but no one stops driving. The chances of an innocent civilian getting in the way of a drug shootout are probably about the same chances you face going into convenience stores which are prone to armed robberies in the States. And if you stay out of the areas where the drug lords are battling it out, your chances of being involved in their battles are extremely slim. You're more likely to be hit by lightning in the US or Canada.

When President Felipe Calderón was elected to his six-year term, 2006-2012, he bravely ordered a crackdown on the narcotics traffickers as a major focus of his administration, vowing to end all organized crime in Mexico as a necessary step in the country's progress, and the drug cartels are not going quietly. As one is arrested, others battle to take over his (or her) turf. The US has voted to send more than a billion dollars to assist Mexico, realizing that it is US customers for the drugs and US guns which are supplying the drug cartels so that they can outgun Mexican police.

How does this affect visitors and those who live in Mexico?

The honest answer is hardly at all. In the years we have lived in Mexico, the drug wars have had no impact on our lives whatsoever, despite the fact that they do occur in our cities and the surrounding areas. Unless you are involved with illegal drugs, or live in the direct path of drug traffic, put drug gang violence near the bottom of your worry list. In only a few cities in Mexico, mostly near the border, are the drug cartels fighting it out.

Crime rates for almost all of Mexico are the same or less than in the US and Canada, impoverished transitory areas of big cities having higher personal crime rates than close-knit smaller communities anywhere in the world.

An interesting study by the US State Department of non-natural deaths of US citizens in Mexico during the three years of 2005-2007 found that 668 died of other than natural causes during 18 million visits to Mexico. This table shows the breakdown of those deaths:

Deaths	Cause	Percentage
389	Accidents	58%
128	Homicides	19%
85	Drowning	13%
61	Suicides	9%
5	Drug overdose	1%
668	TOTAL	100%

About 58% of the deaths were in car and plane accidents. Pedestrians don't have the right of way in most of Mexico, contrary to what visitors from the US and Canada expect. Remove the drowning, overdoses and suicides and you are left with 128 homicides of US citizens in Mexico in three years. That's one murder per 140,000 visits. Two thirds took place along the northern border cities, especially Tijuana, Ciudad Juaréz and Nuevo Laredo, and most of those were drug related. Many involved Mexican-Americans with dual citizenship who were suspected of being involved in drugs in some way.

Depending on which statistics you use, the murder rate for Mexico overall is 11 to 13 per 100,000. If it gets any worse it might get as high as the murder rate for New Orleans and other high-crime US cities!

Yes, of course comparing an entire country's murder rate to that of any big city is apples and oranges, and the murder rate in Cuidad

Juaréz is higher than that of New Orleans. But you get the picture. Vast areas of Mexico are fairly crime free the same way that vast areas of the US are fairly crime free.

An American or Canadian not involved with drug trafficking (or bar fights) has almost no chance of being murdered in Mexico. Drive, walk and swim carefully and stay away from drugs, and your chances of a non-natural death in Mexico are about zero.

What about other crime?

The most likely crimes an expat might experience are similar to the most common crimes in the US and Canada—occasional purse and wallet snatchings, burglaries of your home when you are not there, ATM and credit card fraud by global scam rings, an occasional deliberate case of getting the wrong change (usually poorly educated workers don't do it on purpose), and similar minor crimes. The police in the US don't usually pay much attention to these kinds of crimes, the same way that Mexican police will usually give you cursory attention if someone stole from your home while you weren't there.

Carol and Norma were burglarized five times in their last four years in Los Angeles, and even after the first break-in, when thousands of dollars in electronics and wrapped Christmas gifts were taken, the Ramparts Division police also said honestly to forget expecting anything to happen on their end.

Look at your Mexican neighbors' security measures

If you look around at your Mexican neighbors' security measures, you will see what makes good sense for your neighborhood. Decorative wrought iron window grills, high walls around courtyards, and plain facades that do not call attention to the wonderful homes behind the walls, are all the Mexican way since the Conquistadors brought the Spanish influence, as well as being good security measures. Neighborhood Watch associations, a barking dog, and maybe alarm systems, video cameras and motion detectors if your property is particularly valuable are common sense additions to any home.

Carol and Norma hated the thought of living behind bars in LA but they used their insurance money from that first burglary to install grills on all their windows. Soon they were thrilled at the feeling of security, at being able to leave windows open on hot evenings even if the Night Stalker was out there torturing Los Angeles residents. They have them on their windows in Mexico, too, as do their Mexican neighbors.

If you look at many Mexican homes you will see broken bottles installed along the tops of high walls around the courtyards. This is one precaution that you needn't bother to copy. Broken bottles and spikes are not much of a deterrent—a criminal can throw a heavy blanket or leather jacket over the bottles and scale the wall anyway.

Mexico is far more likely to have an expensive home on a block next to a very poor home, so you can't evaluate neighborhoods the same as you might in the US or Canada. It is good to visit the home late on a weekend as well as during the day to see if there are any gangs in the neighborhood, excessive noise, etc., same as you would in many US cities. Some call graffiti an art form; it is also a way for gangs to send messages and mark territory.

Did gangs and graffiti start in the US and returning young men bring them to Mexico, or vice versa, or some of both? Is it stereotyping to be frightened by what appear to be gangs in a neighborhood? Yes and no—certainly some young men are unfairly lumped into the category of "gang members" by virtue of being a group of Mexican men hanging out together. A gang can be simply a social grouping. But criminal gangs do exist and you will want to avoid moving into such a neighborhood.

With many Mexican homes being very small with no real living room, it is more likely that Mexicans of all ages will flock to the streets, to the parks, to the gardens, for their living room socializing. That is one of the attractions of Mexico—more people are out socializing, not isolated in their separate homes.

We think you'll find that small town Mexico is not all that different from small town USA—close knit, conservative and slow-paced. Likewise, large city Mexico is not that different from large city USA—diverse, impersonal and fast, with many areas that feel very safe and others that are not. Crime statistics are inaccurate anyplace, since especially in Mexico, crimes are rarely reported and police departments anyplace can label the same crime in different categories depending on many factors, not the least of which is to make their department's crime statistics look better.

In Detroit while working as a newspaper reporter, Carol noticed that a man attempting to murder his wife might be charged with simple domestic violence or even disturbing the peace, rather than attempted murder. The teenager of a police officer would be given a verbal reprimand for a burglary while another kid would go to prison. Crime statistics are not accurate anyplace.

The point is that the same things can happen to you in the US or in Mexico. You should take careful precautions when you go out in public in both countries. It seems that some people leave their common sense behind at the border. Always remember that you are instantly recognizable as a *norteamericano* and commonly viewed as being rich.

In any purse snatching anywhere in the world, give up your purse—whatever you have in it is not worth being pushed to the ground and perhaps breaking a limb or suffering a concussion, and you're going to lose it anyway. And don't carry valuables with you. The same is true anywhere in the world.

Mexicans, by and large, are friendly people, but they also tend to be reserved in public, not likely to interact with strangers beyond the expected social niceties.

When someone says "*Hola, buenos dias, como está?*" (Hello, good morning, how are you?) that is expected social protocol in Mexico. In high crime areas of the US, a prospective purse snatcher may be friendly and perhaps ask the time to size you up as a potential victim, while in Mexico these greetings are routine.

But when a stranger suddenly goes beyond these pleasantries to become quite friendly, be on guard the same way that you would north of the border. (Carol and Norma have to add that they developed a strong sense of street smarts in Detroit and Los Angeles, but when they moved back to rural Michigan for a few years, they soon found that on the small town sidewalks, a hello was meant as a hello. And a high crime in rural Michigan was when underwear was stolen off a clothes line, drawing full attention from the tiny police department.)

Our personal experiences

Carol and Norma have never personally experienced any crimes in Mexico or San Miguel de Allende and they live their daily lives without even thinking about it which was not true in Los Angeles.

Rolly states that he can say quite honestly that he feels safer in living in Lerdo than he did living in Los Angeles where his house was burglarized, or in Chicago where his apartment was burglarized and his car stolen. Boston=burglary, Little Rock=mugging, Memphis=burglary and car stolen. Rolly jokes that maybe he had a little dark cloud over his head in the US that went away when he moved to Mexico.

A couple of crimes may be more common in Mexico. Worldwide, tourists are hit every day by the mustard scam, where someone squirts mustard or ketchup on your back or water on your head, then the partner alerts you to it and offers to help you clean up. In the process your wallet slips away.

Kidnappings are very common in the US—remember all those photos on milk cartons. In Mexico they are usually of wealthier Mexicans for ransom, though some poorer Mexicans are being kidnapped lately as well. As the economy worsens, crime increases everywhere. When expats or tourists are kidnapped, it is almost always to get money out of their ATM, as often happens also in the US. In one case publicized internationally, a French tourist who visited a Mexico City airport ATM had many thousands of dollars on hand and he was killed for it, as he might have been if he showed that much cash anywhere.

One scam more common in Mexico is phony kidnappings, where someone, often a prisoner, calls randomly and demands ransom for a kidnapped child—even if the person answering the phone is holding the child safely. Mexicans with family members in the US illegally will often get a phony call saying their relative has been jailed or is in the hospital, and money must be sent to a certain account right away. In case you get any such random kidnapping call, report it to the police immediately. Certainly don't pay without having the call checked out.

To pay a bribe (*mordida*) or not

A few corrupt police use the speed trap scam in the US as well, but in Mexico you're more likely to encounter a traffic cop (*tránsito*) who wants a bribe (*mordida*) rather than writing you a ticket for a real or imagined traffic violation. These stops are rare but knowing about the possibility ahead of time may help you prepare for such a possibility. One place where these speed traps occur is a short distance below the border, where a corrupt cop knows you have money on hand for the trip south. You can insist on following the police car back to police headquarters to receive your ticket in person (and usually the corrupt cop will give up if you do insist on this and let you go), or you can pay the bribe.

Morally, of course, you should resist paying any bribe, and report any such attempt to authorities, to help Mexico fight its corruption problem. But some days you will be in a hurry, you will already be stressed from the entire experience of moving, you don't want to take the chance it might take overnight for your ticket to be issued back at the police department while you cool your heels waiting with a carload of goods, etc.

If you decide to pay the bribe, let the *tránsito* bring it up first— it's a crime, and you might be dealing with an honest cop and you made a legitimate driving error, even if you didn't know the law. Ignorance of the law is no excuse, any side of the border. Often the policeman will offer to take care of the ticket for you if you buy him a Coke, or lunch. Keep only a small amount of money in your wallet so that you can show him you have $50 USD and say that is all you have.

Rolly was stopped several times in Lerdo before 2003 when the city cracked down on police corruption. He once showed he had 20 pesos, about $1.60 USD, and another time he even got away with a five-peso coin, about 40 cents USD. If you're obviously moving down with a carload of goods, ready to pay some $50 USD in tolls and about the same in gasoline for the journey, nobody will believe you have only five pesos in your pocket. If you speak Spanish fluently, you will be better able to "negotiate." Otherwise, it may be better to keep repeating, "*No hablo español*," rather than get caught in an incorrect wording you didn't intend.

Paying a bribe is your choice. Few of us can take the high road all the time. If you accept the ticket, be prepared to have the officer remove your license plate and take your driver's license, which you reclaim at the police station when you pay your fine. That's standard practice for any traffic violation in Mexico, including for parking tickets.

Starting salaries for the various kinds of police officers in many Mexican police departments are $400-600 USD a month. In the past it was expected that police would earn most of their money from bribes and their salaries were deliberately kept low. They were not and often still are not respected by the Mexican people, who usually do not report crimes. In Mexico's 500 years since the Spanish conquest, encompassing centuries of harsh oppression, the police were the agents of the oppressors, and old attitudes die hard. Most cities are now attempting to upgrade their police departments and salaries to fight corruption. Thousands of corrupt police officers have been fired all across Mexico in recent years.

So forget what your well-meaning relatives and friends tell you about moving to Mexico. Take the same common sense precautions you do in any big city or tourist area in the US and Canada, and stay away from drugs.

Differences in the legal system

There are some things you should know about differences between the Mexican legal system and that of the US or Canada.

First, there are different levels and kinds of police officers. *Tránsitos*, the traffic officers, are real police. But they are not the regular police (*policía preventiva*) who deal with crimes. In most cities, the *tránsitos* are a separate police force with their own chain of command and bureaucracy, even different uniforms. They don't deal with criminal matters, and the regular police usually don't deal with traffic matters. Consider US traffic divisions such as the California Highway Patrol.

If you have a car accident, you call a *tránsito*. If you are mugged or feel you are in danger, you call the *policía preventiva*. If you want a crime prosecuted, you go to the Mexican equivalent of the district attorney, not the *policía preventiva*, and all of these departments may not communicate well with each other. In the next section, when we talk about police, we mean the *policía preventiva*, not the *tránsito* force.

Think of the *Law and Order* television series where the law part is the police and the order part is the judicial. In Mexico the lines are somewhat different, and it is important to know the distinctions. *Tránsito* police are involved with traffic. If you hear a burglar you phone the *policía preventiva*. After they check out the scene, if you want to report a crime has been committed and you want it prosecuted, you go to the *Procuraduria Generales*, who have their own police, the *policías judiciales*, and their own investigating agents of the public prosecutor (*ministerios públicos*). Their technical experts are the *peritos*. There are at least 330,000 preventive police throughout Mexico, and at least 25,000 judicial police.

At all levels the Mexican government is seeking to recruit a higher standard of law enforcement officers, train and pay them better, and fight corruption. President Calderón has commissioned a study of the qualifications of current *policía preventivas*, which has found that of those investigated so far, overall, half were corrupt or unqualified. In the worst drug cartel cities like Tijuana and Ciudad Juaréz, that figure was closer to 90%. Corrupt police are being fired as fast as they are discovered, and there is a major push on throughout Mexico to get better qualified police cadets, train them better, and pay them sufficient wages so that they are not tempted by the outrageous bribes offered by the drug lords.

In some major cases such as the current crackdown on narcotics, the Mexican military is called in to supplement local law enforcement. The military has long had the reputation of being the fairest and least corrupt policing agency. But they also have been accused of human rights violations in their stricter enforcement.

In 2009, the Mexican Chamber of Deputies (similar to the US House of Representatives) passed a law establishing a new category of Federal Police who would have the same powers as the *ministerio público* investigative police, as a sort of bridge between the military and the two types of police. They would be able to wiretap and check bank and phone records rapidly as another tool in combating the drug cartels. The law was expected to pass the Senate and be signed in to law by President Calderón, who had asked for the change. At the same time laws were being enacted that would allow more access to cell phone information, and require fingerprinting. It is likely that even more legal changes will be enacted as the crackdown continues on the drug cartels.

The chances you will ever be involved in any sort of crime where you will need to know these distinctions are very small, but be aware that the police system in Mexico is not exactly like the US or Canada.

You should also know that the Mexican legal system is in the process of major reform. A Constitutional amendment was passed in 2008 that will not be fully enforced until 2016, and the major change is that you will be considered innocent until proven guilty.

In the past, Mexico's legal system has come from Roman and Napoleonic Code where you are considered guilty until proven innocent. (Louisiana and the US Internal Revenue Service still operate on the principle that you are guilty unless you can prove yourself innocent.) US and Canadian laws mostly evolved from the British Magna Carta.

When the reform is fully in effect by 2016 (four states have already made the transition), judges will have to hear all cases in public.

Trial arguments will be presented orally, instead of the judge reading written statements behind closed doors. Mexico does not require a trial by a jury of your peers. The judge renders both the verdict and sentence. Decisions can be quick or take years. Certainly in the past and too often today, corruption has been involved at every step. The US is assisting Mexico in training its lawyers for the transition to oral presentations before audiences.

President Calderón in April, 2009, asked for a partial decriminalization of possessing very small amounts of marijuana, cocaine, heroin and methamphetamines, as a way to concentrate drug fighting efforts on the cartels rather than on individual users of very small amounts. This change will be another major difference between the laws of Mexico, the US and Canada.

Another legal issue often a surprise to expats is that the Mexican Constitution forbids foreigners from getting involved in Mexican politics. If you take part in a demonstration against the Mexican government or give a donation to a Mexican political candidate, for example, you could be deported immediately.

Also, the laws on defamation are very different. In 2007 a federal law was passed making defamation a civil crime, where you have to sue for actual damages, rather than simply report someone for defaming your character and that person can be put in jail immediately on a criminal charge.

But in many states defamation is still a criminal offense, and truth is not necessarily a defense. (Libel is defaming someone via the written word, slander is oral defamation.) Mexican culture places high value on saving face, and damaging a person's reputation or business image is serious business.

Until the constitutional amendment explained above is fully in effect, you are still considered guilty until you can prove yourself innocent. The chances are extremely slim anyone would file a formal defamation charge against you no matter what you say, of course, but the law is there.

The Mexican Constitution in general favors the average citizen, such as an employee over an employer, or a renter or squatter over an owner. It is important to realize that Mexican law is in many areas very different from the legal systems of the US and Canada.

When do I need a police report?

If you lose property which is insured—camera, laptop, jewelry—your insurance company is going to want to see a police report. If you lose important papers—passport, car permit, visa—you may need a police report, as well as your report to Mexican Immigration, your Consul, your insurance company, etc. Sometimes it is a major pain to get a police report of what the police consider a minor crime, so you may need to be very persistent. Reports of car accidents are usually forthcoming from the *tránsitos* without undue pain. (More information on what to do if you are in a car accident is in Chapter 11 in Part Four, Living in Mexico.)

If you do have the misfortune to become the victim of a crime in Mexico, be aware that it may feel difficult to report it, and you may even feel as if you are being accused of the crime yourself. Persevere. Bring someone who is fluent with you to make your report. It may take hours, because what you are telling the investigator is what will be the basis for the court case if the criminal is caught.

Pepper spray and mace are legal and can be found in many hardware stores and open air markets. Guns are not. It is extremely difficult to obtain a gun permit in Mexico. Don't even think of trying to smuggle one down with you or you could be spending decades in a terrible jail. US customs officers are now checking cars headed into Mexico for guns and laundered money as well.

Counterfeiting is a problem from time to time. All peso bills have a metallic thread embedded in the paper to foil counterfeiters. If a bill lacks this thread, it is not legit. Mexico is changing over its bills to make them more difficult to counterfeit, and the latest bills are made of plastic and have cellophane windows and other safeguards.

Real estate and other contractual scams will be discussed in the housing sections. Suffice to say, in buying real estate or building a house or any other legal matter, you need to exercise great care.

Scams in these areas are more common than in the US, and often they are hard to detect in advance. "Let the buyer beware" is good advice anywhere.

Are taxis safe?

In Mexico City take cabs from *sitios*, clearly marked secure taxi stands, or have your hotel call one for you, or hire a cab from a kiosk within an airport or bus terminal. Check to see if the identification number on the side of the green and white striped cab matches the number on the back as well, and it should have an L or S in front of the number. The green VW bug taxis are being phased out because they were particularly likely to be unsafe, as well as usually not meeting pollution controls.

In other cities you should have no problems hailing a cab anyplace. You may want to casually note the license inside the cab, and let the driver see that you have noted it, without being so obvious that it appears you are accusing the driver from the start of being a criminal. At airports and bus stations you will have to buy your ticket from a kiosk inside and then go to the lineup of taxis waiting outside with your paid ticket.

Women, gays, lesbians, color consciousness, hate crimes

Some Mexicans have disapproving views of women who go into a bar alone (especially do not go into a *cantina*, traditionally men's territory where unescorted women are usually prostitutes). Take clothing cues from locals—what you wear on the beach back home differs from what you wear in a conservative inland small town, too. You cannot assume that the same signals and assumptions apply in Mexico as back home. Rape happens, of men and of women. It is rarely reported in this country which still places a great deal of emphasis on *machismo*, though that is lessening every day.

Gays and lesbians living in Mexico generally experience no problems but the same kinds of hate crimes can happen as in the US and Canada. Though many cities and areas of Mexico are particularly welcoming to gays and lesbians—the Zona Rosa in Mexico

City, Puerta Vallerta and other popular beach cities, San Miguel de Allende and Ajijíc/Lake Chapala, for example—public displays of gay affection in conservative areas may not be prudent. Mexican straight women are more likely to hold hands and hug in public than in the US, and so lesbians can sometimes "blend in" more easily than gay men.

Mexico is very color conscious. African-Americans and African-Canadians may notice discrimination based on darker skin colors, counter-balanced by their desirable status as Americans and Canadians. Mexican culture freely uses descriptive nicknames including *Negro* (the color black) and *Gordo* (fatso) easily, no slight intended. If someone is putting you down, you will probably be able to tell by body language and tone of voice—words may have very different connotations in Mexico. Some 15% of the population in parts of Mexico is dark-skinned from the slave trade, and Mexico's history includes major contributions by African and Caribbean influences, though not all Mexicans are aware of it, as not all US and Canadian citizens know and appreciate their diverse histories. Hate crimes can happen in Mexico, too, but they seem to be rarer than in the US, at least in the authors' experiences.

Find out the emergency number in your area—066 is a common number for police but it is not used in all areas. In San Miguel it goes to a general emergency switchboard that can summon the police, fire department (*bomberos*), an ambulance or doctors. In other parts of Mexico different numbers are used for different services. In many areas the number for the *preventiva* police is 066, Red Cross 065, fire department, 080, ambulances and urgent medical 086, car theft report 061, or the Green Angels (mechanics who travel the main highways in vans to help motorists whose vehicles have broken down), 078. One of the first things you should do in any new area is to find out what the local emergency numbers are. There is a move to standardize emergency numbers nationwide as the US did with 911.

When you call the emergency number, the switchboard will be answered in Spanish. Be able to give your address in Spanish.

It is good to memorize a few common emergency words or have them by your phone: robber (*ladrón*), rapist (*violador*), fire (*incendio*), intruder (*intruso*), noise (*ruido*), gang (*pandilla*), gun (*pistola*), knife (*puñal*), heart attack (*ataque cardiaco*), no breathing (*no respiración*), copious blood (*mucho sangre*), death (*muerte*), traffic accident (*accidente de tránsito*), need a doctor (*necesito un doctor*), need an ambulance (*necesito una ambulancia*), need the fire department (*necesito bomberos*), need the police (*necesito policia*).

Don't let thinking about such a list scare you off—you learned in childhood how to call the police or fire department, how to make a report clearly, how to give your address. Being prepared for an emergency does not mean you are going to experience that emergency, it merely means you are being sensibly prepared.

In short, you need not fear for your physical safety—or your health— in Mexico any more than anyplace else, once you take the same kinds of reasonable precautions you would take anyplace else.

Don't let fear prevent you from pursuing your dreams

In Part One we haven't sugarcoated any of the three main fears many people have of moving to Mexico: cost of living, health care, and crime. These are the deal-breaker questions for many people as they first begin to seriously consider relocating.

We hope we haven't scared you off as we've given you the full picture to help you decide whether you really can move to Mexico. Now that you know the truth in depth about these issues that were probably your main fears about moving to Mexico, you can assuredly go ahead with your dreams.

In **Part Two** you'll find out the major areas of Mexico you may choose to live, and how life could be like for you in each kind of Mexican area, whether in an expat haven or a city where you are the sole foreigner. **Part Three** will help you make the move smoothly. Part Four will be devoted to your new life in Mexico.

Part Two

Where in Mexico is Best For You?

Chapter 7

What's Your Closest Fit?

*In this chapter: Figuring out what you really want in a new home lo-
cation. How Rolly and Carol and Norma made their decisions. The
varied kinds of lifestyles you can live in a city with many expats, compared to how you might live in a town where you are the sole expat.
A trip around Mexico looking at potential relocation areas in all 31
states and the Federal District (Mexico City) Map (pages 118-19).*

Now that we have talked about the three most common
worries about moving to Mexico—cost of living, health
care, and personal safety—and if you're still with us, you
will probably want to start thinking of what your life in Mexico
could be like.

This will depend largely on you and on the area you choose to
live. There is no one answer to the question of where is the best place
to live in Mexico; there is no one perfect destination for everybody
house hunting in the US or Canada, either. These are some of the
starting questions to ask yourself.

Do you need the ocean nearby and crave a beach city? Will you
be living there year-round and are you able to handle the high heat
and humidity of many beach cities in the summers? Or would you
prefer an historic colonial city, filled with traditional architecture
and culture, even minus a beach? Would Ajijíc/Lake Chapala (about
5,000 feet altitude) or Lake Pátzcuaro (about 7,000 feet above sea

level), two beautiful inland lakes with many expats living nearby, combine the best of both worlds for you? (By the way, you shouldn't swim and engage in water contact sports in many Mexican lakes, which are often polluted, but the lakes may solve your boating and scenery urges.)

Do you think you'd fit best into an area with a large English-speaking expat population, at least to get you oriented to Mexico? Or is living with other gringos the last thing on earth you want—you envision a small Mexican town to live closer to average Mexican people not connected with tourism?

Do you thrive in large cities and want all that a Mexico City or Guadalajara can offer? Do you need to be close to a particular kind of terrain for your favorite sports? Must you be in a city where you can join a chamber music orchestra or a jazz band or pursue a similar specialized interest? Maybe you can't live without horses and must be in horse country. Or can you not imagine living where you can't go fishing on a whim? Do the waves have to be spectacular for your surfing urge? Does the snorkeling have to be great?

Do you need a low altitude for your health? Do you have to have an excellent hospital very close by? Are your prescription needs so crucial that you must be close to the border to ensure you can always get your medicines despite any screw-ups with your meds in Mexico? Are you tied to a specific medical center in the US and you'll need to get to it easily and quickly in case of emergencies?

Do you need to be close to the border, or at least to a major air-port, so that you can get back to family frequently? Do you have a realistic idea of how often your kids and grandkids will come visit you, and how often you can visit them? Many parents and grandparents who move to Mexico find that no matter how much their kids tried to make them feel guilty about "abandoning" them to move to Mexico, once the strings are cut their family members manage quite well and may even come so rarely the parents wonder what happened. (But when they do visit, they may prefer visiting you in Mexico rather than having you come back up north. You'll probably prefer it that way, too.)

Choosing the best place in Mexico for you to live is as individual a decision as choosing a career, or even a spouse. For that matter, how do you choose a career or even a spouse? Are you someone who believes in love at first sight and would marry someone after a few days? You may be one of those who trusts your instincts and falls in love with a Mexican city immediately upon arrival and starts house hunting. Have you stumbled into your favorite jobs in the past, or did you do months of intensive research and careful job hunting to get those positions? The same kind of approach you take to other major decisions in your life will probably be what you will do to find the best place for you in Mexico, maybe with similar outcomes.

It must be said that wherever you go, there you are, personal baggage and all. If you are overall a happy, adaptable person, your chances of finding many places within Mexico that suit you well are better than if you can never find a place to live that you like in the US or Canada, either. If you have a hard time reaching out to make friends where you are now, your personality will come with you here. But it may be easier to make friends with both Mexicans and expats in what is generally a more relaxed environment where family and friends are more valued and they come first when time is allotted.

How Rolly found his home

My first contact with Mexico happened in 1987 when I went to Manzanillo to visit a friend I had met when he lived in Los Angeles. During that ten-day trip, I fell in love with Mexico. I commented to my friend that I felt I had lived there in a previous life. I understood, for the first time, why my grandmother had lived in Mexico City for extended periods in the 1930s and '40s. I returned to Manzanillo many times over the next few years.

During that time, I had occasion to pick up a day laborer on a street near my home to help with spring clean up in my yard. He was a legal Mexican who spoke no English. What happened next is a story for another book. Suffice to say, today he speaks English, is a US citizen, and I live in a little retirement cottage that he and I built in his back yard in Lerdo, Durango. I moved here in the spring of 2000, nine years after I first met Enrique. Today I am an adopted member of his large extended family. My Spanish still stinks, but I get by very well. Of the many adventures in my life, none has been as deeply satisfying as my life in Mexico.

Carol and Norma's discovery of San Miguel

As told in greater detail in their book, *Falling...in Love with San Miguel: Retiring to Mexico on Social Security,* Carol and Norma were living in a senior citizen RV park near Phoenix and going slowly mad from boredom and from irritation at the internecine infighting and rules fetishes of the other retirees.

When Norma was elected to the board and named treasurer, she raised the dues to keep the park from going into the red and made many cutbacks in spending, causing half the park to hate her. One resident in a drunken rage even tried to drown Norma one night in the pool. Norma started to dream of moving to Mexico, something she had been thinking about since she first visited Baja in 1960.

Carol had never been impressed by Mexico in her short visits, but Norma started doing research on the net and stumbled upon San Miguel de Allende and fell in love with the town sight unseen. She convinced Carol to spend three months there studying art to escape the 120-degree Phoenix summer in 2002.

After three days in San Miguel Carol asked, "What do you think about moving here?" Norma responded, "Thank heavens—it had to be your idea." They rushed home, sold their RV park model, and have been happily in love with San Miguel ever since. They've passed the seven-year itch that struck them every other place they've lived in the US and the thought of leaving has never entered their minds.

It was part luck that the town they chose to spend three months at happened to meet all their needs as they analyzed them later. It was medium size, with plenty of activities and organizations, and many liberal and artsy expats to help them settle in. It had art classes and a thriving writers' colony. It was a walking city where they could get out of their dependence on cars. The location was central Mexico to make it easy to do side trips throughout the country. It had a temperate climate year-round because of its 6,400 foot high elevation. Many free or low-cost happenings made it possible to enjoy the city's cultural and entertainment offerings even on a budget.

Most importantly, it was a beautiful colonial city with vivid colors and abundant flowers and an open feeling that made them both respond instantly and even viscerally. They've been in similar-sized colonial cities since that somehow never clicked with them.

Though the love at first sight folks often are very happy with their first choice and never regret it, usually it is better advice to look around, to rent in a city during all seasons of the year and all holiday periods to know it well before you settle down. The usual advice is to stay a year before committing, but you can get a good idea of what a typical holiday is like in your town after having experienced a few, and people will tell you honestly about your town's pros and cons as you get to know them. With this economic market, it may be difficult to sell a home quickly and move on if you change your mind soon.

Like finding the "best" place to live in the US or Canada

We'll give a sweeping overview of some of the favorite expat areas in the 31 states of Mexico, to get your imagination flowing. It is admittedly superficial and incomplete—imagine one chapter attempting to tell someone from another country where the "best" places are to live in all of the US states or Canadian provinces.

The goal of this chapter is to open your mind to all the possibilities in Mexico and get you started in doing further research into any areas that interest you. If one grabs you, do more research before visiting. Google the state and the city or town, set up a *www.news.google.com* alert to get all news stories about the area, go to *www.yahoogroups.com* and sign up for any email lists for the region you are considering and sign up, subscribe to any of the region's publications, start asking around for opinions from those you know who travel extensively in Mexico.

Expats are found in each of the 31 states of Mexico and its Distrito Federal, besides Ajijíc/Lake Chapala, San Miguel de Allende,

Baja, Puerto Vallarta, Cancún and other areas you've probably heard about where expats have settled.

A caveat: we decided not to do much with those areas that the US State Department lists as having considerable drug violence: Tijuana/Rosarita, Ciudad Juaréz, Nuevo Laredo, Nogales, Matamoros, and much of the states of Sinaloa and Chihuahua. The US State Department also warns of political violence in parts of the southern states of Chiapas, Guerrero and Oaxaca. Drug cartel infighting has been reported in parts of Durango, Coahuila, Nuevo León and Michoacán as well.

Though millions of people live in these areas without ever experiencing any kind of violence, and it can be argued that the State Department warnings are overblown and sometimes political, we are not going to feature areas that we know are currently in the middle of drug cartel violence. If you get a job offer or otherwise need to seriously consider one of these areas, carefully research what your daily life will really be like there.

Ordinary people live enjoyable lives even in high crime US areas like Atlanta, Philadelphia, Detroit, Dallas and Houston. No one says, don't go to Disneyworld or settle in Orlando because of drug running off the coast of Miami. No one would avoid Prince Edward Island because of a shootout in Montreal.

All of Mexico is worth discovering, and there is an area of Mexico for everyone looking for their own idea of paradise.

Five very different lifestyles in one city as an example

Let's start with San Miguel Allende in depth, the city Carol and Norma know the best. The 12,000 or so foreigners living in SMA, some 70% from the US and 20% from Canada as well as from 30 other countries, live 12,000 different kinds of lives, each one individual and unique, in the same way that the possibly one million foreigners living throughout Mexico all have their own stories. You will write your own story as well.

But this examination might help you think about how life might be for you in any colonial central community in Mexico where there is at least some expat community—Ajijíc/Lake Chapala, Guanajuato, Querétaro, Morelia, Pátzcuaro, Oaxaca, San Luis Potosí, Monterrey, Puebla, Cuernavaca, Zacatecas, Aguascalientes, and Tequisquiapan are a few others. We'll give highlights and differences for each of these cities later, and then also for many of the beach cities and areas of southern Mexico.

San Miguel and Ajijíc/Lake Chapala have high percentages of expats, though perhaps there are more in Mexico City and Tijuana. There is a reason for their popularity: they are both highly desirable communities.

At the same time, that popularity makes them despised by some who charge that the very presence of 12-15,000 foreigners changes the towns for the worse. Others say that the money, enthusiasm, and volunteer work from these expats have made both areas far richer, in more ways than economically, than they would have been if no expat had ever discovered them. Some note that it has been expats who were largely behind efforts to revitalize San Miguel when it was almost a ghost town around 1930, its history ignored, its 16th century buildings largely in ruins.

The most popular girl in school is also going to be the one most criticized. And yet she is still the most popular for some reason. 12-15,000 happy expats can't be all wrong. As Yogi Berra said of some other place, "Nobody goes there any more, it's too crowded." People are still flocking to both areas, despite the naysayers.

So what are some of the ways expats live in a central colonial city with many other expats like San Miguel? As usual, money plays a large role, as does age, health, interests, and marital/relationship status. An elderly frail woman living near poverty will have a far different lifestyle in SMA than a wealthy, active younger couple. These five stories incorporate many of Carol's and Norma's friends' lives though names and details have been changed and intermixed.

Anna on limited means

Anna is 82 and came to SMA to study Spanish in the late '60s so that she could earn more money as a bilingual teacher in Miami. There she met a vet studying art at the Instituto Allende on the GI Bill and never left. Because she worked in the States for only 20 years when incomes were low, and her late husband's US income was also very low before he moved to Mexico, her Social Security is $650 USD a month. Luckily her husband bought a home near the Instituto for a few thousand dollars way back when, and she still lives there. She's been on *inmigrado* status for decades so doesn't have to worry about visa renewals or income qualifications any more. Her property taxes are less than $100 USD a year. She lives frugally but can't think of a thing she needs.

She putters in her garden and goes to all the activities at nearby St. Paul's Episcopal Church. A highlight of her week is the sociable breakfasts after Sunday services, and she enjoys making mattresses from recycled plastic grocery bags for poor families once a week at the church. The work sessions remind her of the quilting bees her mother used to talk about.

Another favorite volunteer activity is socializing the kittens and puppies brought to the Sociedad de Proteccion des Animales to make them more adoptable. She offers a volunteer foster home for the tiniest kittens and pups who need bottle feeding around the clock until they are healthy enough to live in the shelter. She's got friends from the church and they go to the movies on discount Wednesdays and know all the Mexican holes-in-the-wall where they can get their main meal before 4 pm, *comida corrida*, for under $4 USD.

Brad the perpetual wild child

Then there's Brad, still a bit of a wild child, though he's 41. A messy divorce in Wichita sent him off on the road trip of all road trips to find himself, and somehow he landed in San Miguel. He's not sure if his visa is up to date, and he does odd jobs under the table, not thinking much about getting legal working papers. If he gets deported, no big deal, he'll start up some other place.

He's a pretty good mechanic, he can be a driver and tour guide if asked, he'll cook up a backyard catering feast for a friend's party, he tutors some wealthy Mexican kids in English for a few bucks, he'll videotape a wedding or baptism, he'll help somebody move to a new apartment. Very low-key, word-of-mouth only. He keeps his listing out of the phone book.

He's got a Mexican girlfriend whose father hates gringos and doesn't trust Brad in particular, though Brad doesn't understand why. Lately he's been living at her parents' house in Colonia San Rafael—he built a small room on the back of the two-room family home for him and his *novia*, which assuaged the father a bit. He keeps making repairs and renovations to the house to further win over the father, though Brad is not sure why he bothers, he's probably not going to be around long.

Last winter was kind of cold, he's thinking about hitting the beach around Zihuatanejo next November. Or maybe Baja, or Quintana Roo. He won't tell his girlfriend until shortly before he goes—if he tells her at all. Sometimes he wishes somebody would turn him in to Immigration so that he'd get a free ride back to the border and never have to worry about deportation again—it would be over with. Maybe the oil rigs are hiring in New Orleans.

Chris, into everything

Chris is a retired policewoman from San Francisco who has enough of a pension and savings to hold out until her Social Security checks start coming in four more years. She's got a sweet one-bedroom apartment in Colonia Guadalupe for $600 a month and she keeps an old VW Beetle with Mexican plates for running around.

And she does get around. She's into everything—a bit part in any play, ceramics and beading classes, mentor for one of the girls on scholarship through the Biblioteca, tour director for the *Patronatos por Niños* walking tours around the historic Centro to raise money for children's medical needs, and volunteer for the Biblioteca House and Garden tours. Hospice volunteer to relieve caretakers who need a break, voter registration for every US election, fundraising for the local Red Cross ambulance program…let her know and she'll be there. Her life is a whirl, and she has plenty of friends who are very much like her, living life to the fullest, loving San Miguel.

Tad and Rich, not missing the "gay ghetto"

Tad and Rich lived in a mostly-gay area of Ferndale, Michigan, and now their old friends can't believe they live in a town without a single gay bar. They say it's the price of finally achieving full equality in a community—who needs gay bars and clubs when they are totally accepted in their very integrated circle of friends? This is what they were fighting for all those years in gay organizations in Detroit, the gay men's professional groups, the activist groups, the political movements.

Tad lost his job as a graphics designer for General Motors and now works online for clients all over the US, most of whom don't even know he's in Mexico. Rich teaches English online for an international language school and often is before a camera hooked up to his computer listening to a student in India practicing her pronunciation at an hour that is morning to her, evening in San Miguel.

They sold their luxury condo in Michigan before the housing bubble burst and were able to buy a four-bedroom home in Colonia San Antonio for $300,000 which is now Party Central for their wide circle of friends.

Denise and Gerard, torn between Montreal and San Miguel

Denise and Gerard still call Montreal home though they find themselves spending more and more months each year in their million-dollar Colonia Guadiana home in San Miguel. They don't really care about keeping up their Canadian residency for at least six months a year to maintain their health care. They've got the best international health insurance in the world and would prefer to fly to Mayo Clinic or Johns Hopkins or ABC Hospital in Mexico City when they have a medical problem.

Gerard is weeding out his remaining architectural clients, Denise rarely accepts another assignment designing dental suites. They've earned their retirement and they want to enjoy it while they can.

Denise doesn't want to use her artistic talents for dental suite renderings and choosing upholstery fabric any more, she wants to loosen up and experiment with watercolor when she's in San Miguel.

She still considers herself a dilettante, but she hopes someday to have a gallery in Fabrica Aurora, or at least an occasional show.

Gerard is finding to his surprise that he likes working with his hands in actual construction instead of designing architectural plans. When he's in San Miguel he volunteers with Casita Linda, an organization that builds very low-cost homes for the poorest Mexicans living in shacks and under tarps in outlying San Miguel. He always admired Habitat for Humanity, and now Gerard is helping to build basic small homes himself.

They could live anyplace in the world and sometimes think Portugal or Greece might have been good choices, too. But San Miguel always feels like home when they arrive each October, and more and more they hate to go back to Montreal in June.

These sketches represent five possibilities out of 12,000 lifestyles of San Miguel de Allende, or other Mexican towns with large expat populations. None of them sound like the "thundering gringo hordes" some critics, both Mexican and foreign, say are out to destroy Mexico. They're people, as diverse as in any US or Canadian town, building their own unique lives.

Why some people leave

Not everyone stays in San Miguel or any other part of Mexico forever. Those who leave mostly do so for health reasons, or to move back with their families. One gay man came to San Miguel from a very conservative small Midwestern town with no other open gays to find a lover, and when he didn't, he moved back home. Another woman came to find a Mexican boyfriend, and when none of them worked out and she was lonely in the home she bought far from Centro, she moved back in with her daughter NoB. Another couple who have lived all over the world finally had it with all the inconveniences and problems of daily living and are moving back to the US, "tired of living in a third-world country." Another man started to feel insecure walking on cobblestones and irregular streets as he aged, and he returned to a US city where all the sidewalks and streets are paved and smooth. For some, San Miguel is too big, or too small, or too poverty-stricken, or too wealthy, or too cold, or too hot, or too dirty, or too gentrified, or "too Mexican," or "not Mexican enough." If it were perfect for every taste SMA would have a million expats. Traffic is congested enough as it is.

If you want an out-of-the-way town that hasn't been discovered yet, then you'll have to discover it yourself, possibly starting out in a town without all the comfortable expat resources and learning along the way about you and your surroundings and what little town makes you happy, before you can escape into expat oblivion.

A very different lifestyle with few or no other expats

Read Rolly's website descriptions of his life in Lerdo and his involvement in an extended Mexican family. He has come to share their interests, their excitement, their fun, rather than coming with any expectations of how his new life should be. He teaches English to high school kids in his neighborhood to help them get a head start on college and careers. He documents the daily lives of the people around him, such as the major event of a pig slaughtering and all the kinds of foods that come out of the occasion.

He has come to understand and appreciate the hard but fulfilling lives of these Mexican families in a far more intense way than an expat in a town where there is so much to do in the expat community that it is easy to never come into deep contact with any Mexicans. He is embedded in his town more than most expats manage to achieve in an expat enclave. (But learning Spanish is still hard for him even when nobody around him speaks much English. It is not necessarily true that being immersed in Spanish means you will soon become fluent.)

These are a few examples of how expats might live in any community. There are a million (or however many the expat population is in Mexico) more stories, all different, from all the expats in this vast and diverse country. You can write your own.

Choosing a new home is totally individual, and once you've decided what kind of city or town you want and the approximate region, you are on to the next stage of your research—exploring.

Spend time in the area that interests you—maybe a year

Even if you think online or in books you've discovered the perfect spot, or one town caught your attention on a previous vacation, spend considerable time in the area before making a major move, preferably in different times of the year.

Look at an area late Saturday night as well as on a Sunday morning and a weekday afternoon. Don't invest all of your savings or your home-sale nest egg in the first house that appeals to you. Rent for awhile and get to know more about your chosen destination and the neighborhoods within that area that might be the best fit.

You may even decide to rent the rest of your life, either because you can't afford to buy a house for cash in a cash society, or you simply prefer the freedom of renting. Your choice, it's your dream.

Now for an overview of today's Mexico, starting with the Baja Peninsula. We'll look at the various states, cities and regions of Mexico to give you some starting points. We'll do a giant lopsided W, beginning on the west coast below the California border, traveling down the Baja peninsula, swinging up to the northwestern part of mainland Mexico and down the Pacific and Sea of Cortez coast, visiting lower Mexico and the Yucatan Peninsula, and then swinging back up the Atlantic/Caribbean coast before examining the central states.

This is not by any means a complete look at Mexico, only the highlights of possible areas of interest to potential expats. The descriptions and opinions of each area are solely the authors, and the three of us don't agree on all of them. And we make no claims to have visited every area. Where we have, you will know from our deeper descriptions. Where we haven't, admittedly this book may sound like an abstract travel brochure. This section is only a tasting. The feasting will be yours.

You may find your perfect home in an area we don't even mention that truly is undiscovered. And then you probably won't tell anybody else, much less the authors.

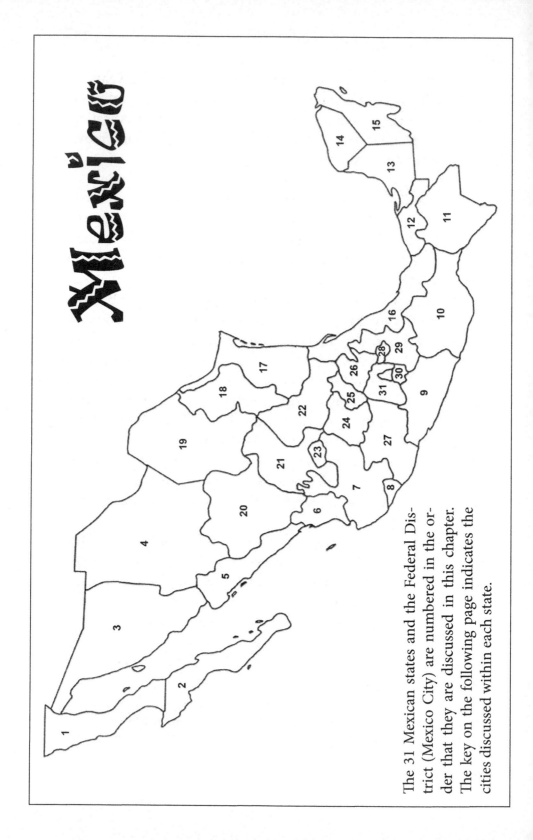

Mexico

The 31 Mexican states and the Federal District (Mexico City) are numbered in the order that they are discussed in this chapter. The key on the following page indicates the cities discussed within each state.

1. **Baja California (North)**
   Tijuana, Mexicali, Valle de Guadalupe, Ensenada, Rosarita Beach, Punda Banda, Tecate, San Felipe, Punta Colonet

2. **Baja California Sur**
   Guerra Negro, Santa Rosalia, Mulegé, Loreto, La Paz, Bahía de Palmas, Todos Santos, Santo Tomas, San Jose del Cabo, Cabo San Lucas

3. **Sonora**
   Puerto Penasco (Rocky Point), Kino Bay (Bajia de Kino), Guaymas/San Carlos

4. **Chihuahua**
   Barrancas del Cobre (Copper Canyon), Chihuahua, Ciudad Juaréz

5. **Sinaloa**
   Mazatlan

6. **Nayarit**
   San Blas, Sayulita, San Francisco (San Pancho)

7. **Jalisco**
   Guadalajara, Lake Chapala, San Antonio Tlayacapa, Ajijic, San Juan Cosalá, Jocotepec, Tonalá, Tlaquepaque, Puerto Vallarta, Nueva Vallarta, Mismaloya, Boca de Tomatlán

8. **Colima**
   Manzanillo, La Manzanilla, Tenacatita, Melaque

9. **Guerrero**
   Zihuaterejo, Ixtapa, Troncones, La Majaia, Acapulco, Taxco

10. **Oaxaca**
    Escondido, Puerto Angel, Huatulco, Oaxaca

11. **Chiapas**
    San Cristóbal de las Casas

12. **Tabasco**
    Villahermosa

13. **Campeche**
    Campeche

14. **Yucatan**
    Mérida Chichén Itzá

15. **Quintana Roo**
    Cancún, Puerto Moreles, Cozumel, Isla Mujeres, Playa del Carmen, Akumal, Puerto Aventuras, Tulum, Cobá, Chetumal

16. **Vera Cruz**
    Xalapa, Veracruz

17. **Tamaulipas**
    Reynoso, Nuevo Laredo, Tampico, La Pesca, Ciudad Victoria

18. **Nuevo León**
    Monterrey

19. **Coahuila**
    Saltillo, Torreón

20. **Durango**
    Lerdo, Gómez Palacio

21. **Zacatecas**
    Zacatecas

22. **San Luis Potosí**
    San Luis Potosí, Matahuela, Real Catorce, Xilitla, Las Pozas

23. **Aguascalientes**
    Aguascalientes, Azientos, Tepezalá

24. **Guanajuato**
    Guanajuato, San Miguel de Allende, Dolores Hidalgo, Atotonilco, Mineral de Pozos, Salvatierra, Salamanca, León, Irapuato, Celaya

25. **Querétaro**
    Querétaro, Tequisquiapan, Bernal, Sierra Gorda

26. **Hidalgo**
    Tula de Allende, Pachuca

27. **Michoacán**
    Morelia, Pátzcuaro, Tzintzuntzan, Urupuan

28. **Tlaxcala**
    Tlaxcala, Xochitecatl, Cacaztla

29. **Puebla**
    Puebla, Chohula

30. **Morelos**
    Cuernevaca, Cuautla, Chalcatzingo, Xochicalco, Las Grutas de Cacahuamilpa, Tepoztlán, Tlatacapan

31. **Mexico, Federal District**
    Toluca, Lerma, the Federal District, Mexico City, Valle de Bravo, Ixtapan de la Sal

BAJA CALIFORNIA (north)

Nearly a thousand miles long with nearly two thousand miles of beaches, Baja is two Mexican states, named Baja California and Baja California Sur, north and south. Some 75% of the population of the northern state of Baja population lives in Tijuana below San Diego, or in the capital city Mexicali.

Baja California to the north includes beaches, forests, deserts, and the Sierra de Baja mountain range that divides the climate of the state into the more semi-arid northwest, the moderate and more humid central section (one of the central valleys, Valle de Guadalupe, is a major wine producer, indicating its Mediterranean climate), the Sonoran Desert to the east, and the dry southern region, including the Vizcaino desert and many islands.

It is probably true that Tijuana has more expatriates than any other part of Mexico besides perhaps Mexico City. Since it is one of the cities hit hardest by the drug wars, we won't go into much detail, but because of the size of the expat population it does deserve mention.

Many US citizens living along the south side of the border continue to work in the US, while many Mexicans cross the border every day in every border city to work as domestics, hotel and restaurant staff—and business owners and professionals and every occupation in-between.

To live in the city of Tijuana is like living in any large border city in the world—you can make yourself at home anywhere, but there will be a sense all around you that things are in flux. The population is transitory, so many people are *flotillas*, temporary residents from all over the globe waiting for visas to enter the US. (Tijuana and the rest of Baja to the north also have one of the largest Asian populations in Mexico, with many Chinese settling in Mexicali.)

Tijuana has been hit hard by the drug wars, and even some middle class Mexican families have moved their businesses north of the border to escape the violence. Tourism and business authorities have initiated many programs to restore economic stability and a feeling of security. The bustling shopping and tourism area of downtown Tijuana, once noted for its zebra-painted burros waiting for you to photograph them for a fee, street vendors hustling gaudy ceramic vases and statues to those in line at the border crossing, and drug stores filled with Americans purchasing cheaper prescriptions, has had its problems. Outlying shopping areas are often as busy as ever, however.

The majority of Tijuana residents will never be affected in any way by the fights between police and narcos, and among drug lords seeking more markets. They create their own daily lives as in any city, drawn by the convenience of Tijuana's location, opportunities, lower cost of living and climate. But many Mexican families tell reporters they now live in fear.

As noted in the health care chapter, Tijuana is the destination for considerable medical tourism and investment in health care facilities. High rise condos and golf course communities aimed at US and Canadian citizens were springing up all over the region, but many are on hold because of the global economic crisis.

Expats who live in Tijuana cite the ease of returning to the US for shopping and every other convenience, and it is far easier for family members on the West Coast to come visit you in Tijuana than in anyplace farther south. Expats who choose Tijuana consider it an ideal destination, with all the benefits of a large city and the additional convenience of ease of travel back to the US. For many working age expats, Tijuana might still make the most economic sense.

But when you think of retiring to the northern state of Baja California, you're probably envisioning one of other four major municipalities: Ensenada, Playas de Rosarita, Mexicali or Tecate. Most likely you're thinking the beach. You're thinking Pismo clams and a pina colada at sunset. And Rosarita Beach down to what is called the Punda Banda is one such an area, some sources claiming it includes 25,000 US residents. The drug wars extend that far down as well. Much of what was said about Tijuana applies to Rosarita Beach, too.

Ensenada, which is the Spanish word for cove, has a total population of about 300,000. Carol and Norma used to spend long week-ends at a rented beach house in Ensenada when they lived in LA. Norma remembers the deep-sea fishing trips, coming home with burlap bags of red fish with bulging eyes hauled up from the depths. Carol remembers stupidly eating fish tacos off the street stands and somehow escaping food poisoning, and dipping into Hussong's and other tourist-oriented wild bars when her younger sister visited and wanted some night life.

A town which is growing in popularity among expats is San Felipe on the Sea of Cortés side. A good paved road for the 120 miles from the border has transformed the small fishing village into an RV and retirement destination, at least in the winter. In the summer it can be as hot and dry as Phoenix, but more and more hardy souls are calling San Felipe home year-round, the same way Phoenix retains most of its residents all summer long now.

A few years ago the federal government announced plans for a huge port to rival LA and Long Beach to be built 150 miles south of Tijuana. Punta Colonet, a village of 2,500, is expected to grow to 200,000—if the port ever comes through. Consider that possibility when you're evaluating Baja Norte. Right now the plans are on hold due to the economic slowdown.

BAJA CALIFORNIA SUR

It is a long, mostly empty drive down to the most popular areas of southern Baja using the two lane blacktop Trans Peninsular Highway 1 completed in 1973, but there are pleasant stopovers in the small villages of Guerra Negro, Santa Rosalia, Mulegé, and Loreto. The Green Angels, Mexico's patrolling car mechanics in green vans who will repair your vehicle for only the cost of parts (though a donation is welcome), drive the length of the highway at least once a day. Put up your hood, call 066 which is becoming standardized as Mexico's emergency number, or try their two 24-hour toll-free numbers: 01-800-987-8224 and 01-800-903-9200. Their website in English is *www.sectur. gob.mx/wb/secturing/sect_eng_angeles_verdes*. If asked on the phone where you are, look at your last toll booth ticket for an address. It is always a good idea to carry spare parts that may be scarce in Mexico, such as an unusual belt, and fill up frequently since it can be as much as 100 miles between Pemex stations in deserted stretches.

The northwest coast of Baja tends to have rocky beaches with pounding waves, while the east coast on the protected Sea of Cortés tends to have sandier, quiet beaches.

Mulegé, Norma's son's favorite RV beach hangout, and Loreto, towns before you get all the way to Cabo, are known for relatively undiscovered beautiful beaches where you can be alone and perhaps scuba dive or fish. In little towns throughout Baja Sur you may find a few expats living their own ideal lifestyle. If that sounds like your thing, you may want to spend some time exploring off the highway.

La Paz is the capital of Baja Sur and it benefits from late spring through the rest of the hot summer from an afternoon breeze called the Corumel wind. La Paz is at the narrowest part of the peninsula where mountains do not stop the cooler Pacific winds from crossing the desert to the warmer Sea of Cortés side. It's an up-and-coming retirement destination.

Bahía de Palmas, Todos Santos and Santo Tomas closer to Cabo are also small towns being discovered by expats. These regions may very well grow in popularity among expats in coming years.

But more likely you will be driving to the very bottom of Baja Sur to check out "Cabo," more properly called Los Cabos, the capes, and the two main cities of San Jose del Cabo and Cabo San Lucas, both booming tourism and retirement destinations. A busy four-lane highway runs 32 kilometers between the two cities making up the cape's Tourist Corridor. They have four outstanding golf courses and are sometimes called the Pebble Beach of Baja. Deep sea fishing is a major draw.

If you choose to live in Baja California Sur you can enjoy often watching the gray whales in the winter on the south end of their 10,000 mile annual journey between Baja and the Bering Sea. You can live as luxuriously as you like, or do the club scene, or play hermit on a deserted beach a few miles away. If a beach resort area is your image of perfect Mexican living, check out Baja Sur.

SONORA AND CHIHUAHUA

The sprawling region from Baja to the Gulf of Mexico's lower states includes two of the largest states in area, though they are not densely populated. In Sonora, Puerta Penasco, called Rocky Point by those north of the border, and considered a party town, is a five-hour drive from Phoenix. It is as hot in the summer, which will limit many expats from considering it as a year-round home. It is still popular because of its proximity to Arizona, New Mexico, West Texas, and eastern California, though the economy has cut tourism severely. In choosing a Mexican town to live, especially if you have family in the southern US states, your main criterion may be proximity to the border—location, location, location.

Other towns in Sonora to research if this area of the country interests you are Kino Bay (Bajía de Kino), with its white sand beaches, and Guaymas/San Carlos with its fine natural harbor and water temperatures of about 80 degrees year-round. (The entire area is very hot much of the year to achieve that average beach temperature.) Guaymas, a city of 100,000, the second largest port after Mazatlán on this coast, is the starting point for a ferry to La Paz in Baja Sur. (A more popular ferry farther south leaves Mazatlán for La Paz.)

Chihuahua is the largest state in area but includes only about three million residents. Its main claim to fame is Barrancas del Cobre, Copper Canyon, seven canyons that are in many areas deeper and wider than the Grand Canyon. The "train ride in the sky" will surely be on your list of sights to see, passing through 86 tunnels and over 39 bridges and trestles, some a mile high. It's an area where some expats are developing ecotourism services. But the state of Chihuahua is another where drug wars are being fought, though tourists taking the Copper Canyon train or staying at ecotourism resorts are unlikely to ever notice.

After the rainy season ends the landscape is harsh and spare through the winter and into spring. The Chihuahua desert is the largest in North America. The only two major cities are the capital of Chihuahua and the border town of Ciudad Juaréz, across the Rio Grande from El Paso.

Ciudad Juaréz is fighting an image as a city of hundreds of un-solved murders of young women, many factory workers in the 330 or so *maquiladoras* erected across the border by US firms to utilize lower-paid Mexican workers, and as a site of considerable narcotics violence in recent years. It and Tijuana have the highest narcotics-related murder rates in the country. This is the city from which many of those horror stories in the media originate. Since the Mexican army has been deployed to Ciudad Juaréz in large numbers, the drug violence has decreased dramatically. Still, you're not likely to want to settle there without great incentive, such as a corporate job transfer too good to refuse.

However, it is an important business city, sixth largest in Mexico, and expats who are employed in the city's industries create their own life styles around all the offerings of a metropolis. Chihuahua is an historic city where the leaders of the 1810 Independencia war were beheaded and Revolutionary war hero Pancho Villa is the subject of a museum. Violence is not new to Mexico's history.

THE NORTH PACIFIC COASTAL STATES: SINALOA, NAYARIT, JALISCO AND COLIMA

Moving down the Pacific Coast of Mexico you will find some of the most popular expat destinations in the Gulf of California.

Sinaloa is another state known more for its drug cartel infight-ing, particularly in its capital city of Culiacan, but that should not outweigh the draw of the city of Mazatlán, the largest port between Los Angeles and the Panama Canal. It is also the largest uninter-rupted beach in the country. When some German developers im-proved the port in the early 1800s, a rush of wealthy German, Span-ish, French and Filipino merchants built fancy monumental homes whose influence can be seen today.

Mazatlán has many attractions for expats, including the fact that it is not as highly developed as many beach cities, though it does have a high rise resort beach area, the *Zona Dorada* (gold zone). If you want a city that retains much of its Mexican character, check out its central historic section. Norma and Carol loved Old Town and could envision living there at least part of the winters, some areas reminiscent of historic San Miguel de Allende. They like funky, and parts of Old Mazatlán are funky. It has one of the largest Mardi Gras celebrations in the world where anything goes, though prices skyrocket for the week before the Ash Wednesday start of Lent.

Luxury resorts and condos dominate the *Zona Dorado* beachfronts, but there are more shops and casual restaurants along the beach in Old Town. Expats can live a short walk from the water in pleasant communities. Considerable English is spoken—beware the timeshare salespeople in all these popular beach cities on the lookout for overwhelmed gringo newbies—so it could be a good spot to ease into Mexican living until you become more comfortable with the language and culture.

Carol and Norma met expats who loved it and others who couldn't wait to get back to places like San Miguel, or Santa Fe, kept there by love for their partners who would not leave. They said they didn't like the hot and humid summers. Coastal areas are more susceptible to hurricanes and typhoons. The summer rainy season can feel worse along beaches. Working expats that Carol and Norma met held jobs in real estate, in the arts and tourism, and in businesses serving the expat community. With the economic slowdown, they were having a hard time of it. (Educated young Mexican men throughout the country will often ask a tourist where they might find a job today, as the tourism industry is so hard hit.)

The ocean, climate (it is more moderate than the beaches to the north), lower costs, and seafood could be enough of a draw for you to check out Mazatlán further. There is the summer heat, humidity, and the possibility of hurricanes. But people all over the world who live in similar temperatures learn to do their errands in the morning and hole up by day, emerging after the sun goes down for social life. That's not all an impossible way to live. Carol and Norma did it for years in Phoenix.

You might never get tired of walking along the *malecon*, the beachfront walk, which has some of the sexiest statues in all of Mexico. Chesty mermaids and lusty muses wooing fishermen abound along the lengthy stroll. Carol and Norma discovered a little hole-in -the-wall restaurant bar where they danced till midnight to a local band's versions of rock and roll hits among a crowd so expansive as to include both young Mexican men and other *gringas* who must have been over 80.

Moving down the coast, the next major beach town that many call an expat destination is San Blas in the state of Nayarit, but potential year-round expats should know about the mosquitoes and tiny biting flies each summer. Carol still remembers being bitten so badly in San Blas that her eyes were swollen shut. It's a cute little fishing village, though, with many charms, not the least of which is its beauty. Surfers know it as the home of a mile-long surf break. Crescent-shaped Matanchen Bay south of San Blas is a vast stretch of unspoiled coastline, wide beaches, rolling hills, and jungle vegetation.

What are really booming in Nayarit are the towns of Sayulita and San Francisco (also called San Pancho). Both have populations of only a few thousand but were recently discovered by expats. *USA Today* has called Nayarit the up-and-coming Mexico. If that region interests you, read Barry Golson's book, *Gringos in Paradise*, about his home-building experience in Sayulita as part of your research.

Carol and Norma took a bus to Sayulita from Puerto Vallarta and were dropped off half a mile from town amid construction of a new highway. That was their first impression of Sayulita: hiking in dirt and mud. But the town itself was charming and reminded Carol of Venice Beach in LA in the '70s. They guessed the older expat couples who seemed right at home in the town were entertaining their grandkids on the beach, treating them to surfing lessons in the pleasant coves.

Working expats were selling real estate, renting motorcycles, *cuatromotos* (four-wheeled all-terrain vehicles), surfboards and fishing equipment, offering palm readings and massages, and in general looking as if they were having great fun.

JALISCO

Puerto Vallarta in Jalisco is an expat beach paradise for those who can handle the summers. The state of Jalisco also has several other major expat concentrations farther inland in Ajijíc and Lake Chapala, along the north shore of the largest lake in Mexico and the source of water for Guadalajara and the region. (Jalisco has given the world tequila and mariachi music, formerly the main entertainment for weddings in PV.)

Inland from PV is Lake Chapala, a beautiful large fresh water lake with a popular expat stretch of homes and towns along its north beach. The mountains close behind the beach moderate the temperatures and protect the stretch from cold breezes, giving the area bragging rights to the best climate in Mexico. (The south shore of the lake gets the chilly winds and is less developed.) The lake, a major source of water for the region, is the site of extensive ecological preservation efforts. It's an ongoing struggle to keep water plants from taking over the lake surface.

The highway from Guadalajara to the lake ends at a new Super Wal-Mart that has brought expat complaints but also vastly improved neighborhood shopping to the area. Turn left at the Wal-Mart and you're headed to Chapala, which has a charming dock and walkway. The Braniff Mansion (Braniff airlines fortune), now a restaurant, dominates the view. It is a most pleasant way to relax, for expats and for *Tapatios* (residents of Guadalajara) as well.

Turn instead to the right at the Wal-Mart and you're headed to a dozen towns, the largest being San Antonio Tlayacapa, Ajijíc, San Juan Cosalá, and Jocotepec, each with its own character and its own fans among the 15,000 or more expats living in the region. (We've read estimates as high as 40,000.) Even in these numbers, expats do not overwhelm the towns, which are definitely Mexican in character despite the expat-oriented businesses. Expats are divided not only by which town is the best, but whether to live in the flat lower areas or up in the hills. Chula Vista is the largest of the numerous gated communities tucked into the hillsides.

Besides the proximity to Guadalajara, the beauty of the lake and mountains, and the moderated climate, this area is considered cheaper than San Miguel de Allende and some other popular expat centers. And Ajijíc has an outstanding welcome center for newcomers, the Lake Chapala Society. LCS is a former garden home that is now the site of a 30,000-volume lending library, classrooms to learn Spanish or take computer classes, an outdoor café, information centers about the community and about government programs such as immigration and health care, patios for card games and conversation, and rotating medical services such as hearing and vision specialists.

Ajijíc includes many retired military and Western Canadian immigrants, although its earliest expat reputation was as an arts community. Both free spirits and conservatives mix in the approximately 50 community organizations, ranging from Daughters of the American Revolution and American Legion to New Age groups. (Probably at least a few expats belong to both kinds of groups.) Its colorfully decorated storefronts on streets near the pier are fun to explore. Expats may work in the usual tourist and arts businesses or servicing other expat business needs, or tuck themselves into their own compact social group, or take on the problems of the world and their community in dozens of service organizations, or reinvent themselves as artists and writers, or simply learn to be themselves, free of any expectations or pressures.

Your biggest problem each day may be figuring out how to cross the busy main highway. With the piers and boardwalks at both Ajijíc and Lake Chapala providing focal points for activities, weekend visitors from Guadalajara may enjoy the beaches and restaurants even more than local expats.

And then there are those beautiful mountains behind you, keeping bad weather at a minimum. Ajijíc claims to have the best climate in all of Mexico, and the residents do have a point. San Miguel can get a little hotter in April and May, and a little colder in December and January. Ajijíc is a little lower in altitude as well, around 5,000 feet, perhaps enough to make a difference if altitude is a problem for you. (San Miguel and Ajijíc have a longstanding rivalry, some San Miguel residents calling Ajijíc boring, some Ajijíc residents considering SMA snobbish. Oh well.)

For many decades Guadalajara itself was one of the largest centers for expat living in Mexico, and many US and Canadian citizens still live in the metropolis, the second largest city in Mexico. Its metropolitan population is often cited as seven million, almost as large as Manhattan. It has all the civilizing amenities such as good theater, dance, and music of Mexico City—as well as the smog and traffic.

Both cities are doing much better with both problems in recent years. Carol and Norma were pleasantly surprised at how attractive both cities are for expat living, if you're a big city person. An estimated 5,000 expats live in Guadalajara, most employed in corporations. IBM and Motorola pour millions into the local economy. Carol and Norma found it more manageable than Mexico City, 22 million compared to seven million, and easily found their way around to the fantastic cultural offerings and shopping.

The arts and crafts factory town of Tonalá and the high-end arts and crafts shopping town of Tlaquepaque are major attractions for many expats, though few live in either suburb. These days more expats live around Lake Chapala. They take the bus or drive the 45 minutes in to town to enjoy Guadalajara's attractions. One of the renowned Ken Edwards ceramic dinnerware and sculpture factories is in Tonalá, where the artisans who sell their goods at much higher prices in Tlaquepaque are manufacturing their goods on back roads with factories located next to middle class homes. The main street turns into a huge arts and crafts shopping strip on Thursdays and Sundays. English speakers were packing up sculptures, stained glass, and stuffed animals for shipping to gift shops and other retail outlets around the world, in wholesale stores along Tonála streets.

Tlaquepaque is wonderful. Carol and Norma felt they were walking through Scottsdale's art gallery stretch, or along a Greenwich Village shopping street, enjoying window shopping at the high-priced galleries and stores, interspersed with excellent restaurants offering Margaritas at the door. Taxi drivers and store owners told us not many expats live in Tlaquepaque, but the city looked like someplace where someone could hunker down and build a life that revolved around perhaps international marketing of arts and crafts.

You don't even have to think about how expats might live in Puerto Vallarta, you see them all around you. The city of 300,000 includes several thousand year-round expats and many times that many seasonal residents. It is located on Bahía de Banderas, the largest natural bay in Mexico, more than 100 miles of coastline, the winter home of 500 humpback whales. It's often called the San Francisco of Mexico.

The entire town is about 12 blocks wide in parts and the beaches run for 20 miles, but the historic center retains its cobblestoned charm— and less expensive prices. You can get away from the tourists fairly quickly. The hillside housing perhaps eight blocks from the beach also includes less expensive homes, but there is the very expensive Nuevo Vallarta development north of town. PV has one of the largest gay communities in Mexico as well. If you're gay, head for Playa del Sol, Los Muertos Beach, or Olas Altas and look for Blue Chairs and Green Chairs.

Carol and Norma had a ball in Puerto Vallarta, enjoying the *malecon* but also exploring the *Zona Romantica* and beyond, the old town off the beach. Expats can live any kind of lifestyle they want in all the varying neighborhoods of Puerto Vallarta, from inexpensive homes tucked into hillsides to million dollar condos along the beach. Like the five sketches of possible expat life in San Miguel earlier in this chapter, similar diversity is found in this expat haven as well, though you'd have more beach-oriented lifestyles, too. The town is a riot of bougainvilleas, deep blue sea and skies. And if you need a Baskin Robbins or Dreyer's ice cream fix, or a Señor Frog's, or a Burger King, they're on the *malecon*.

Night of the Iguana was actually filmed in Mismaloya south of PV. John Huston brought Elizabeth Taylor and Richard Burton together for the 1964 film that drew a rush of sightseers to this paradise setting. Many expats have followed and never left. Boca de Tomatlán ten miles south of PV has another small expat community that hopes no one else discovers it.

Leaving Puerto Vallarta going south, you'll enter the state of Colima, most notably the city of Manzanillo. Manzanillo, like several other cities, calls itself the "sailfish capital of the world." It's more laid back and inexpensive than many other beach cities, and it is home to fewer year-round expats.

The north coast is the biggest concentration of both expats and luxury resorts. Or, you can jump right into the Mexican neighborhoods and find your own way to love Mexico.

Rolly's website has photos of his friends who live the equivalent of 14 stories off the road—not too handy for hauling groceries or a refrigerator home. The downtown can be off-putting if you're one who wants to escape, and the port is as much of an economic base as tourism is for Manzanillo. Some expats live in large self-contained expensive gated communities, year-round or for the winters, while others have found their own little paradises off the highways and on their own secluded beach areas.

The capital of the state of Colima is the city Colima, about an hour east of Manzanillo in the mountains, giving it a mild year-round climate. It has been voted the city with the best quality of life in the country. Real estate is reasonable, music and other cultural experiences are of high quality, the lifestyle is relaxed and intellectual. Expect Colima to draw more and more expats in the future. The area around Colima and Manzanillo is an earthquake zone and there is an active volcano near Colima, however. Check out the earthquake record and other possible natural disasters in any area of Mexico you're considering. Hurricane season is June-October, on both coasts.

North of Manzanillo about 40 miles is a horseshoe bay with the villages of La Manzanilla (note the "a" that distinguishes it from the much larger Manzanillo), Tenacatita, and Melaque, the area drawing few expats now but a likely spot for more in the future. Like most of the coast, the region is hot and steamy during the rainy season of July to September.

The area is called the Costa Alegre (happy, sunny coast). Melaque, population around 6,300, includes the tourist town of Melaque to the west, the business center and town plaza of San Patricio, and the residential Villa Obregon to the east. The beach is oriented east to west, so the sun rises on one end and sets on the other. The area is too sparsely populated and too hot in the summer for Carol and Norma, but it might be exactly what you are looking for. They have friends who load a suitcase or an ebook reader with light fiction and rarely leave their hammock all winter. Carol and Norma would die of boredom.

Michoacán is the next state down the Pacific coast, but its popular expat destinations are well inland and will be discussed in the Central Bajía section at the end of our trip around the coast of Mexico. The next expat coastal destinations are in the state of Guerrero, particularly Zihuatanejo, Ixtapa, Troncones, and Acapulco.

THE SOUTH PACIFIC COASTAL STATES: GUERRERO, OAXACA, CHIAPAS

About six hours south of Manzanillo on good highways is the start of the Costa Grande, Big Coast, and the town of Zihuatanejo, nicknamed Zihua (Zee'-wa). It's a 60,000-population fishing village (with other industries) about halfway between Manzanillo and Acapulco, on a half-moon bay, and is one of the up and coming expat destinations, now reachable by the same highway that brought tourists in droves to Acapulco.

Carol and Norma have decided Zihuatenejo is their favorite beach town and it is someplace they think they could live, at least in winters. Neither one is much for summer heat, especially after seven years in Phoenix. This beach town also reminds them of Venice Beach in the '70s.

More funkiness—they loved finding bars a wee bit seedy with entertainers singing songs from the '60s who close up turned out to be in their 60s, dancing with the same mix of young Mexicans and old gringos as in old Mázatlan. They enjoyed meeting two sisters who call themselves The Happy Hookers who run deep sea fishing charters, running into pony-tailed dudes on loud Harleys, feasting on seafood pizza in a beach dive where you have to squeeze past the pizzas coming out of the oven to get to the restrooms, judging a diving contest among the pelicans and cormorants....yeah, they could live there.

Most of the tourism is deflected to nearby Ixtapa, a glitzy high rise condo and beach hotel resort area a few miles away, so Zihua's prices have remained lower. The entire coastline is spectacular, as is most of Mexico's coast. (The cover photo for this book is of a stretch near Ixtapa.)

Ixtapa began as a manufactured government project designed to draw tourists, and it succeeded mightily. Its tourist brochures point out that it has ten beaches, two championship golf courses, world-class resort hotels, a marina, high-end shopping, restaurants and other amenities. Few year-round expats live there unless they are working in the tourism industry but it is a draw for those who choose Zihuatanejo and want all those extras close by. We met an expat who was expanding his Ixtapa fresh seafood restaurant to include gourmet delivery pizza, and we think he hoped to use his motorcycle to do the deliveries himself to get out of the kitchen and into that beautiful sunshine more often.

Troncones about 20 miles north of Ixtapa was developed by the Mexican government at the same time as Ixtapa but it never became as popular. The beach runs from the village of Troncones to La Majajua north, and the best beach is Playa Manzanillo. Troncones is also now a three-hour toll road drive from Pátzcuaro and Morelia in inland Michoacán, so that expats can get quick access to major shopping in a cooler area. Carol and Norma have friends who swear by Troncones as their ideal getaway, and some expats live there, involved in the tourism industry.

Acapulco may be the most famous Mexican beach city, thanks to a big push by the Mexican government in the '50s to make it one of the world's first jet-set resorts. Movie stars who flocked to the beaches made Acapulco even more famous.

As other cities developed their tourist attractions, Acapulco slipped in desirability and so did its prices, as government ad campaigns moved to attract middle class Mexican tourists rather than the international set. It is now a city of about two million, with the gamut in neighborhoods from affordable expat homes to luxury houses high in the hills with amazing views. Many expats leave in the summer heat. While Mexico City and Guadalajara seem very livable big cities to Carol and Norma, somehow Acapulco didn't grab them, despite its beach. How many times can you watch Acapulco's famed divers leap off the cliff? Not to say that it won't grab you. The gay beach area is Playa Condesa.

The state of Oaxaca is known in expat circles more for its city of the same name, but Puerto Escondido on the coast has a famous beach known for gigantic surfing waves. A few expats live full-time in the area, though more choose PE for the winter months. It isn't as highly developed as many beach cities and so prices remain somewhat lower.

Puerto Angel and Huatulco are other beach towns in this stretch of coast that remain fairly undeveloped and fairly undiscovered by expats, though the Mexican government attempted to make Huatulco a major resort destination with a Club Med and many luxury high-rise hotels. It didn't take off as much as other government-planned resorts did. Again, the beach cities are spectacular but are too hot and humid for many expats to consider for year-round living. But if you survive well in steamy Washington, DC on down to Florida in August, you could probably enjoy the beach, jungle and desert areas of Mexico as well.

Oaxaca the city is one of the most beautiful towns in all of Mexico. As many as 2,000 expats have settled into this arts community. The state of Oaxaca has perhaps the most varied Indian populations in all of Mexico, with about 15 separate languages being spoken and 200 varieties of native dress being worn today for fiestas. (In Mexico as in much of the world, standard daily street wear today is more likely to be jeans, T-shirts, blouses and tennis shoes rather than native costumes saved for celebrations.)

The richness of these cultures and the proximity of the 2,500-year-old Monte Albán archeological site, founded by the Zapotec Indians and once a city of at least 25,000 residents, make Oaxaca a city that feels like untouched Mexico, even as it has grown to a population of 300,000. A teachers' strike made its Zócalo the scene of political strife a few years ago, but expats' lives were largely untouched other than detouring around parts of Centro. The expat community publishes a newspaper and supports an excellent bookstore, many concerts, and other cultural events. This could be the town for you if you want to be close to the richness of diverse indigenous cultures and an expansive arts and cultural scene, and still be able to get an excellent cup of cappuccino in an expat-oriented coffee shop. It's a politically active region—remember that the Mexican Constitution forbids foreigners from getting involved in Mexican politics. This is the place where you could be really tempted to do so.

It has some of the most beautiful churches and walking streets in all of Mexico—stand in the midst of the gilded Santo Domingo church interior and think of how the military used the golden church as a cavalry stables during the Cristeros wars in the late 1920s. Monte Albán museum is close by, preserving an ancient pyramid region that began development around 800 BC and reached its zenith in 500 AD. You can feel enriched by Oaxaca's culture and history merely by breathing in the air.

The next Mexican state as we move down the Pacific coast is the last before Guatemala, Chiapas. The beautiful city of San Cristóbal de las Casas is a favorite tourist destination for knowledgeable expats wanting to experience "the real Mexico," though fewer live there. There is a small community, however, and expats who have settled in Chiapas believe they have found paradise. Probably the poorest Mexican state, and one of the least visited by tourists, it has a history of political struggle that could be off-putting to some. They remember Subcomandante Marcos leading an indigenous army New Year's Day 1994, fighting for land, recognition, and their rights as native Indians. The Mayan ruin Palenque that was flourishing around 600 AD, vast rainforest jungles teeming with wildlife, six national parks, and wild rivers make this an ecological paradise for those eager to explore the untouched Mexico and find their own way. It is likely that more expats eager for another aspect of the "real" Mexico will discover Chiapas despite its distance from the US border.

THE YUCATAN PENINSULA: CAMPECHE, YUCATAN, AND QUINTANA ROO

The next state as we head north into the Yucatan Peninsula is Campeche. Its capital, also named Campeche, is a pretty city of cobblestone streets, pastel-colored homes with ornate wrought iron balconies, and street cars. Few expats live in this area—though they are plentiful a bit farther north in the states of Quintana Roo and the Yucatan.

The peninsula is largely limestone with underground rivers, caves and jungles to lure explorers. The beaches are white sand, the resorts luxurious. The capital of the Yucatan is the colonial city of Mérida, founded in 1542 on the site of the ancient Mayan city of Tho, in Mayan called the city of five hills, or pyramids. Mérida is probably the oldest continually occupied city in the Americas. Its colonial historical center is second in size to Mexico City's. With all those years of civilization it is indeed a highly civilized city, hosting 16 universities and a vibrant cultural and arts scene.

Mérida is a draw for expats, possibly as many as 3,000, who can tolerate the humidity and heat (high temperatures are often in the 90s and even over 100 F) and who appreciate the city's laid-back and artistic nature. It is nicknamed both the Paris of the West for its European flair and the White City because much construction is of limestone.

About 80 miles east is Chichén Itzá, originated in 600 AD, the site of outstanding archaeological ruins including a 272-foot long ball field that tells much about the civilization that utilized it 1,400 years ago. It is a UNESCO World Heritage Site, and a worldwide vote in 2007 chose it as one of the New Seven Wonders of the World. It is a favorite side trip from Cancún. Expats who have an interest in world history can spend years exploring this region.

It is Quintana Roo that is the tourist success story of the Yucatan. The totally planned resort community of Cancún is now the number one tourist draw in Mexico, some three million visitors a year in good times. It has also been called the most expensive city to live in Mexico. But a few blocks off of the beach resorts, condos, houses, and rentals can be as affordable as other expat destinations. Gay readers might want to search out Playa Delfines, the longest and widest stretch in the Hotel Zone.

Cancún is close to Mexico's second busiest airport, has three million travelers a year, and its economy is usually healthy because of the influx of tourist money. With the Yucatan jungle and the Caribbean ventilating the city (and keeping its average highs to 80 degrees F., 300 sunny days a year), Cancún has clean air for a city its size.

The fishing village of Puerto Morelos 20 minutes south of Cancún is close enough to the big city to meet expats' needs for services and yet remote enough for seclusion. The coral reefs and mangroves nearby are ecological preserves. The 30-mile-long island of Cozumel is another popular resort draw, gaining its popularity when Jacques Costeau called it one of the best diving sites in the world. Isla Mujeres and other islands in this region have their own personalities and small expat populations.

The area along the Caribbean Sea to the south is sometimes called the Mayan Riviera and includes dozens of smaller beach cities that attract expats. Playa del Carmen, Akumal, and Puerto Aventuras are some of these highly desirable towns. Tulum is a walled city built by the Mayans on the Caribbean and filled with history, as is Cobá, the largest Mayan city ever discovered so far. Chetumal, the capital city on the border of Belize, is also a popular expat destination. Maroma Beach near Tulum, south of Cancún, is consistently listed as one of the top ten beaches in the world by the Travel Channel.

Carol and Norma have not yet been able to explore much of Southern Mexico themselves so these descriptions are not as complete as other areas of Mexico. You'll have to discover the region for yourself. They'll be right behind you.

TABASCO

Bordering Chiapas to the east is Tabasco, a narrow state that stretches from Guatemala to the Gulf of Mexico. It is oil-rich, and therefore more prosperous than much of the region outside of the Yucatan resort cities. This is the state of the giant awe-inspiring Olmec stone heads. You can get to the fascinating Mayan ruins of Palenque more easily from the Tabasco capital of Villahermosa than from any place in Chiapas.

VERACRUZ

This is a long narrow state along the Gulf, 600 miles of coastline bordering seven other states, including numerous ports and a history befitting all of that space used by explorers to land through the centuries. It is the third most populated state and a favorite tourist destination for Mexicans. Its altitude ranges from sea level up to 19,000 feet at the active volcano of Pico de Orizaba, nicknamed El Pico, second highest volcano on the continent.

Its capital is Xalapa, population around 400,000, with all the expected symphonies and other cultural attractions, for both Mexicans and expats, of a university town. Xalapa has the best symphony in Mexico and the best anthropology museum outside Mexico City. Since it's surrounded by mountains its climate is milder. Ecotourism is big in this region, along with white river rafting. If your interests are both intellectual and athletic, this may be your place.

The city of Veracruz has half a million people, making it the second largest metropolitan area on the Gulf Coast, and is famous for fighting off four invasions and numerous pirate attacks in its history. It was the major seaport for the shipments of silver and gold sent back to Spain during the 300 years of conquest. Veracruz is also the home of marimba, and is closer to Caribbean island culture than to Mexico. Its population of African descent is about 15%. Its great influxes of foreign influences, including the slave trade, have given Veracruz a reputation as one of the most open, accepting areas of the country today, while much of Mexico is considered culturally conservative. The region has not yet attracted numerous expats, though it is a business center. It is a city known for seafood, fish, and culinary dishes unique to the area. Whatever your expectations are of Mexico, Veracruz can expand them.

TAMAULIPAS

The last state north along the Gulf of Mexico, Tamaulipas, extends a long finger west from the Golf across the Texas border to encompass the popular crossings at Reynoso/Brownsville/McAllen and Nuevo Laredo/Laredo. Tampico is the northernmost port on the Gulf side, and the little fishing village of La Pesca between Tampico and Brownsville is a popular tourist attraction drawing some notice from expats.

Like Tijuana and Ciudad Juaréz, the border locations of Reynoso and Nuevo Laredo offer serious economic incentives for settlement by both Mexicans and expats. Many Mexicans and Americans and Mexican-Americans cross the border daily or frequently to work. These border cities are also often sites of drug violence.

McAllen is a major medical center and shopping focus for both Mexicans and Americans, making the Reynoso area across the border a particularly attractive destination. This region of Texas is one of the poorest US areas, and its population is more than 90% Mexican-American. This may be the area of Mexico where the border feels most porous and irrelevant—sometimes you may not be sure which side of the border you are on. Housing prices on the US side are lower than many expat enclaves in Mexico. It has all the advantages of being in the US for Medicare availability and safety net programs. US citizens who are looking solely for an inexpensive area to live and who are not equally influenced by an attraction to living specifically in Mexico may want to consider remaining in the US in a low-cost area such as southern Texas.

Carol and Norma visit McAllen for a shopping run at the end of most summers to snap up clothes and shoes on sale, and the Mexican side would be convenient for expats who need to stay close to the US while enjoying the economic benefits of Mexican living.

Farther to the west along the border, Nuevo Laredo is also considered one of Mexico's major drug trafficking centers and has been the scene of considerable drug cartel violence. For the majority of its law-abiding residents, these battles don't impact them. There is a great deal to be said in terms of location, climate, lower prices, shopping, and economic opportunity for almost all border cities, though again, almost all border cities also share similar problems due to their transitory nature. The obvious advantages of location may outweigh any possible disadvantages for you.

Ciudad Victoria is another major city in Tamaulipas. Home to a quarter million people, including a few expats, it is prosperous and modern.

Now we will head across the remaining northern inland states of Mexico bordering the US, Nuevo León and Coahuila, and then crisscross the middle of Mexico to take in the rest of the country, including the populous Central Bajio, which has many favorite expat communities. We will end in Mexico City, a fitting conclusion of this brief overview.

NUEVO LEON AND COAHUILA

Nuevo León has a nine-mile border with Texas. It is an industrialized state with one of the highest per capita incomes in the country. Its capital is Monterrey, home to some three million people, the third largest city in Mexico, and a highly desirable place to live for many expats and Mexicans alike. It is a major center for education (some 26 colleges), health care, culture, sports and industry. The Sierra Madre Oriental mountains provide the backdrop to city views. Carol has shared art classes with a watercolorist from Monterrey who filled her head with its mountainous beauty and its extensive art scene as he painted scenes from his memory, so that she can easily see why expats would consider living there.

Coahuila's capital is Saltillo, population about 650,000, 240 miles south of the Texas border and 54 miles west of Monterrey. In 2006 *Inversionista* magazine named it the best city in Mexico to live. About a third of all cars and two-thirds of all trucks manufactured in Mexico were made near Saltillo, earning it the name of the Detroit of Mexico.

Torreón is in Coahuila, and it adjoins Gómez Palacio and Lerdo which are in the state of Durango. The total three-city municipality is called Comarca Lagunera, totaling more than 1.1 million people.

Torreón is an educational and health care hub for the region. It is becoming very much like a US city in terms of its commercial appearance. One of its landmarks is Cristo de las Noas, a 71.5-foot-tall statue of Christ that is the third highest in Latin America. It is said to symbolize the faith and iron will of the people of Torreón.

DURANGO

Rolly lives in Lerdo, which adjoins Gómez Palacio, also in Durango, and Torreón in the state of Coahuila, and he believes he is the only gringo in Lerdo. His website, *www.rollybrook.com*, gives a sample picture of daily life in Mexico for those who choose to expatriate to someplace other than communities with large numbers of US and Canadian residents.

Durango has the reputation of being a Wild West kind of place. A low-density state, it is heavily forested. (It is also known for its abundance of scorpions.) The city of Durango has a population of about half a million and has not attracted many expats. Because a major highway runs from El Paso down through the Durango/Coahuila border, rival drug cartels have battled for control of this passageway.

ZACATECAS

East of Durango is Zacatecas, a state which sent more than $800 million in silver to Spain during the conquest. The total state population is about 1.5 million, and it has the smallest percentage (0.3%) of indigenous people in the country. Half the people at any time are working in the US. Its mining days are long gone—what was once the major silver mine is now a tourism attraction. An underground cave is now the site of a disco. The center of the city of Zacatecas, abounding with highly decorated churches, is a UNESCO World Heritage Site and a popular tourist destination for Mexicans and expats, who usually enjoy shopping at the numerous silver shops.

SAN LUIS POTOSI

The state is bordered by nine other states and is mostly on the high Mexican plateau, 6,000 feet altitude or more, that gives the central plateau a moderate climate and a higher concentration of population. The city of San Luis Potosí includes a million people and was cited by *Investor* Magazine as Mexico's third most desirable place to live. The colonial centro retains the Spanish architecture, pedestrian promenades, and malls, while the outer edges of the city are industrial and have all the same giant chain stores that are springing up in major cities throughout Mexico. The American Society is an umbrella organization that assists San Luis Potosí expats.

Matahuela is another large city in San Luis Potosí on a major highway, though it has not drawn many expats. Two other towns are tourist draws if not that suitable for permanent expat living. Real Catorce three hours away is a ghost town that Hollywood rediscovered for the filming of the Brad Pitt film, *The Mexican*. At 9,000 feet, it is cooler than its surroundings. The buildings are constructed of stone from the surrounding mountains. You get in through a 1.5 mile one-lane tunnel alternating traffic with those leaving. Xilitla is known for mountaineering but nearby in Las Pozas is the Enchanted Garden of the English author, Edward James, an important tourist attraction.

AGUASCALIENTES

Aguascalientes means hot waters. The hot springs and baths are a major lure for tourists and residents alike. The city of Aguascalientes is called el Corazon (heart) of Mexico because it is in the geographic center of the country. It has retained its attractive colonial center, but the biggest draw is the San Marcos Fair, hundreds of years old, called the national fair of Mexico. It runs from mid-April to mid May and attracts some seven million visitors. The former mining ghost towns of Azientos and Tepezalá are also tourist destinations. The Natural Protected Reserve of Sierra Fría at 9,000 feet altitude is a place to hike, camp, see wildlife and even experience snow in the winter.

GUANAJUATO

Two of the most beautiful and popular colonial cities in all of

Mexico, Guanajuato and San Miguel de Allende, both major expat draws, are located in this central plateau state. Along with the city of Dolores Hidalgo and the metropolis of Querétaro in the neighboring state of the same name, this area is the heart of Mexico's historic Independencia, the war for independence from Spain from 1810 to 1821. Mexican tourists flock to these beloved cities to celebrate their roots in far greater numbers than do US, Canadian, and other international visitors.

Dolores Hidalgo, which has a metropolitan population of about 140,000 and a city population of about 70,000, has the fewest expats of these cities, but it has an international reputation for its colorful talavera ceramics, manufactured and sold throughout the city. (The competing state of Puebla claims to produce the only truly authentic talavera from glazing methods brought from Spain.) It is also known for its ice cream vendors in the main square selling flavors such as corn, avocado, tequila, prune, and shrimp ice cream cones.

Guanajuato means "place of frogs" and indigenous tribes thought it was nothing more than a place where frogs should live. Silver mines changed all that. The Valencia mine once yielded two-thirds of the world's silver. The main streets are underground, following the Guanajuato River bed that used to flood the city until it was dammed.

A major drawback for those who want to live downtown is that most houses and apartments are up narrow, steep alleyways called *callejones* so that you'll be hauling groceries home up hill on foot. One is so narrow that lovers are supposed to be able to kiss from balconies on opposite sides of the *callejon*. Outside of town the same "big box" chain stores of every large Mexican city dot the suburban residential and industrial areas. The city has at least 140,000 residents.

Besides its historical significance as the site of the first major victory by the ragtag peasant army against the Spanish hiding in the Granary, Guanajuato has one of the most important historic universities, particularly for law and the arts. Strolling student musicians in Renaissance costumes brought the custom of Las Tunas from Spain to Mexico. It is also host each October to one of the most important musical events in Mexico, the International Cervantino Festival. Some sources still say there are about 200 expats living in Guanajuato but that figure is rising rapidly. Others say it is now 1,000 or more. As usual with most Mexican statistics, it is impossible to know for sure.

Possible San Miguel de Allende expat lifestyles are presented earlier in this chapter, but here is some more information. SMA has as many as 12,000 expats (70% US, 20% Canadian, 10% from about 30 other countries) living in the town in high season. At least 7,000 are permanent residents. But by walking a few blocks from the main square it immediately becomes obvious SMA is still very much Mexican. It is one of the Puebla Mágicas, cities featured by the Mexican government for their special feeling of magic and beauty.

After seven years Carol and Norma are still totally besotted with San Miguel and recommend you read *Falling...in Love with San Miguel: Retiring to Mexico on Social Security*, reporting a calendar year in SMA and sharing the history as they learned it and their day to day experiences as expats. Though SMA has a reputation as an expensive city, by Mexican standards, it is still possible to live there on the minimum monthly FM3 income requirement from the Mexican government.

To include at least some of the highlights of San Miguel, it is host to an international chamber music festival, international jazz festival, international short films festival (shared with Guanajuato), and hundreds of concerts, gallery openings, plays and other cultural events each year. The Biblioteca Publica (library) includes about 50,000 books, half in English, and includes a bilingual newspaper, a computer center and theater, numerous art and computer classes and films for children, and scholarships that have put thousands of Mexican students through college. Feed the Hungry provides a hot meal each school day for more than 4,000 children. Mujeres en Cambio helps Mexican women improve their lives, Casita Linda builds very inexpensive homes for the rural poor, Patronatos por Niños and other groups provide free medical care and surgeries, a midwife training program assists those giving birth unattended out in the campos, three animal rights groups improve the conditions for local street dogs and cats, and much more.

Atotonilco 15 minutes away is also part of the UNESCO World Heritage designation for SMA, its Santuario the starting point for religious pilgrimages for the past 250 years. More and more expats are building or remodeling homes in the countryside along the way to Atotonilco and Dolores Hidalgo. The road between San Miguel de Allende and Dolores Hidalgo and past Atotonilco, which is being expanded to four lanes for the 2010 anniversary of Independencia, has been called The Golden Corridor for its new development plans. Hot springs in the area are favorite destinations.

Mineral de Pozos less than an hour from San Miguel is a ghost town rediscovered in recent years by a small but flourishing artists' community, primarily expats, some of whom are also working on arts projects with local school children. (In any abandoned former mining town, check out water quality and any remaining toxic wastes that may impact a home you are considering. Mining businesses around the world have not been concerned with the ecology until recently.) Real estate interests in Pozos promote it as the next San Miguel. If you dream of starting an art gallery on a budget with fresh talent, this could be the place for you.

Another colonial city in Guanajuato is Salvatierra, population 35,000, which took over the annual Running of the Bulls (also called the Pamplonada and the Sanmiguelada) when San Miguel de Allende city officials decided in 2007 that it was too much like a disruptive spring break than an event befitting a UNESCO World Heritage site. In this economy, SMA may reinstate the tourist draw.

Salamanca, a city of 145,000, has the largest Pemex refinery in Mexico and the world's 11th largest crude oil refinery. (Note: there are four cities called Salamanca in Mexico.) Much larger Guanajuato cities are León (the leather capital of Mexico), Irapuato, and Celaya, and some expats have settled in all these areas. León in particular is a very nice large capital city with much to recommend it, including universities, fine shopping, a beautiful 1,300-seat theater, La Casa de la Cultura Diego Rivera, and even a zoo.

QUERETARO

A bustling metropolis of a million, Querétaro has been called the second best place in Mexico to do business, only Monterrey surpassing it, and the fifth best business location in Latin America. It has one of the highest per capita incomes in the country and boasts numerous leading universities and a thriving arts community. Such international corporations as Nestlé, Gerber, Kellogg's, Daewoo, Michelin, Samsung and numerous automotive suppliers have made Querétero home, along with major medical and shopping centers that draw expats from San Miguel de Allende and throughout the area.

Outside of its colonial center and numerous churches, the most striking landmark is a 74-arch aqueduct that is the focal point for many areas as it stretches. The French-appointed Emperor Maximilian tried to fight off Benito Juárez in 1867 but was captured and executed here. One of the best bilingual private schools in the region, John F. Kennedy, is located in Querétaro. This is a city which could continue to draw more and more expats, as well as employees of the international corporations who have made Querétaro at least a temporary home for many years.

One of the other cities in the state of Querétaro that is drawing some expats is Tequisquiapan, known for its thermal waters and for its local wines and cheeses. The region includes about 55,000 people and is a tourist destination for European as well as Mexican visitors. Bernal is a pretty little tourist town built around an impressive rock formation, the third largest of its kind in the world.

On the northern edge of the state of Querétaro is the Sierra Gorda—rivers, deserts, jungles, mountains, canyons, beauty—running for 383,000 acres. Sierra Gorda rolls through missions established in the 1750s by Fray Junípero Serra—Jalpan, Landa, Tilaco, Tancoyol and Concá. A biosphere reserve aims to maintain the endangered species found uniquely in this region. As ecotourism grows in popularity and more people yearn to see the remaining wilderness and jungles of the world in their untouched state, expect more public attention to come to the Sierra Gorda.

HIDALGO

Few expats live in the state of Hidalgo, though the archaeological ruins at Tula de Allende that date back to 804 AD draw many tourists. The capital, Pachuca, is becoming more and more of an industrial center, especially for companies that want to leave Mexico City. The government provides economic incentives for industry to decentralize, to reduce pollution and congestion in Mexico City.

The region was filled with silver mining communities under Spanish rule. Their beautiful colonial homes are still a reminder of that history. Pachuca is also has a popular photography museum.

MICHOACAN

This state has several very popular expat communities, particularly the capital city of Morelia, and Pátzcuaro and other arts and crafts towns around Lake Pátzcuaro. It may be best known globally as the state where Monarch butterflies migrate in the hundreds of millions each winter to forests in the northeast part of the state.

Morelia is often called one of the most beautiful cities in Mexico, the predominant construction material of the 1,000 historic buildings being a soft rose cantera stone that gives the city a pink glow. Friends of Carol and Norma who are into classical music chose Morelia over San Miguel to live because of the music and cultural scene. The city also has four golf courses, including a 27-hole Jack Nicklaus court, Tres Marias, that hosts the LPGA each year. The striking aqueduct that brought water into the city for nearly 200 years has 250 arches. Morelia is primarily a colonial city developed by the Spanish while Pátzcuaro, long its rival, has pre-Hispanic Indian roots from centuries earlier.

A priest, Vasco de Quiroga, sent to the region to protect the Indians from brutal treatment by the Spaniards, shaped the economic and cultural future of Pátzcuaro and the towns surrounding the lake when he urged each town to develop its own craft specialty. He wanted each town to be part of a larger economy, so that the towns could trade with each other and with other regions, and each town could concentrate on becoming really good at its own craft.

This tradition continues to today, so that one town is known for its copper work, another for furniture, another for weaving. Carol and Norma's favorite is Tzintzuntzan, "Place of the Hummingbirds," in the lower reedy shores of Lake Pátzcuaro, which became famous for its reed-sculptured animals, baskets, and Christmas ornaments.

Pátzcuaro and much of Michoacán have a distinctive and charming look of deep brick red paint along the bottom of the one-story buildings and a crisp white for the top. Even their lettering style on signs is unique to the region. Fishermen using butterfly-shaped nets can still be seen on the lake, though they are often now posing for photographs rather than fishing.

Pátzcuaro is famous for its Day of the Dead celebrations involving boats sailing at night to an island in the lake. The area including small towns all around the lake continues to be discovered by expats. Because it is above 7,000 feet, the area can be colder and wetter than other parts of the central plateau.

Urupuan, now a major avocado growing area with a city population of about 250,000, also has a lengthy pre-Hispanic history, partly because of its choice location along the Cupatitzio River, now preserved through the National Park Eduardo Ruiz. The Paricutín volcano made itself known in 1943 and scared off many local residents—and perhaps future expats. A few are venturing into this area, however.

TLAXCALA

Not much larger than Rhode Island, Tlaxcala is Mexico's smallest state, dissected by three mountain ranges. It was never defeated by the Aztecs. Its leaders made an alliance with Cortés to bring down the Aztecs—a good move short range. The area is rich agriculturally and is considered part of the Central Breadbasket. The name means, "place of corn bread." The city of Tlaxcala has classic colonial features as well as pre-Hispanic murals dating back to 600 AD. Nearby are ancient ruins at Xochitecatl and Cacaztla. The town celebrates its own running of the bulls like the Spanish Pamplona, but here the bulls roam through closed-off Centro streets while would-be bullfighters taunt them.

PUEBLA

Cinco de Mayo, celebrated far more in the US than in Mexico, commemorates the day in 1862 when a small Mexican army at Puebla defeated a much larger French military force—even though France later conquered Mexico and installed Maximilian on the throne. Puebla was the second most important city in Mexico during the Spanish conquest, located halfway between Mexico City and the port of Veracruz where silver was shipped back to Spain.

Many European immigrants settled in Puebla in the late nineteenth and early twentieth centuries, so that German architecture, traditions, and even an Oktoberfest are still prominent today. Puebla is also a rival with Dolores Hidalgo on who makes authentic talavera ceramics according to techniques brought from Spain. The town is largely industrial, known for its textiles and automobile suppliers. Its automotive museum contains one of the Popemobiles used by John Paul II. At 7,000 feet altitude, it is a little cooler than some central plateau cities. Its horizon includes four snow-capped volcanoes, including Popocatepetl, nicknamed "Popo," 17,845 feet.

Tourism is important enough that the industry utilizes red double-decker *turibuses* in the historical center. Most visitors come to see the nearby pyramid of Cholula, the largest in the world depending on how archaeologists measure it against Egypt's, and the 365 chapels of Pueblo, one for every day of the year, or so it is claimed. It is the birthplace of the classic Mexican dishes *mole poblano* and *chiles en nogado*.

Today the city of Puebla has 200,000 people and several times that depending on where you draw the metro boundary, people flocking back into the area since after the 1985 earthquake. (When Cortés arrived, nearby Cholula, which had begun possibly around 1,200 BC, had about 100,000 people, second to Tenochtitlan, now Mexico City.) Yes, there are many expats in Puebla, enjoying the European feel of the colonial center. Carol and Norma consider its Centro even more beautiful than San Miguel's. This is another city where they think they could live, though their Spanish would have to improve considerably.

Taxco, in Guerrero but closer to Mexico City

The state of Guerrero was covered in the Pacific Coast section of this chapter, but Taxco is far inland, on the far border of the state, closer to Morelos than to the ocean, so we're placing the town of Taxco in this section. Taxco is called the silver capital of the world. It is a tourist attraction, with more than 200 shops in the city specializing in silver. It is also known for its roses grown locally and then sold all over Mexico. The city used to be on a major route between Acapulco and Mexico City but was bypassed by a new toll road. It is built on the side of a mountain with very steep narrow cobblestone streets lined by whitewashed houses with red-tiled roofs. Expats have settled there in small numbers for nearly 80 years.

MORELOS

Morelos is another very small state, though it encompasses pine-covered mountains, sub-tropical jungles, and cactus-filled deserts. It is also the mostly densely populated state after Mexico and the Federal District. The largest city, and home to many expats, is Cuernavaca, nicknamed the City of the Eternal Spring because its average year-round temperature is 80 degrees F. The city stretches from those cool mountains on the north to more tropical temperatures on its lower south side.

It's a 45-minute drive to Mexico City. Taxco is also close by, across the state border of Guerrero. The state is filled with archaeological ruins, thermal spas, and palatial haciendas. The city is famous for its language schools, and it is also one of the major science and mathematics centers of Mexico.

Some famous expats who chose Cuernavaca included Woolworth heir Barbara Hutton, gangster Sam Giancana, actress Helen Hayes, philosopher Erich Fromm, jazz musicians Charlie Mingus and Gil Evans, and English writer Malcolm Lowery who based *Under the Volcano* on Cuernavaca.

Artist Robert Brady left behind a 1,400-piece museum that includes works by Diego Rivera, Frida Kahlo, and Paul Klee. Emperor Charles V gave Cuernavaca to Cortés, who introduced the sugar cane that is still a major agricultural export, although the city's economy is also based heavily on industry and tourism.

Cuautla, a city known for its hot springs, is another important city in Morelos. Some of the other noted areas are the archaeological sites of Chalcatzingo and Xochicalco, the caverns of Las Grutas de Cacahuamilpa, the village of Tepoztlán and the Tepozteco pyramid that overlooks it, and Tlatacapan, a pottery town. (Carol and Norma haven't explored this area yet, either, and so our descriptions are sorely lacking in the kinds of details that could help you decide on any of these cities. You'll have to explore on your own, and Carol and Norma will be right behind you.)

MEXICO, MEXICO CITY, and the FEDERAL DISTRICT

And now we arrive at the state of Mexico, the city of Mexico, and the Federal District that is synonymous with the country's capital. For city lovers, this is saving the best for last. If you've never lived in one of the great capital cities of the world you may want to work up to Mexico City, making plenty of visits first. But you know who you are if you're ready to make the plunge.

Toluca is the capital of the state itself. Toluca and Lerma are cities in the central valleys of the state that host prosperous industrial parks. But the capital of the country is *el Distrito Federal*, the Federal District.

In 1824 the Federal District was created as a separate district and made the equivalent of its own state, much like the District of Columbia in the US, so that the nation's capital would not be part of any state. For decades it was not clear what was the DF and what was Mexico City. The issue was settled in 1993 by an amendment to the 44th article of the Constitution stating that Mexico City and the Federal District are the same entity.

Beware, to most Mexicans, Mexico City is called simply Mexico. If someone says he or she is going to Mexico, don't ask where in Mexico—Mexico City is intended.

Thousands of books and billions of words have been written about Mexico City, and any guide book will tell you DF has more museums than anyplace in the world, its historic Zócalo is right up there in size and importance with Red Square in Moscow and Tianneman Square in Beijing, it's the fourth largest center for theater in the world after New York, London and Toronto, and it boasts 16 concert halls. Its National Autonomous University of Mexico is the highest-ranking Spanish-language university in the world. The National Anthropology Museum has the world's best collection of surviving pre-Conquest art and artifacts.

Population estimates vary depending on what you consider greater Mexico City—it is 20 million or more, somewhere among the contenders for largest city in the world, and the region ranks as the world's eighth richest urban metropolis. The city on its own would be the 30th largest economy in the world, ahead of Sweden and Switzerland.

But this massive population also comes from millions of indigenous country dwellers who seek economic improvement in this economic powerhouse, settling into shantytowns around the city for which government officials must provide decent housing and adequate utilities as fast as possible. Along with the impressive wealth comes depressing poverty—as well as the expanding middle class.

Like LA, Mexico City is located in a valley and surrounded by mountains that do not allow easy dispersal of pollutants. Mexico City has been infamous for its smog, though much is being done, such as encouraging heavy industry to locate outside the valley. Among the aggressive measures to combat this problem is the *Hoy No Circula*, "A Day without a Car" program, whereby the last digit of a car's license plate determines what day of the week that car cannot be driven in the city. (Wealthier residents simply bought additional cars so that they could always have one with a license plate allowing it to be driven each day.) Forewarned, no foreign plated vehicles may be driven inside the city from 5-11 am on weekdays. Read Chapter 11 and the Appendix for details.

Where do expats live? US and Canadian citizens have flocked to Mexico City through the centuries; but its foreign population represents the world, with sizeable contingents from all of Central and South America, Europe, the Middle East and Asia. At various times the US expat population in DF has been estimated as high as half a million, though as always, these kinds of figures are impossible to confirm and may include children who were in the US only long enough to be born.

DF has 16 boroughs and hundreds of *colonias*, or neighborhoods. The middle and upper class *colonias* are more to the south and west. The areas many expats settle include Polanco, Chapultepec, Santa Fe, Zona Rosa, La Condesa, Roma, Los Lomas, and El Pedregal, any of which or the Historic Center would be a good place for a new expat to settle temporarily to explore the city and find your own niche.

Polanco has a large Jewish population. Zona Rosa, long a nightclub and entertainment district, includes many gay residents. (Mexico City has legalized same-sex marriage, as has the state of Coahuila.) San Angél was an independent city that became encompassed by the growth and includes excellent restaurants and a Saturday art market. Coyoacan is also known for its markets.

One of the two main streets that will help a newcomer get oriented is Paseo de la Reforma, ordered by Emperor Maximilian to imitate the Parisian Champs-Elysées. It connects the National Palace on the Zócalo with Chapultepec Castle which was the official emperor's residence. The gold Angel of Independence statue soaring in the air is one of the major landmarks of the city.

The other most important street is the 18-mile-long Avenida de los Insurgentes. To choose between the historic center and the colonias around Chapultepec Park, the glitzier, more European-feeling communities are nearer the Park. The Alameda Park area containing Belles Artes, one of the finest concert halls and museums in Mexico and the site of famous murals by Diego Rivera and Mexico's other leading muralists, is also a convenient central neighborhood.

The Mexico City subway system is a quick and cheap way to get around the sprawling metropolis. Carol and Norma, who have been pick-pocketed on subways in Paris and Rome, know now to take more precautions on subways and were very impressed by the Metro. The city has started some women-only cars for those who have experienced harassment, particularly when traveling alone. The Metro transports 4.5 million people a day, for about 20 cents USD, and seniors ride free.

Though some expats take any cab they want and have never experienced any problems, it is recommended to choose a cab from a *sitio*, a marked space on the largest streets specifically for licensed cabs, or have a hotel call one for you. The city is gradually phasing out the green VW bug taxis that have the front passenger seat removed because they were the most likely to be the cause of complaints.

Settle on a price before starting out and look for a working meter. Carry a map with you so you can follow the driver's route. A ride within the city is usually under $10. Some of the smaller green buses are not part of the city's official transit system but Carol and Norma found them as safe and sometimes more convenient. The double-decker red Turibuses are a good way to get oriented. The price includes your own headset that you can plug in for a guide of the sites you pass, given in several languages. The Turibuses take nearly three hours to circle their route through many of the colonias mentioned above.

Carol and Norma rode the Turibuses for several days to get a feeling for these neighborhoods. In their usual daydreaming about what life would be like in the cities they visit, they decided that if they could afford it they'd move to La Condesa but more likely they'd pick Zona Rosa. It is a city for younger expats, they eventually concluded. But if there are 12,000 ways to live for expats to emulate in San Miguel de Allende, there are a half million possibilities in D.F.

Tourist attractions, for Mexicans who want to experience their own roots even more than for foreigners, include the pyramids at Teotihuacán 31 miles northeast of the city, and the floating gardens of Xochimilco to the south. Right by the Zócalo is the Templo Mayor museum, displaying the Aztec temple ruins that were accidentally discovered in 1978 by utility workers laying underground lines—another example of the Conquistadors building a city on top of famous Aztec temples to extinguish the earlier pagan religions and culture.

The Cathedral on the Zócalo and the shrine of the Virgin of Guadalupe are the heart of the country's predominantly Catholic religion. (Mexico has been called the most Catholic country in the world and also the least Catholic because so much of pagan traditions and beliefs remain barely below the surface.)

Many of the city's most beautiful statues and buildings were ordered by Porfirio Díaz for the 1910 one-hundred-year anniversary of the Independencia and also to glorify his reign. Ironically, 1910 was then the start of the Revolution that knocked him from his dictatorial presidency. Another recent key date in Mexico City's history is 1968, when it hosted the Olympics but many hundreds of student demonstrators were murdered shortly before the opening ceremonies. That period of repressive history is still being investigated by those trying to find out exactly how many protestors were "disappeared." And in 1985 a giant earthquake destroyed 100,000 homes and killed somewhere between 5,000 and 20,000 people.

Do not be shocked to see naked men and women demonstrating in the Zócalo occasionally, among the hundreds of protests in the square each year. Indigenous residents of an area of Veracruz come to DF regularly to protest what they say is a land grab some 15 years ago. The men are in the streets wearing only a skimpy flag with a photo of the governor of Veracruz, while the women with no clothes at all are on the sidewalks distributing pamphlets and collecting donations. The taxi driver taking Carol and Norma into DF during one of these demonstrations couldn't wait to see their reactions as he rounded the corner to the Zócalo.

In recent years the Mayor of Mexico City has turned part of the Zócalo into an ice skating rink in the winter and a beach of sand (though no water) in the summer. This is a city of continual surprises and delights, no more unsafe than similar great cities of the world if you take the same kinds of common sense precautions. DF is nearly a mile and a half high, a factor to consider for those with breathing problems.

Valle de Bravo and Ixtapan de la Sal are nearby cities worth considering for visits and possible residency. Valle de Bravo is 90 miles west of DF. The residents enjoy golf, tennis, hang gliding, and water sports, including sailing and fishing, utilizing the large artificial lake. The beautiful cobble-stoned city on a hill with Spanish architecture tends to be expensive. Ixtapan de la Sal, 70 miles from Mexico City, is known for its thermal springs and water parks, and private pools.

And this concludes our trip around all 31 states of Mexico, starting with Baja on the west, coming back up around the mainland and down the Pacific coast to the Yucatan Peninsula, then up the Gulf Coast and down the center of the country to take in the central plateau. Admittedly it is an incomplete overview, designed to give you a feel for all the possibilities of Mexico, besides the areas where many expats have already settled.

We hope this brief overview of Mexico's 31 states and the Federal District/Mexico City, and how the authors decided where to live, has helped you to start thinking about all the places in Mexico that might suit you.

Part Three will deal with making your move. In **Part Four** we'll talk about living in Mexico.

Part Three

Making the Move

Passports, Visas, Pet Permits

In this chapter: Passport requirements today. What is a visa and which one is right for me? Everything about FMTs, FM3s, FM2s, inmigrado status and Mexican citizenship. What if I know from the start that I intend to become a dual citizen? Should I get the most common residency visa, the FM3, while in the US or Canada, or when I arrive in Mexico? What is this about having apostilles *for some documents and how do I get them? What paperwork do I need for my pets to cross the border? How to find a pet-friendly hotel.*

The Mexican government requires that all US and Canadian citizens present proof of their citizenship and a photo ID to enter Mexico. Besides passports, certified copies of birth certificates or naturalization certificates, or a Consular Report of Birth Abroad may work. Here is the website that states that you do not need a passport to enter Mexico: "In accordance with dispositions by the National Immigration Institute, in order to enter Mexico US citizens should show any US official ID. Passports are not required." *http://portal.sre.gob.mx/usa/index.php?option=displaypage&Itemid=111&op=page&SubMenu*

But you are going to need a US passport to get back into the US, or a Canadian passport if you are passing through the US on the way back to Canada, and passports will be important many times if you are moving to Mexico, such as for your visa applications. It can take weeks or even several months to receive a new passport,

161

although sometimes services can be rushed for an additional fee. Here is the US State Department link to all of the information needed to apply for or renew a US passport: *http://travel.state.gov/ passport/passport_1738.html*. Note the 2009 changes in fees and in the process to obtain a passport for a minor.

If you are obtaining or renewing your US passport while in Mexico, here is the link to the Embassy information: *http://mexico. usembassy.gov/eng/eacs_passports_general.html#first*

For Canadians, a Certificate of Canadian Citizenship is not a travel document. A Canadian passport is the only reliable and universally accepted travel and identification document available to Canadians for the purpose of international travel. Canadian citizens returning to Canada who present other documents, such as a Certificate of Canadian Citizenship, birth certificate, provincial driver's license, or foreign passport, instead of a Canadian passport, may face delays or be denied boarding by transport companies. A Canadian passport will be required to pass through the United States.

Here is the website for information on applying for or renewing Canadian passports while in Mexico: *www.canadainternational. gc.ca/mexico-mexique/consul/ppt.aspx*. From within Canada here is the basic passport information website: *www.ppt.gc.ca/*.

For both US and Canadian citizens, if you do not have a passport and already are in Mexico, or if yours is lost or stolen or you need a renewal, it is possible to obtain one at a US or Canadian consulate or embassy. A list of these offices is in the Appendix.

While we are talking about crossing the border, it should be noted that if you are bringing a minor child across the border without both parents, the other parent must have provided a notarized permission, and the original of that notarized permission must be with the child. The permission must include the name of the parent, the name of the child, the name of anyone traveling with the child, and the notarized signatures of the absent parent(s).

Here is the official wording for the permission from the US State Department: *http://travel.state.gov/travel/cis_pa_tw/cis/cis_970. html#entry_requirements*

"The State Department recommends that the permission should include travel dates, destinations, airlines and a brief summary of the circumstances surrounding the travel. The child must be carrying the original letter—not a facsimile or scanned copy—as well as proof of the parent/child relationship (usually a birth certificate or court document)—and an original custody decree, if applicable. Travelers should contact the Mexican Embassy or the nearest Mexican consulate for current information."

The child must also have an individual passport to reenter the US by air. Under the June, 2009 changes, children under age 16 are able to continue crossing land and sea borders using only a *US* birth certificate (or other form of *US* citizenship such as a naturalization certificate.). The original birth certificate or a copy may be used. Check on the latest passport requirements for your country at least a couple of months before you are planning to move.

An overview of visas versus your migratory status

There are at least 17 kinds of visas with various kinds of provisions, but most expats will use either the FMT tourist visa which is good for up to 180 days; or an FM3 *No inmigrante Visitante Rentista* immigrant visa which is renewable every year, for those who have sufficient verifiable monthly income from sources outside of Mexico such as Social Security. (The word *rentista* has nothing to do with whether you rent or own, it has more of a connotation of wealth, of sufficient outside income to live on money not earned in Mexico.)

Your visa is your approval to enter another country, which is different from your migratory status once you are in the country. You can be a tourist on an FMT visa, an immigrant on an FM3, a resident immigrant on an FM2, or after five years on an FM2 you can apply to be either an *inmigrado* or a nationalized Mexican citizen who no longer has to apply yearly for visa renewals.

In 2009 these were the government fees for the various visas: FMT 262 pesos; FM3/New 1,785 pesos, FM3/Renewal 1,294 pesos; FM2/New 3,291 pesos, FM2/Renewal 2,800 pesos.

Most expats won't even think about five years down the road and the possibility of becoming a dual citizen or going for *inmigrado* status, but we will very briefly discuss those choices as well. The right decision now could save you years of waiting later—only five years on an FM2 qualifies toward the five years for applying for *inmigrado* status or nationalization.

If you are coming in on one of the other kinds of visas, for athletes, business travelers, distinguished visitors, students, ministers, scientists, media correspondents, etc., the sponsoring institution will assist you in obtaining the appropriate visa. There is also an investor migratory status for those who will be investing in Mexican commerce or industry with funds from outside the country. The amount to qualify for an investment visa is 26,000 times the Mexico City minimum daily wage, or about $110,000 USD at 13 pesos to the dollar.

The General Law on Population has two additional migration categories for immigrants, which seem to overlap:

"Family Members (*Familiares*)—applies to spouses and/or direct blood descendants (sons, daughters, nephews, grandchildren and brothers/sisters)"; and "Assimilated Individuals (*Asimilados*)—granted to those who do not fit into any of the preceding categories but are assimilated (fit in) to Mexico and will perform some licit, honest and productive activity in Mexico, or for those that are the spouse of or descendent of a Mexican national."

If you think you may fit into either the *familiares* or *asimilados* category, you may wish to consult an immigration attorney to see if it would be advantageous for you to apply for a visa under those categories instead of through an FM3 or FM2.

But most readers will only need to consider whether to stick with the FMT 180-day visa you get at the border, or whether you should apply for an FM3 visa. Then you will need to decide whether to get your FM3 while still in the US or Canada or when you get to your new home in Mexico.

Everything about FMTs, tourist visas

The FMT is the common tourist visa issued as you enter the country. If you fly into Mexico, you will be given the simple FMT visa form on the plane where you can fill it out between turbulence bumps, so you'll have it ready for Immigration when you get off the plane.

Keep that insignificant-looking piece of paper—you will have to return it when you leave Mexico by plane or pay about a $40 USD fine for losing it. The cost of the FMT is included in the price of your ticket. (If you have an FM3 or FM2 and find that you have been charged for an additional FMT visa on an airline ticket, you can apply for a refund from the airline.)

If you walk, drive or boat into Mexico, you will be given the FMT form at the Immigration office at the border. You will have to pay a charge of about $20 USD for your FMT.

The amount of time given on your FMT is at the discretion of the Immigration agent, up to a maximum of 180 days. When driving into Mexico, 180 days is the usual amount given. When flying in, you may be given a lesser time. If your FMT is for less than 180 days, you can get an extension for up to a total of 180 days at any Immigration office within Mexico. After that you must apply for a new one at any Mexican border, including Guatemala or Belize.

If you happen to be asked how much time you will need, tell the border agent that you will be taking a Spanish class for six months and need the entire 180 days—who knows, maybe you will.

The Immigration offices within Mexico usually go by the initials INM (*Institución Nacional de Migración*). Occasionally you may see INAMI, which is the old name. It was changed to INM a number of years ago, but some offices have never gotten around to changing their signs. Forewarned: Immigration offices are often open only 9 am to 1 pm, and often there will be a wait of an hour or more to be seen. Bring a book. They will be closed on Mexican legal holidays, which of course are not the same as in the US or Canada. (To save you checking, the Mexican legal holidays are January 1, New Year's Day; First Monday in February, Constitution Day; Third Monday in

March, Benito Juarez's Birthday; May 1, Labor Day; September 16, Independence Day; Third Monday in November, Revolution Day; and December 25, Christmas.)

The pros of an FMT are that it is easy to get, the fee is only around $20 USD depending on the exchange rate, there is no income requirement or complex paperwork, you need no assistance to get one, and you can change residencies anyplace within Mexico without telling Immigration of your change of address.

You're supposed to turn in your FMT when you leave the country before it expires, and definitely it will be collected if you leave by plane. If you have lost it the fine is about $40 USD. You can get a new one back into Mexico again, even the same day. You can repeat the process forever, at least for now.

If you drive in you can get a temporary vehicle importation permit connected with your FMT at the *Aduana* about 20 miles below the border. (The process of getting a vehicle importation permit is the subject of Chapter 10.)

This next part of the law is not clear and you will get numerous interpretations. Some officials will state that your car is supposed to leave with you when you next exit Mexico and you are to get the hologram you received at the border removed from your windshield when you exit. Keep your receipts.

You are not supposed to fly out of Mexico, leave your car behind, and come back in on another FMT. Your car is not now magically connected with your new FMT. It is possible you will be in serious trouble if at some point *Aduana* realizes that your car is now in Mexico illegally, and your car could even be impounded. But many expats do this routinely, taking advantage of the fact that rarely does anyone at the border take the trouble to check exiting FMTs and remove the vehicle permit holograms. If you didn't turn in your FMT when you exit by driving, don't worry, it is dead once you leave Mexico, and you can still reapply for a new FMT when you next enter.

Here's one con to having an FMT if you have a temporary vehicle importation permit for a vehicle: the law states that you can only have a car in Mexico under an FMT for up to 180 days a year. The law is rarely enforced now—as Mexico's computerization of its car importation records becomes more thorough, it may be enforced more frequently in the future.

One way around this law is to have two names on the car's ownership documents, and on the second 180 days switch the person whose name is being used to apply for the temporary vehicle importation permit. You can then alternate forever. It isn't the car being in the country more than 180 days that is the potential problem, it is one person on an FMT having a car imported for more than 180 days in a year that is the potential problem. But so far this rule is rarely enforced.

Another big con to sticking with FMTs forever is that you can never obtain work papers to work legally on a tourist visa. And if you do decide to buy property you will not be able to take advantage of some tax benefits at resale time. You will also not be able to get an INAPAM/INSEN senior discount card even if you are over 60 if you do not have an FM3 or higher visa.

For those who want to live in Mexico forever but do not qualify under the income requirements for a higher visa, figure out how you can get to the border every 180 days to get a new FMT. Mexican buses to the border are much cheaper than US buses. A round trip fare from the center of the country is about $100 USD depending on the quality of bus you take, and the ride to Texas from the center of Mexico may average 12-15 hours. You can do it overnight both ways and sleep away most of the time, and do a little shopping in Texas while you are there, avoiding the cost of a hotel. McAllen, TX, has particularly nice shopping and good medical facilities.

You want an FM3 if you plan to stay in Mexico for more than 180 days up to the rest of your life, with no restrictions on your coming and going, and you have a Mexican address with proof such as a utility bill in your name or a letter from your landlord, and you aren't thinking already of becoming a dual citizen.

FM3, *"No Inmigrante Visitante Rentista"* visa

An FM3 is a little harder to come by and costs more than an FMT, but it is good more or less forever—so long as you renew it before your expiration date each year at the Immigration office that serves the area where you live. The application and renewals for an FM3 involve a nuisance amount of paperwork, but you don't have to go back to the border every six months. If you move at any time while you are on an FM3, or any other residency visa, you must notify the Immigration office serving the area where you have moved of your new address. There is a small fee to change your paperwork.

When you get your FM3, you will be issued a little olive green book that is like your passport for Mexico. It is useful in opening a bank account, signing up for utility services, and getting some discounts, as well as going in and out of the country.

A big advantage of having an FM3 if you are over age 60 is that you can apply for a Mexican senior discount INAPAM (formerly INSEN) card. It grants half-price bus tickets, movie and museum discounts, discounts on medicines, reductions in some utility bills, and more. (How to get an INAPAM card is discussed in the last chapter of this book in the part on living in Mexico.) And if you own a house, an FM3 may be helpful to you in lower taxes and other real estate transactions. (These benefits apply to the FM2 as well.)

Once you decide an FM3 will be better for you than getting new FMTs every 180 days, you have a major decision to make:

Should you get your FM3 in the US or Canada before you move down, or should you come across the border on an FMT and get your FM3 in Mexico at the immigration office serving your new home?

Pros and cons of getting your FM3 in the US or Canada

Carol and Norma recommend that you come in on an FMT and get your FM3 in Mexico because you'll have to register with your FM3 in the Immigration office closest to your new home anyway, and the process is largely a duplication of paperwork.

But it is usually quicker to get one in the US or Canada, often the same day or a few days compared to as long as three weeks if you get it in Mexico. You may be required to furnish a letter from your local police department that you are of good character and have no outstanding warrants. It's fairly easy to get such a letter, however—you go to your local police department and pay a small fee and they'll check you out and write the letter. If you are applying for your FM3 NoB, some consulates ask for a letter stating you are in good health from your local physician, depending on the consulate's requirements. If your consulate wants this additional time-consuming paperwork to accompany your FM3 application, you may not have any savings in time getting your FM3 NoB.

In the US or Canada you won't be able to take advantage of a reduced FM3 income requirement for owning property in Mexico.

Some Mexican consulates in the US and Canada set age requirements such as no one under age 55, while there is no age requirement to get an FM3 in Mexico.

Each consulate and Immigration office can make its own requirements, including for the amount of income required for the application. So the requirements at the nearest Mexican consulate to you in the US or Canada may be harder or easier than the ones at the Immigration office closest to your new address in Mexico. If you are applying for your FM3 NoB you will be doing all the paperwork yourself; if you apply for it in a Mexican area with many expats, you will be able to find someone to do most of the work for you, for a small fee.

In any case you can make the decision after checking with your closest Mexican consulate to see what their exact requirements are. One thing you will find about moving to Mexico and living here: you may often do some shopping around to take advantage of differing requirements for many things.

One pro of getting your FM3 in the US or Canada is that you can then immediately apply for a *menaje de casa* to bring down one shipment of your household goods at one time with no duty. Chapter 9 includes more about the *menaje de casa* and ways to bring down whatever you want to bring to Mexico for your new home duty-free, whether in a commercial moving van full or a carload.

If you use a commercial moving van, you may not need to apply for the *menaje de casa* yourself anyway; many companies handle all the paperwork.

(If you get your FM3 in Mexico, you can still go back to the US or Canada to get a *menaje de casa* within six months, if you will need one. In some consulates you can obtain a *menaje de casa* within six months after any renewal, not only the initial FM3. You will then have 90 days—or six months, depending on the consulate—after receiving the *menaje de casa* to complete your move of your household items to Mexico.)

To get an FM3 while in the US or Canada, you will have to visit your closest Mexican consulate in the US or Canada in person. Surprise, they can change frequently—a list current as of early 2009 is in the Appendix, along with the US and Canadian consulates in Mexico. Phone calls, letters, and e-mails don't work. You will find that few Mexican business or agencies respond quickly if at all to emails, letters or calls—it is best to do business in person.

You will meet with someone at the Mexican consulate in the US or Canada who handles FM3s and *menajes de casa*. Your line will usually be shorter than the other lines at the Mexican consulates for Mexicans with their own visa applications and problems moving the other direction.

There you will learn about the application form and fee (less than $150 USD) and exactly what other paperwork you need to get your FM3. Here is the Mexican Immigration website, in Spanish, with the current fees for various services including the many types of visas and work permits: *www.inm.gob.mx/index.php?page/ DerechosconsultaDSMO.*

Here is another government site in English, with the requirements for various visas: *http://www.inami.gob.mx/EN/index. php?page/I_would_like_to_live_in_Mexico*

FM3 income requirements from consulate to consulate

One thing all consulates require is proof of financial responsibility to be sure that you are not going to become a burden on

Mexico. Mexico has enough trouble trying to provide any kind of security net for its own citizens. But the income required varies from one consulate to another—usually $1,000 to $2,000 USD per month with 50% more for a dependent—spouse or child—on the same FM3 application.

A spouse is considered a dependent under Mexican law, though you can both apply for your own separate visas if you both have the income to qualify. You will get your own little green booklets either way, but a dependent's will be tied in the system to the main visa if you come in as a dependent.

The official federal requirement is 250 times the current Mexico City minimum daily wage, which is 54.8 pesos in 2009, so 250 times that is 13,700 pesos a month. At 13:1 the minimum monthly income to qualify for an FM3 thus would equal $1,005 USD.

The conversion rate varied all over the place in 2008, from a little below 10:1 to almost 14:1, and it hit 15:1 in early 2009. The amount required for an FM3 thus varied in US dollars from nearly $1,400 a month to less than $906 a month.

It is likely that the peso-to-dollar rate will continue to vary somewhat. We're guessing 13:1 will be the average exchange rate for the near future. Know that if the rate is higher than 13:1, the amount in US dollars required will be less, and if it goes below that, the amount in US dollars will be more.

But even with this rate set in federal law, each Mexican Immigration office in Mexico and each Mexican consulate in the US and Canada has the power to adapt that figure to local conditions, as do the Immigration offices within Mexico if you apply for your FM3 in Mexico.

In San Miguel de Allende, for example, the requirement was set at the beginning of 2009 at $1,200 USD a month, much higher than the federal law requires. At the Mexican consulate in Seattle, it was $1,000, as another example. If you do not qualify at the amount your Immigration office specifies but do qualify at the current exchange rate, ask to see a supervisor and ask that the current exchange rate be used. (Your request may or may not be honored.)

As usual for all our advice in almost every situation, with almost every law and regulation, check with your closest Mexican consulate in the US or Canada or the closest Mexican Immigration office within Mexico for current requirements. These figures should give you a guideline, however.

If you have a dependent entering on your FM3, the monthly requirement is half that of the primary FM3 holder. Be prepared to show a marriage license, birth certificate, or adoption papers to prove the dependent's status. If you have a year's income in the bank, that may qualify for that year instead of monthly income.

Vehicle importation permit

If you drove into Mexico, you got a temporary vehicle importation permit and a hologram window sticker when you came through the border—more on that in chapter 10. If you came in on an FMT, that car permit which you got with your FMT will still be valid when you change to an FM3. You will not be required to get a new car permit at that time. Your original car registration continues to be valid so long as your FM3 is valid.

However, if you ever drive out of Mexico after your FMT would have expired and now you are on an FM3, at the border you might be asked to turn in your FMT-issued car permit and get a new one tied to your FM3. You are not breaking the law by driving with the old permit (read Article 106 in Chapter 10) but at the border they may want you to correct the inconsistency. You will find that many Mexican officials are sticklers for consistency—and inconsistency.

Activating your FM3 at the border

Before you apply for your FM3, you need to consider the time line (and limits) imposed by the Mexican regulations. If you acquired it in the US or Canada, your FM3 is not activated until you cross into Mexico for the first time, and the Immigration folks stamp it. (Oh, how they love to stamp papers in Mexico.) Furthermore, you must use it to cross into Mexico within the first 90 days after you receive the FM3, or it will be invalidated. That means you will have to make a quickie trip to Mexico for this chore unless you are ready to make your move within the first 90 days.

That date when your FM3 is activated is your renewal date for coming years—you can apply for your renewal not more than 30 days before the expiration. There is usually a grace period of up to 60 days for late renewals, especially if you were out of the country at the time. Again, each Immigration office's policies may differ. Generally you will be able to renew your FM3 only in Mexico, although a few Mexican Consulates may do FM3 renewals for you under certain conditions. Check at the Mexican consulate nearest to where you are staying in the US or Canada at your FM3 renewal time and see what they say. If you do find one that will renew your FM3 for you in the US, you may still have to get back to your home in Mexico within 30 days to have it validated.

Once you have crossed the border and had your FM3 stamped at the border, you have only 30 more days to register at the Immigration office serving the area where you will be living. If you fail to meet this 30-day deadline, you will be fined about $300 USD. Norma misunderstood the rule, thought it was 90 days after arrival in Mexico, and was hit with about a $300 USD fine as a result. You are not reregistering your FM3, you are actually registering yourself in your new home Immigration office. A new file will be started on you there that is pretty much a duplicate of your original FM3 application.

If you intend to work in Mexico or start a business, there are additional rules that will be discussed in Part 4, *Living in Mexico*. If you already have a job offer in Mexico, your prospective employer will help you go through the process to obtain a work permit from the beginning.

So what do you need to apply for an FM3?

Whether you apply at a Mexican consulate in the US or Canada, or wait to apply for one when you reach your new home in Mexico at a Mexican Immigration office, the requirements will be similar—with variations possible at whatever office where you apply. The number of copies required may be two or three, depending on the office. You will probably need:

• Original and copies of every page of your passport, including the blank ones.

• Original and copies of your FMT if you came into Mexico on one.

• The application form and cover letter that must be typed, not written, plus copies.

• Proof of residency such as a utility bill or lease or letter from your landlord (probably including voter and/or tax ID), or your deed if you own property in Mexico. (Even if you own a house you may also still have to provide a current utility bill that you are living there.)

• Marriage license and/or birth certificate or adoption papers for any dependents if you are claiming an income requirement reduction for a dependent.

• Original and copies of your proof of income that you meet the minimum monthly financial requirements for an FM3. Usually bank statements for the most recent three months will be enough. Some offices may want the letter from Social Security each year saying the amount of your monthly check, or something verifying the source of your monthly deposits. If you have sufficient funds in a Mexican financial institution the officers will usually write a letter for you to that effect. If you have a full year's income in a bank equal to the 12 months' requirements, a financial statement to that effect may be sufficient to qualify, depending on the consulate or Immigration office.

• Four photos of specific dimensions and requirements—no glasses or jewelry, no hair in your face, ears visible, etc.—so it is best to use a photo studio that is used to making visa photos to these criteria. Taking your own photos and making copies on computer photo paper are not supposed to be acceptable.

If you get your FM3 in Canada or the US you will need about the same papers to register at the Immigration office in your new home. You will also need about the same papers to renew your FM3 in Mexico each year. You won't need more photos until your fifth year renewal, or until or if you switch to an FM2, when you will receive a new passport-like booklet for either the FM3 or FM2.

For renewals other than the fifth year renewal, it is possible to do most of the work yourself by using an *escritorio público*, someone who is authorized to type up government forms for you for a small fee, and who may have the application form and invoice form for you rather than having to stand in line at Immigration to get the forms.

In San Miguel Carol and Norma need only go to an *escritorio público* across the street from the Immigration office with all of their paperwork. He types up the application form, checks to see the paperwork is in order, and types up an invoice to be paid at Banamex. His cost is around $20 USD, paid to him, in addition to the government fee for the visa.

Carol and Norma take the invoice for the government fee to Banamex and pay it and get the invoice stamped paid. Next, they take all the paperwork to Immigration themselves, saving a few steps. The SMA *escritorio* also will make any needed copies and take the proper sized photos when necessary for any kind of application.

In many Mexican offices, even at hospitals, you will see manual typewriters still being used, especially for government forms, rather than computer software that can generate the correct form with a client's information where needed. But it is also true that computerization—and shared files between offices and departments—are coming fast to Mexico.

Some consulates will allow computer printouts of your financial statements if you use internet banking. You may need to include a letter in Spanish explaining why your statements are computer printouts. Carol uses these words:

> *Delgado Regional de Servicios Migratorios*
> (address at which you are applying)
> (date, in day/month/year format
> *Yo,* (your name exactly as it is on your passport and visa
> application), *cuidadano/a de los Estados Unidos de America
> (o Canadá) y residente de (city where you are going to live in
> Mexico), aplico por FM3 visa con cuentas de mis bancos a
> probar mi ingreso, adjunto.*
>
> *Uso operaciones bancarias en internet y mis cuentos son
> de impresora de computadora. Mi banco usa cuentas de in-
> ternet porque es mejor por ecologia no usar papel, y es mas
> rapido y mas barato a usar internet.*
> (Your name and signature)

Translated loosely, the letter says that your banks use the internet for business rather than paper mailings because it costs less, it is better for the ecology to not use paper, and it is quicker.

If you already own the Mexican home you will be living in, you can have the income requirements halved, but you will need to apply for your FM3 in Mexico to get that lower amount—and you will need your deed as proof.

Getting your FM3 in Mexico

You can also get your FM3 in Mexico at the Immigration office nearest to where you will be living in Mexico. There are many reasons you might choose this route: The requirements at the Mexican consulate near you in the US or Canada may be more restrictive. The consulate may be very far from your home. You may not yet know for sure whether you want to stay so you want to come in on an FMT while you travel around and check out areas. You may want to go directly for an FM2 which can only be obtained in Mexico and so you decide to come in on an FMT and avoid the middle step of an FM3. You want to save the duplication of registering and starting a new file in Mexico that requires almost as much work as the original FM3 application if you did it in the US or Canada.

The requirements and paperwork needed will be about the same whether you apply for an FM3 in the US or Canada or in Mexico, with the possible additional requirements for NoB mentioned above.

Immigration assistants

If you are moving to an area with many expats, there will be assistants who can do this process for you for an additional fee of perhaps $50 USD. Immigration attorneys will also gladly do the work for you for much more. We recommend you get help your first time, and also for your five-year renewals. For other renewals you may want to try to do it yourself and save some money.

That is the story of Mexico—we cannot say exactly what any one person's experiences will be because the rules can be enforced differently from one office to another, from one official to another, and even from one time of day to another.

As an aside, President Calderón's campaign to eliminate red tape utilized a national contest to find the worst example of bureaucracy in Mexican government. Top prize in 2009 was $22,000, awarded to a woman who had to visit four different doctors each month to get signatures for the medication she needed for her disabled child. All of the repetitive hassles she documented made it impossible for her to work full-time to pay for the child's care. Expats could have entered the contest with all of the duplications in paperwork we face. (But compared to the problems the average Mexican finds in trying to become "legal" in the United States, we have it easy.)

Why go for an FM2 right from the start? It's the path to *inmigrado* status and/or to Mexican citizenship

If you already have decided that you want to apply for *inmigrado* status or for Mexican citizenship in five years, you may wish to enter Mexico on an FMT rather than getting an FM3 at a consulate in the US, and then go for an FM2 when you get to Mexico.

The rules for obtaining *inmigrado* status and for Mexican citizenship keep changing. At the start of 2009 you needed five years on an FM2 to apply for either, and neither is granted automatically.

More income needed to qualify for an FM2

The application qualifications for the FM2 require a higher minimum monthly income requirement (400 times the Mexico City minimum wage, or 21,920 pesos a month, which in 2009 is equal to about $1,686 USD a month at a 13:1 peso/dollar conversion.). Again, each immigration office can set its own minimum monthly income requirement for an FM2 as well as for the FM3. San Miguel de Allende Immigration office in 2009 set a minimum monthly income requirement of $2,000 USD to qualify, though if you ask for the supervisor you may be able to qualify on the $1,686 figure instead.

You are not allowed to be out of Mexico for more than 18 months out of the five years you are on FM2s, or six months in any one year. If so, you must start over from the beginning. (But you will find that not every trip out of or into Mexico is documented by a stamp in your passport if you drive, so you may be able to be gone longer. Still, it's best not to count on having the extra time.)

Technically you are responsible for having your visa stamped each time you leave and reenter Mexico, but sometimes it can be impossible to find anyone who will stamp it for you. If your visa ends up containing a stamp for one direction and not the other, keep track yourself to be able to explain the discrepancies if you are ever confronted at the border.

For a brief period in 2006-2007, it was possible to apply for Mexican citizenship (also called naturalization) after only five years on an FM3. Then the rules were reinterpreted to say that an FM3 was not really an immigration visa, it was more like a glorified tourist visa, not conveying the necessary resident immigrant status.

Only on an FM2 visa that conveys resident immigrant status do you start to accumulate the five years residency required to apply for Mexican citizenship. You can change your FM3 over to an FM2 at any time to start building up the five years, if you didn't go for the FM2 from the start. Awhile back you had to be on an FM3 for five years before upgrading to an FM2, but that is no longer true.

There are other paths to Mexican citizenship, such as marrying a Mexican citizen or having a child born in Mexico, that have shorter residency requirements—currently two years in these two examples.

The agency that determines citizenship is the *Secretaria de Relaciones Exteriores, SRE,* separate from Immigration. The website for current Mexican naturalization requirements and all the ways to qualify is *http://www.sre.gob.mx/english/services/nationality/default_nationality.htm*

The naturalization process can take a few weeks or, more likely, a year, so apply early, as soon as you have renewed your FM2 the fourth time. Suggestion: keep the office where you file your application informed when you make your future FM2 renewals, if the process continues through a renewal date and you have to renew your FM2 while waiting. We know of a case where the process took more than a year and the office threw out the application because someone in that office decided the FM2 hadn't been renewed and the applicant was no longer interested. She had to start all over.

There will be an oral history and culture test in Spanish, and currently five questions are selected randomly from a list of 100 that require you to know such facts as the Mexican states and their capitals, the major presidents, key eras in Mexican history, five noted Mexican authors, musicians or film directors, federal parks and landmarks, and the author and first verses of the Mexican national anthem (you don't have to sing it). One person was asked the motto of UNAM university. One person accidentally and automatically gave an answer in English first, but even though he immediately corrected himself, he was told to come back in five years when his Spanish was better.

Here is the link to the questions used for the citizenship exams for July-December 2009: *www.sre.gob.mx/tramites/nacionalidad/guia_estudio09.pdf.* These questions are easier than previous years, hopefully a trend.

Different cities will have differing degrees of difficulty for the test. A few applicants haven't been tested at all! Using an immigration lawyer makes the process much smoother. If you're rejected at one city, apply at another, though the fees and the process will start over.

When you are close to the time of applying for citizenship, if you choose to do so, do more research then on what are the requirements, since probably they will have changed.

Why apply for *inmigrado* status or naturalization?

Why apply for *inmigrado* status, and why apply for naturalization? Once you have *inmigrado* status, you never have to renew again, or meet the financial requirements. You will be able to work without a special work permit (a few jobs are not allowed to the foreign-born such as high security positions). You have to formally file for permission from Immigration to work at a job but by law you cannot be refused that permission once you are on *inmigrado* status. You cannot vote or get involved in Mexican politics, but otherwise you have almost all the other rights of a Mexican citizen.

With *inmigrado* status, you do have one time limitation: you can't be out of Mexico for more than 36 consecutive months or five years accumulated absences in ten years, or you forfeit your status. The only Immigration office that issues *inmigrado* cards is in Mexico City. You may want to use an immigration attorney, especially one from Mexico City, for this application process, granting *carta de poder* (power of attorney) to save you many hassles.

With citizenship you can also vote and take part in the political process. (Article 33 of the Mexican Constitution of 1917 forbids non-citizens from influencing Mexican politics, such as by contributing to candidates in Mexican elections or by taking part in demonstrations against any level of the Mexican government, under punishment of immediate deportation).

The same as in the US, a naturalized citizen cannot hold some elected positions. The same way that the US requires its highest elected officials to have been born in the US, the requirements to run for president and vice president include that the candidate be born in Mexico. Requirements for those offices in Mexico also specify that even the parents of the Mexican-born citizen must have been born in Mexico. Mexico does not have fond memories of foreign intervention in Mexican politics.

Although you will be asked to renounce your US citizenship at the time you become a citizen, this is a technicality and is not considered valid by the US. To actually renounce your US citizenship you must make a formal declaration of renunciation before an official of the US State Department such as a consular agent, or take similar official action. If you do have to hand over your US passport, simply apply for another copy from the US later.

Possible tax repercussions

If you have US or Canadian income, check with an international tax consultant before deciding to apply for naturalization, to see your tax implications. In general, if your Social Security income was not taxable in the US, it won't be taxable in Mexico, either.

Of course any money earned in Mexico is taxable in Mexico. Even if you are working online for a foreign company or clients, if you are physically doing the work in Mexico, the law says you should apply for a Mexican work permit and register with *Hacienda* (the equivalent of the US IRS) and file tax forms on that income. (Not many expats in that situation do.)

Which country you will have to pay taxes on that income can vary depending on many circumstances, so you will need to discuss this question with a tax accountant acquainted with your case and with both countries' tax laws. Norma, a former tax specialist, states emphatically that it is very important to get advice from tax specialists rather than relying on the internet or on generic books that don't address your exact situation.

*Apostille*s and translations into Spanish

It is possible but not likely that you will be required to have some documents for any of these application processes translated into Spanish by a designated official translator wherever you apply. And it is also possible that some documents will require an *apostille*, a legal verification that the document is what you say it is, and then it may also need to be translated into Spanish. The office where you apply will explain these procedures if they are needed

The Hague Convention of 1954 established an international system for verifying the authenticity of official documents that might travel from one country to another. This guarantee of authenticity is called an *apostille*—a French word meaning "certification." It is a governmental act by which a designated public official certifies to the authenticity of the signature, seal, and the position of the official who has executed, issued, and/or notarized a document.

Typically after a document has been notarized, it is sent to a state office where the signature and seal of the notary is verified, and the *apostille* is issued. The *apostille* may be a letter attached to the document or be placed on the document itself by means of a stamp.

You may someday need to have your birth certificate, college diplomas, professional credentials, marriage certificates, divorce decrees, adoption papers, or death certificates *apostilled* for some use in Mexico, such as for work permits. The process will be easier if you gather all of your documents together while you are still in the US or Canada, before your move.

Where do you get an *apostille*?

When you need to have an *apostille* for a document and you are in the US, ask at your county clerk's office; they will know the procedure for your state. And your notary may be able to direct you.

In Canada the procedure is different. Canada is not a signatory of the Hague Convention; thus, it does not issue *apostilles*. You will need to take your Canadian documents to a Mexican consulate in Canada where they will issue the necessary papers for you.

If you are already in Mexico, you may be able to send your original document back to the state office which issued it, or you may choose to use a private company that will obtain *apostilles* for you. Private firms are especially helpful if you have documents from several states and institutions that you need in a rush for something like a work permit application. Google for names of many such firms—Carol and Norma used *SFBayNotary.com*.

The state office or the private company will use an official stamp or attach a formal sealed letter to the document verifying its authenticity, usually at a cost of $125-300 USD per document from a private firm. It's much less if you go through the original issuing state office. Especially with a private firm, you will probably be asked to pay for FedEx charges each way, perhaps another $35 USD.

The *apostille* process can take only a few days or perhaps weeks depending on the lag time in a particular state office. If you need one for anything in your visa application, start working on it the minute you find out you need it. You may not need anything *apostilled* unless or until you go for a work permit attachment to your visa later on, or for such applications as for a marriage license to marry a Mexican or for adoption papers.

Proof of residency

Here's a little more information on that proof of residence that is required for so many applications in Mexico. If you don't have a current electric, phone or water bill in your name and you don't have a deed or a lease, you may have to provide a letter from your landlord. That letter may require additional information other than merely a statement you are indeed a renter from the landlord at that address.

Some offices may be cooperating with *Hacienda,* the Mexican equivalent of the Internal Revenue Service, and may want the letter or lease to include a Mexican landlord's voter ID and tax ID number, to prove the landlord is paying taxes on the rental. An expat landlord may have to include visa information and also documentation that the rental property is registered with *Hacienda* and taxes are being paid.

The letter may need to specify that the landlord is paying the utilities, with details on the names the utility bills accounts are in. Carol and Norma have an additional problem in meeting many requirements for proof of address. Not only does their landlord pay the basic utilities but the phone is in the name of a relative of the landlord, and the phone number for the apartment somehow is not the same number as is on the phone bill records! You can imagine the confusion they have run into when applying for a Mexican bank account, for example. Sometimes a cable TV or internet bill will suffice, sometimes not.

The name game

As another example of bureaucracy, be sure to always sign your name exactly the same way as it appears on your passport on all Mexican documents. Make sure your bank accounts and other documents also match your passport and FM3 signatures—even a missing middle initial or nickname can cause a problem. Carol is really a nickname that she has used since grade school, but she has learned to use her full legal name that is on her passport for everything legal now. Always check to make sure that your name is in the correct order on any document you get in Mexico and that the spellings are exact and either full middle names or initials are used consistently. Robert Edward Lee cannot be on one document and Bob E. Lee on another.

In Mexico, name order is different. Expats' middle names are often confused with our last names. In Mexican telephone books, expats may find themselves listed under their middle name. The reason is that in Mexico, people's first names are followed by their father's surnames (possibly with many assorted saints names in the middle), and then at the end is their mother's surname.

To add to the confusion, if a Mexican woman marries, she may choose to add *de* and then her husband's surname after that. Here's an example. A woman whose father's name is Juan Jesus Rodriguez Juarez and whose mother's name is Lupe Maria Santos de Rodriguez and whose parents name her Maria Guadalupe Rodriguez Santos (Maria=first name, Guadalupe=saint's name, Rodriguez=father's father's surname, Santos=mother's father's surname) may or may not choose to change her name to Maria Guadalupe Rodriguez Santos de Gomez (Gomez=husband's father's surname) when she marries Filipe Jose Gomez Ortega. To make it even more confusing, somebody's name could really be something like Maria Guadalupe Rodriguez Rodriguez de Rodriguez if all parties involved shared the same common surnames.

Like in the US and Canada, many Mexican women now never legally change their names to their husbands. It is not surprising that often Norma is called Señora Jean and Carol becomes Señora Lucy, their middle names confused with their fathers' surnames. (Mexico is not alone in doing this—Carol and Norma encountered continual problems on a short trip to Morocco when their visas showed their last names as Lucy and Jean.)

These are the kinds of annoying little problems you may run into in Mexico when someone is being a stickler on rules, such as a new office manager who is trying to do everything perfectly. You may also find the rules get tighter if you have irritated someone—remember those social courtesies and stay pleasant and respectful. Never accuse a Mexican of being wrong, even if he or she clearly is. It is a major cultural no-no. Choose your words carefully assigning no blame, only presenting the problem and possible solutions that might magically solve the problem. Magical thinking is a keystone of the Mexican culture, just as magical realism is a key tradition in Mexican literature. A novel's heroine may cry tears that flow for miles reaching the hero who will come to the rescue. If the official will only change this one word that somehow was translated wrong, no one's fault, magically all the problems will be solved! It may work. (We know of a nationalization process that is at an impasse because one word on a marriage certificate was translated incorrectly and registered incorrectly, thus changing the nationality of the husband. The translator will probably never admit to having made a mistake. Check all paperwork carefully at all stages.)

Possible renewal problems

After your documents have been accepted by the INM, you will get a receipt that shows your renewal is in process. Hold on to that! You may need to show that document if you're driving and are stopped by the police who want to see your FM3 and it is in renewal.

If you need to leave the country suddenly and Immigration still has your original FM3 or FM2, you will be able to get a letter from Immigration that they have your documents during renewal, and that letter will be accepted at the border. But such a letter probably will not be enough to help you with a vehicle importation permit. You are forewarned.

If you are out of the country when your FM3 or FM2 expires, you can get your renewal up to 60 days late, once you can show up at your local Immigration office. Sometimes an immigration lawyer may be able to help you deal with special problems such as not being in Mexico during the 30 days ahead of time and the 60 days grace period afterward for a renewal. But if you miss the deadline, you may have to start all over again, year one on your FM3 or FM2.

It really isn't as complicated as it seems—after your first renewal you may be able to breeze through the entire process on your own. There's always that paid assistant if you can't.

Bringing in pets takes paperwork, too

If you are bringing a dog or cat, you'll need an international health certificate and a current rabies certificate not more than a year old. The health certificate says it must not be more than 72 hours old when you cross the border. If you are driving and you live more than three days drive from the border, this is an impossible task using your home veterinarian.

Some places say the certificate can be five days old, other places will tell you it must not be more than ten days old, or a month, or six months. Whenever Carol and Norma have obtained the certificate, it has said 72 hours. They had to get one signed for each of their three animals the morning they were leaving for the border from Arizona, and they drove long hours each day to make sure they crossed in time. And then the certificate was ignored entirely, the usual case, after all that effort and expense.

Your vet may even fill out and sign the certificate and leave it undated for you to complete when you reach the border. If worse came to worse and someone quibbled on the date of your pet's health certificate, you could get a vet on the US side of the border to fill one out for you. Carol and Norma didn't bother getting certificates the next times they brought their pets across the border. All three pets had health records proving current rabies shots and vaccinations, though. They were prepared to find a vet near the border to get international health certificates if stopped. Rarely will you be asked.

The rule that only two pets may be brought in is also generally ignored. Carol and Norma have heard of no one being refused to bring in more than two. Don't push your luck with a menagerie! This is for driving in, of course. The rules for planes are much stricter on pets.

Here is the government website on bringing pets to Mexico: *http://148.243.71.63/default.asp?id=623*

If you are flying into Mexico with a small dog or cat that can fit in a carrier under your plane seat, you can probably arrange with an airline to bring your pet with you in the cabin. There is a charge, the carrier must be approved, and most airlines have rules as to how many pets may be on any one flight. Friends have had to arrange for someone to take their second pet on a different flight because only one pet was allowed in the cabin per flight on some airlines.

If the dog is too large to fit under your seat, and you must fly, you will have to transport your dog in a carrier in baggage, also at an additional charge. Be sure you indicate that you will be on the same flight as your pet, which requires different steps than shipping a pet on its own.

Airlines generally will not accept pets in the cargo hold during the hottest and coldest times of the year. Each airline has its own rules on pets. When you reach Mexico you will present your pet at the same time you are presenting the rest of your luggage, and agents may be more thorough in checking to see that you have the rabies and international health certificate.

Pet supplies and veterinarians

While we are discussing pets, here is more information on bringing your pets to Mexico. You will be able to find some of the major pet foods in most Mexican grocery stores, and veterinarians will have the some of the most popular prescription brands as well. Purina, Beneful, Whiskas, Friskies, Mainstay, Science Diet, and

IAMS all are available in many stores and vet offices. But a friend of Carol and Norma pays nearly $200 a month to have her vet import a special hypoallergenic dog food for one sickly animal.

Veterinarians are abundant in Mexico, and you will be able to find one who is highly recommended and who offers excellent care. You will be able to hire dog walkers, groomers, pet boarders, and, in cities with wealthier residents, even day care providers and doggie spas.

For their move to Mexico Carol and Norma packed large bags of their spoiled Shih Tzu's favorite Mother Hubbard dog biscuits, but when they eventually ran out, the dog adjusted to Purina Dog Chow after a few days of pouting, and later learned to accept a required IAMS prescription diet. (She never bothered to walk around the house with her empty dish in her mouth reminding us of dinnertime once the Mother Hubbard ran out, though.)

There is also a natural tranquilizer for pets called Rescue Remedy, available in many Mexican health food stores, to help your pet adjust to the move, and to the fireworks and thunderstorms once they arrive. Your vet may also prescribe melatonin drops or a tranquilizer for the move and for fireworks later. Some dogs and cats will adjust soon to fireworks, others will always head for under the bed or a closet at the first bang.

Finding hotels that take pets

Finding a hotel in Mexico that will accept your dog is not easy. Here is a website listing a few places where Fido is welcome: *http:// gringodog.home.comcast.net/pet-friendly.htm*. If you find a hotel website that says the hotel does welcome pets, make a copy of the page and bring it with you in case the manager doesn't know anything about the policy.

One kind of lodging that may take pets and also provide security for your packed car is an auto hotel, often a "no tell motel," usually located on the outskirts of a town. Sometimes the motel's name gives a hint— Las Vegas, Hollywood or Paradise. Look for signs like big red lips in the sign. Or the motel may look as ordinary as a Motel 6.

Besides taking pets, these motels are ideal for cars full of your moving "stuff" because each unit has its own garage and entrance, with total privacy and security. Room service is delivered through a rotating dumb waiter where no one will see who is in the room. Be sure to specify how many hours you want the room for! And don't turn on the TV—it's probably x-rated. These units are perfectly safe—many politicians and business leaders use them.

Birds—the problem is getting them back into the US

Friends who have tried to bring in pet birds with the hope of being able to bring them back into the US if things didn't work out were so stymied by the paperwork and delays that they left their birds with relatives. The problem of smuggled birds coming into the US is a serious one, and the laws don't differentiate between a pet parakeet and a wild macaw. Getting your bird into Mexico isn't the problem, it's getting back in later if you ever have to return that will be the problem. Are you willing to think of leaving your pet bird in Mexico in such a case?

If you want to tackle the move, contact your avian veterinarian for the appropriate forms to document that your bird is in good health, and then contact the US Department of Agriculture. Having this documentation may help you to get your bird back into the United States later, although there will be a 30-day quarantine for the bird at the border. Here is a website explaining the lengthy process for bringing pet birds back into the US: *www.internationalparrotletsociety.org/importnot.html.* We have not been able to determine the process for bringing pet birds back into Canada.

This chapter has described the paperwork involved in becoming a resident of Mexico—both all the kinds of visas and how to obtain them and also the paperwork required for your pet to cross the border. Lists of the embassies and consulates for Mexico in the US and Canada, and the US and Canadian embassies and consulates in Mexico, are in the Appendix.

Chapter 9

Moving Your "Stuff" Isn't Easy

In this chapter: To use a menaje de casa *or not. Bringing all your household versus having a garage sale and buying new in Mexico. Dealing with a moving company. What you can't include in your packing for a moving company. Duty-free items. Prohibited items. Passport regulations. Which lane to choose at the border if you're driving—to declare or not. Customs brokers if needed. Should you take a chance and drive through the Nothing to Declare lane? Shipping by sea.*

Now we can talk about a *menaje de casa*, the permit that allows you to move your used household belongings to Mexico without paying any import duties. If you decide you need one, you will probably get yours from the same office that prepared your FM3, if you got it in the US or Canada. It can only be obtained from a Mexican consulate in your home country, not from an Immigration office within Mexico. If you get your FM3 in Mexico, you'll have to return to the consulate nearest to the address from which you will be moving your household goods. Or, if you're using a professional mover, the company will probably handle all of this for you.

The word "used" is defined as at least six months old. We've heard many stories of how expats have made new items look used—bread crumbs in the toaster, dust on the TV screen, grass in the lawn mower. Rules for the *menaje*, like the FM3, vary among the consulates, so get the instructions on your first visit along with the FM3 instructions.

You may decide you don't need one if you are bringing in only a carload of belongings—the *menaje de casa* application may cost about $150 USD, more than the duties you may have to pay on anything that border officials decide is above your limit for duty-free importation. And if you do move a trailer filled with goods, you'll also need a customs broker at the border to verify your *menaje de casa*, another charge of possibly $300-450 USD.

If you are using a moving company, the firm may deal directly with the Mexican authorities and handle everything. You may still need a *menaje*, a list of the contents of each box with especially the model and serial numbers of all electronics and appliances, but it may be possible to have your list in English rather than have it translated. Check on the requirements at your consulate and at the moving companies you consider.

Carol and Norma's moving experience

Carol and Norma moved everything they wanted to bring to Mexico in their car in two trips, the first one when they came down they thought for only three months. They left all of those things in their newly rented apartment in San Miguel de Allende and went back to Phoenix and applied for a *menaje de casa*. They struggled with the Spanish translations but did the best they could for the 19 Office Depot file boxes they squeezed into their small SUV.

They had sold their RV park model furnished and so did not have to make a decision on shipping furniture. They used a *menaje de casa* because they had two desktop computers with all the accessories, two computerized sewing machines, and many other electronics that they wanted to bring. At that time, 2002, only laptops could be brought in without duty. Now desktops can also be imported, with the restrictions to be given below.

In retrospect, since they had only a small car load, they should have entered without a *menaje de casa* and paid any duty, which probably would have been less than the cost of the *menaje*. Since all their goods were in their car and they really didn't have that much of value, they were not required to hire a customs broker at the border, even with the *menaje de casa*. In fact, the border agents looked surprised they'd bothered and waved them through. Norma even pulled over and attempted to talk to an agent and show him the *menaje de casa* but he wasn't interested.

They were not questioned at all at the border or at the *aduana* about 26 miles farther south. (If you are driving, the border agents and the customs agents are in two different stations and you will go through a red light/green light choice at two places. Carol and Norma got the green light both times. Most people do.)

Agents can still choose to inspect your luggage or car contents even if you get a green light but it is highly unlikely. Even if you get a red light the chances are that your inspection will be cursory. Remember the social pleasantries and a smile with everyone you deal with, to start off on the right foot.

If you are bringing in truly a household full of items, you will want to use a professional international mover, though it could cost $10,000 USD or more depending on the size of your home. Friends have paid $20,000 and thought it was very much worth it.

One alternative to using a moving company is to use a rental trailer to move your small household of goods to a storage facility in Laredo, McAllen, or wherever you want to cross. Turn in the rental trailer to U-Haul or whatever once you've unloaded it into the storage facility, and then take a carload of your items down with you on numerous trips across the border in the future, taking the chance you will get the green light on most if not all of those trips and save a bundle that way. You probably won't want to use this method if you have large appliances and furniture that only a moving company can handle easily.

On the US side now, US agents are checking cars for guns and laundered money headed for the drug cartels. The checks are supposed to be random and they vary in their thoroughness. Be prepared for the possibility your car or trailer may be searched even before you hit the Mexico side.

How Rolly made his move to Mexico

When I lived in Los Angeles, I used to go down to Venice beach to watch the crazies along the boardwalk. The craziest of the bunch was the guy who juggled running chain saws. I thought of him several times while I was trying to map out my move to Mexico.

Before I got my FM3 I knew exactly where I would be living—Lerdo, Durango. So I studied the ways in which I might move my household to Lerdo. I wanted to avoid the expense of a moving company. My first idea was to rent a U-Haul truck to take my things to El Paso, and there transfer them to a truck owned by a Mexican friend of a friend. I learned that no rental trucks are allowed to cross into Mexico, and my Mexican contact could not bring his truck into the USA, so that idea was out.

Then, I thought I would take a U-Haul trailer to a storage place in El Paso, so I could take things across in my pickup, making several trips to my friend's big truck. But that idea was shot down when I learned that the rules say everything on the *menaje* must cross the border in only one shipment. Foiled again! (With many smaller trips in your own vehicle and not using a *menaje de casa*, this is a possibility.)

I did not explore the idea of U-Hauling to El Paso and then hiring a Mexican commercial company to complete the move. My information search did not turn up that option. Since then I have heard from several people who have done this successfully.

Strom Moving (*www.strommoving.com/id28.html*) has a warehouse in Laredo, TX, where you can deposit your shipment, and Strom will then move it through customs and to your new home in Mexico. **Mexico Forwarding, Inc.** (*www.mexico-forwarding.com/*) in Harlingen, TX, offers a similar service, as does *www.moving-tomexicoguy.com*, which offers door-to-door service moving your household from the USA or Canada to any place in Mexico. These kinds of companies can also expedite getting your FM3 as well as doing your *menaje*. **San Miguel Moving** also offers door-to-door moving to or from Mexico. Their website, *www.sanmiguelmoving. com*, includes an online estimating form. Another moving company recommended by friends is **Golden Bear Moving**, Mario Ortiz, South San Francisco, *mario@goldenbearmoving.com*

Here is a website to find licensed movers for your zip code: *www. movingmatrix.com/moving.php*

I have learned that taking your *menaje* stuff across the border yourself is not as easy as it sounds even after you have solved the transportation problems. You can pull a trailer behind a pickup or van, so it is possible to bring quite a bit of stuff. If you do, you'll probably have to engage the services of a customs broker to walk the paper work through Mexican customs.

I've talked to some people who have been through this, and their experiences vary from a minor nuisance to a major hassle. I recommend this do-it-yourself approach only to the stout-hearted. (If you use a trailer, it will be treated like a vehicle; you'll need papers for it—see chapter 10. You won't be able to sell it in Mexico but will have to bring it back to the US at some point, with the same vehicle that brought it down.)

After several weeks of phone calls and internet searches, I gave up on the do-it-myself idea and started interviewing moving companies. I selected United Van Lines because their agent seemed, more than the others, to know what she was talking about. A couple of the agents were less informed than I was. You may find a different "best" mover in your city. Talk to all you can find because the prices, services and experience do vary.

(One of the questions to ask is whether the mover will provide their own employees to pack your goods into their van, or whether they plan on hiring temporary local workers—who may or may not be available in your neighborhood if you are not in a big city. Also ask when negotiating whether a customs broker will be hired and paid for by the mover as part of your costs. It is highly unlikely a mover would insist you be at the border when the truck crosses, but verify to be sure when you are selecting a moving company.)

Having worked out all the mechanics of the move and having most of my *menaje* done, I was finally ready to make the application for the FM3. I planned to have everything in place to complete the move within the first 90-day time window, so I would only have to make one trip to the border—the real trip. I completed my *menaje* a couple of weeks after I got the FM3. Then I was ready to go.

Getting ready for the movers, living out of boxes

Now, preparing the *menaje* and getting ready for the movers is where the real nightmare begins. It's almost a catch 22. You must have your belongings packed in boxes, and the boxes must be numbered and inventoried for the *menaje*. My living room was my box room. But you also have to keep on living in your house while doing all this. Some things you can't box until the day of the move unless you want to move into a motel or with family or friends.

I solved this problem by packing those things for the inventory and box numbering, and then unpacking them for continued use until moving day. I also attached labels to each box listing contents in both Spanish and English. This was a big help when it came time to unpack 54 boxes.

All this inventory and box numbering has to get turned into the *menaje de casa*, which, sigh, must be in Spanish—an original and five copies to be submitted to the consulate for approval and stamping. The fee was around $150 USD.

In the Appendix is my *menaje* with side-by-side English and Spanish to help you translate. I had translation help offers from several of my Latino friends—some from Mexico, some from other Latin American countries. I quickly learned that even simple things are not always called by the same word in various Latin countries. I came to rely only on the Mexicans. I had trouble finding names for some less common items. I never did find the word for "wind chime"—*espanta espiritus*, I learned after I moved. On my *menaje* I called it "music by the wind."

Then there is the matter of who packs the boxes. The moving company must prepare a manifest which the Mexican customs folks can use to compare with your *menaje*. The moving company can't (won't?) list the contents of the boxes you pack—their manifest will say "owner packed." (Friends of Carol and Norma found North

America Van Lines did do a manifest that included the contents of each box, though dozens of boxes had general names like "Misc. Kitchen." The border agents accepted that from the moving company but it is not recommended if you are doing it yourself.)

I was told that this would increase the chances of the boxes being inspected. I was completely honest in what I packed and listed, but I wanted to avoid the time delay of a protracted inspection.

I also was told that if an inspection is triggered, the authorities would find something to charge duty on to pay for their time, a thought that I find believable. So we agreed that I could pack the boxes and leave them unsealed so the movers could verify the contents and then seal the boxes. They charged me an additional $160 USD to seal the boxes. $160 for 54 boxes = $3 per box. I thought that was excessive.

But in the end, it all went well. The head of the moving crew was from Gomez Palacio, the town next to Lerdo, to which I was moving. He was so surprised, and asked, like so many others, "Why?" We had a nice chat.

Two copies of my approved *menaje* were attached to the mover's manifest, and my stuff was loaded on the truck and taken away. The trailer part of the truck was loaded on a train and taken to Laredo where it was attached to a Mexican company's rig and taken through customs and on to my new home in Mexico. The move went off without a hitch, and my stuff arrived a couple of days early and with only minor damage—one cracked glass.

No credit cards for the mover

The bill was $8,000 USD (in 2000—it would be more today). I discovered to my chagrin that United (and others) will not accept a credit card for an international move. $8,000 was only $3,000 more than I had calculated would be the cost of doing it myself—helpers on both ends, U-Haul, gas, motels, Mexican truck, etc. In retrospect, I'm glad I used a moving company.

If you choose the moving company route, your cost might well be different than mine. As you can see from my *menaje* in the Appendix, I brought umpteen boxes of books, kitchen cabinets, file cabinets, two refrigerators, even the kitchen sink, and other heavy items. The cost was about $1 USD per pound, so some of my decisions were based on the simple question, "Can I replace this item for a dollar per pound?" I now wish I had brought several things that I decided I could do without. I also brought stuff I have no use for—wine glasses, fancy serving bowls and platters, etc.

Somewhere along the planning for a move to Mexico, you really should carefully address the question of moving your household furnishings vs. having a giant garage sale, moving to Mexico with personal items and a few treasures that will fit in your vehicle, and buying all new for a new life in a new land. (There is also the question whether your English chintz floral print loveseat will fit into a Spanish colonial or rustic Mexican home.) What you save by not doing the big move plus the income from the yard sale could very well furnish a house in Mexico. You might even rent a furnished apartment or house for a while.

I chose to bring a lot of stuff because the move would be cheaper than replacing my stereo recording system and my graphics-enhanced computer system—replacing them in Mexico would cost more than $8,000 USD. So I brought everything that would fit in my new house and then some. If it were not for those big ticket items, I think I would have come with no more than would fit in my pickup.

Moving your household goods by water

If you happen to be moving from one coastline home to another, such as Seattle to Acapulco, you may want to check out shipping your household contents by water. Here is the contact information for one such company that handles such moves, at somewhat less expense than moving vans: World Cargo International, Robert Blankenship, Managing Director, Tukwila WA 98168, phone 800-839-5003

Friends of Carol and Norma who moved their household from Phoenix to San Miguel de Allende chose a company that promised to use a locked shipping container for their household furniture and combine land and sea transport. The container went to Los Angeles, was shipped by sea to Manzanillo, then sat in that port on the west coast of Mexico for many days. The hefty daily storage charge kept mounting until they tracked down the container and got it routed inland to San Miguel. The items arrived no longer in a locked shipping container, which had been a big selling point when they chose that company, but in the back of a regular moving van.

Most people have very smooth experiences moving their goods, others have assorted horror stories. One woman who didn't have a car or much money learned through a friend of a man with a big truck who would move her household goods and also let her ride down in the cab with him.

He knew nothing about a *menaje de casa*, and neither did she. At the border they had to get a customs broker and couldn't find one—it took five days at the border to resolve this problem, stuck in the border parking lot. She chose to sleep on the small bed in the back of the cab because it felt safer while he slept inside the back of the truck—in her bed.

When they arrived at the outskirts of her new town, the van could not navigate the narrow streets and hills. She ended up sleeping in the cab of the moving van another night while the driver slept in her bed in the back, while they used *mixtas*, taxi pickups, to transport the goods to her new apartment. Neither of them had showers or decent meals during this week. She can laugh now.

Most likely you will have smooth sailing, but this period may be the most worrisome of your move.

What can you bring in on a *menaje de casa*?

The law says you can bring in a household of used personal belongings one time duty-free. If you are just stuffing your essentials in your vehicle, you must make a formal declaration when entering Mexico and you may be subject to IVA (value-added tax) and duty.

You are going to have to declare if you are bringing in cash more than $10,000 USD. You are allowed to do so, but the government wants to know about it. Drug dealers are laundering money across borders every day. Individual border agents may be more or less inquisitive about other aspects of your border crossing. The border officials are fighting a huge war against drug and arms dealers.

A commercial mover will tell you what not to ship

If you use a commercial mover, you will be given a list of what cannot be included in your shipment, which may be more extensive than the list of prohibited items in general later in this chapter. Most likely the moving company's instructions will tell you not to pack any guns, ammo, or drugs, including prescription and over the counter medicines. Bring your medicines with you, with accompanying prescriptions.

Probably you will be told not to pack food, spices, oils (even cooking oils, engine oil, skin or hair oils, lamp oils, etc.), flammable items, alcoholic beverages, only one computer and TV per FM3, live plants, or pornography (loosely defined by any agent and possibly including gay and lesbian books).

Anything that looks as if you are going to sell it in quantity will probably be a no-no, along with taxidermy—leave the mounted deer head with your brother. Valuables like good jewelry and coin collections will be safer accompanying you. In reality, we've never heard of anyone's canned goods, spices, moisturizing oils or quilting fabric stashes being confiscated from a moving company shipment.

You can check for more unusual items—like bales of straw—that cannot be imported at this site: *www.sagarpa.gob.mx*. Most countries have similar rules against importing any item that could harbor diseases or insects.

What if I'm flying into Mexico?

You obviously won't be carrying much with the recent crackdowns on luggage. Check on what the airlines are allowing closer to your departure date. At the airport Mexican officials will still use the red light/green light button to determine who gets a close inspection, and even if you get a green light, if you look "suspicious" or show an attitude you could still be inspected.

You will present your identification at check-in, and on the plane you will be given two forms to fill out. One is for your FMT, tourist visa, and the other is the Customs Declaration Form.

No matter how you come into Mexico, if you do not use a *menaje de casa*, here are the restrictions on what you can bring in duty-free. Another list follows of what is totally forbidden no matter how you enter Mexico.

If you get the red light and you are found to have larger amounts than are allowed of the duty-free items, you will probably have to pay import duties.

If you have prohibited items, the goods will be seized. If you have illegal drugs, guns or ammo, you will be taken directly to jail.

Duty-free items

Again, this is what the Mexican law states. But you will almost never be checked thoroughly even if you get the red light. If the particular agent you get chooses to charge you duty on any item, you really have no recourse. Decide whether you would rather leave the item there or pay the duty.

Each person may import the following items without paying an import duty:

• New or used goods for personal use, such as clothing, foot wear, hygiene products and beauty products, including wedding party items, so long as they are in accordance with the duration of the trip, and their quantity does not suggest that they can be the object of commercialization.

• Two photographic cameras and one video recorder, and, when appropriate, their power source; up to twelve rolls of unused film or video cassettes; printed or filmed photographic material; one cellular telephone apparatus and one pager; one typewriter; one new or used portable computer (laptop, notebook, or similar items); a copier or portable printer; a portable projector, and their accessories.

• Two pieces of sports equipment; four fishing rods; three surf-boards (*Aduana* translates the word *deslizadores* as speedboats which doesn't make sense) with or without sails and their accessories; tro-

202 The Best How-To Book on Moving to Mexico

phies or recognitions, provided that they can be transported normally and commonly by the passenger; one stair climber and bicycle.

• A portable radio for the recording or reproduction of sound or mixed tapes; or a digital sound reproducer or portable reproducer of compact discs and a portable reproducer of DVD's, such as a pair of portable speakers, and their accessories.

• Five laser disks, 10 DVD disks, 30 compact disks (CDs) or magnetic tapes (audio cassettes) for the reproduction of sound, and five storage devices or memory cards for any electronic equipment. (We have never heard of anyone with more than 10 DVDs or 30 CDs having them confiscated but that's the law, enforced or not.)

• Books and magazines, whose quantity does not suggest that they can be the object of commercialization.

• Five toys—included those that are collectible—and a video game console and videogames.

• One device that permits measurement of arterial pressure and one for glucose, as well as medications of personal use. In the case of psychotropics (tranquilizers, mood alterers, morphine-based pain medications, etc.) the medical prescription should be available to be shown if asked.

• One set of binoculars and a telescope.

• Valises, trunks, and suitcases necessary for the transportation of goods.

• Passengers over 18 years of age may introduce a maximum of up to 20 packs of cigarettes, 25 cigars or 200 grams of tobacco, up to three liters of alcoholic beverages, and six liters of wine. These items in excess of the above cannot be imported without complying with applicable regulations and restrictions.

• Baby travel accessories, such as strollers and baby-walkers.

• Two musical instruments and their accessories.

• A camping tent and camping equipment, as well as all accessories required for them.

• Handicapped or senior travelers may introduce items for personal use for a better performance of their activities, such as walkers, wheelchairs, crutches, and canes.

• A set of tools including a case; it might have a hand drill, wire cutters, wrenches, dices, screwdrivers, current cables, etc.

• Bedding, including a set of matching sheets and pillowcases, a set of towels, a set of bath towels, a set of table linens, and a set of kitchen towels.

• Up to two dogs or cats may be introduced as well as their accessories, provided that the corresponding import certificate issued by SAGARPA is presented to the customs officials. (Again, many expats bring in more than two pets and are never questioned.)

• If you bring a desktop computer, you may pay duties and taxes by filling out a payment form as long as the value of the computer and its peripherals and accessories does not exceed US$4,000. If the total value of the computer and its peripherals and accessories exceeds $4,000 USD you must hire the services of a customs broker. (In real life, we have never heard of ordinary individuals being asked to hire a customs broker for their personal computer equipment, whether desktops or laptops. If you have enough to open your own retail outlet, that case would be different.)

The amount of goods beyond the above list of duty-free items is not supposed to total more than $75 USD a person, raised to $300 USD before Christmas to allow for Christmas gifts crossing the border. Or, the total value of non duty free items is not to exceed $1,000 USD per car (not including the desktop computer as described above).

If the border agent decides you have too much, beyond his easy calculation of extra duty, you may be required to hire a customs broker to handle your paperwork. This decision, like so much of Mexican law enforcement, can seem arbitrary.

It's not likely you will ever be required to hire a customs broker for a carload. Carol and Norma have often crossed the border with carloads of new stuff far beyond $75 each, or $1,000 per car, and have never been hassled, even when they have gotten the red light. They have always gotten only cursory glances. Their friends generally bring everything in their cars that can fit, they make new items look used if possible, and they pay any duty they might be charged.

Prohibited items no matter how you cross

There is some variability among border agents of what will be prohibited. Some items are sometimes allowed, such as spices, frozen meat and cheese. Live plants, seeds, and fresh fruits and vegetables that could carry agricultural diseases will be stopped. If prohibited items are found, they will be confiscated, generally without any penalty—except in the case of guns, ammunition, and illegal drugs, in which case you will go directly to jail.

To make this point once more as firmly as possible, firearms and ammunition are strictly forbidden, except for hunting purposes when the rules indicated in section 4 of the Manual of Tourist Entry are followed. Apply at your area Mexican consulate if you wish to bring a rifle for hunting at one of the game preserves near the border. When you make reservations for the camp ask how to handle the gun issue. An unauthorized attempt to bring a gun or ammunition is one of the most serious offenses one can commit in Mexico. Possession of as much as a single bullet can result in your being jailed for a very long time.

Don't count on being able to get any kind of permission for a gun but you can try. The narcotics wars in Mexico are being supplied by US arms dealers who often smuggle in one gun at a time with innocent-looking travelers. Pellet guns, holsters, toy guns—anything that looks like guns to a border agent can mean big trouble. A friend of Carol's spent 36 hours of hell in a Nuevo Laredo jail when he forgot he had some ammo left in his car from a shooting range session. It cost many thousands of dollars in fines and legal fees and a few bribes to court clerks to get his case moved up before he was finally cleared. He will never enter Mexico again. He knows he is lucky to not still be in prison for a decade.

Items prohibited for import and/or export

Here is a list of additional items you can be sure are strictly prohibited for import or export, in accordance with the Law of the General Taxes of Import and Export:
• Alive predator fish.

- Totoaba, fresh or cooled (fish).
- Frozen totoaba (fish).
- Turtle eggs of any class.
- Poppy seeds (narcotic).
- Flower of poppy seeds (narcotic).
- Seeds and spores of marijuana (Cannabis indica)
- Marijuana (Cannabis indica).
- Juice and extracts of opium, prepared to smoke.
- Extracts and juice derived from marijuana.
- Mucilage and condensed products derived from marijuana.
- Stamps or printed transfers in colors or in black and white, displayed for their sale in envelopes or packages, even when they include chewing gum, candies or any other type of articles, containing drawings, figures or illustrations that represent childhood in a degrading or ridiculous way, on attitudes of incitement to violence, to self-destruction or in any other form of antisocial behavior, such as the Garbage Pail Kids, for example, printed by any company or commercial denomination.
- Thallium sulfate.
- Insecticide (Isodrin or Aldrin).
- Insecticide (Heptaclor or Drinox).
- Insecticide (Endrin or Mendrin or Nendrin or Hexadrin).
- Insecticide (Leptophos).
- Heroin, base or hydrochloride of diacetylmorphine.
- Medication prepared with marijuana (Cannabis indica).
- Medication prepared with acetylmorphine or its derivatives.
- Skins of turtle or loggerhead turtle.
- Goods that have been declared as archaeological monuments by the Secretariat of Public Education.

Customs brokers

What is a customs broker? This non-government employee usually has an office very near the border on the Mexican side, and, if you're driving a large load across the border, such as in a trailer, you may even be approached first by a hungry-for-business customs broker. At other crossings you may have a short walk to a customs broker office. Don't hire one unless you are told specifically by the border agent that you need one, no matter what a customs agent who approaches you first might say.

Not all crossings are geared for large loads. If your load is large enough you may be told to go to another border crossing geared to large importations where there are customs brokers.

Like border and customs agents, customs brokers can differ on what they charge and how long they take. Some may not even want to deal with your small load. Ask ahead of time what the probable cost will be—some expats haven't even been charged because the broker didn't know what to do for such a minor load and was perfunctory about the inspection; others have paid $450 USD.

If you are asked to provide an estimated value for any of your items, use garage sale prices. If the items do indeed look used, border agents may assign an even lower price than that. Many flea market dealers cross the border every Monday with their weekend purchases from the US for resale. Parking lots at discount stores near the border are often littered with boxes and packages of new items that are going to be passed off as used. You can be sure they give garage sale prices for items they will sell for much higher in Mexico.

Which lane should I use at the border?

Often you will have a long wait at the border and will have to plan ahead as soon as you can see the lane signs, to make sure you will be in the correct lane once you reach the border. Which lane you use depends on what you are bringing in.

Lanes will be labeled *Nade que Declarar* (nothing to declare), and on the far right, *Carril de Declaración* (declaration lane).

There is no question that you should use the nothing to declare lane when you have only your personal luggage that fits into the duty-free categories and other merchandise up to $75 USD per person. (This amount is usually increased to $300 each at Christmas time.) Save the receipts if you are bringing in something new that will qualify under this exemption.

Your car's weight will trigger the red light/green light as you pass through the lane. (Very rough eyeball guess—at least 75% of cars get the green light.)

The law states that if you are bringing in items that are not duty-free that total more than $75 per person, you are to self-declare them by using the declaration lane. An agent will direct you to where you are to park and then inspect your vehicle and its contents. If you are told to, you may have to go into the customs facility to fill out a declaration form.

You also are to use the declaration lane with a *menaje de casa* to show officials your paperwork, in which case you should not have to pay any duty. That is the whole point of going through the process of obtaining a *menaje de casa*.

If you are bringing in goods without a *menaje de casa*, duty may vary depending on the age of the item and on where it was manufactured—NAFTA-made goods from the US or Canada are supposed to be charged less. The duty will most likely be a flat 15% of the chargeable amount over what you are allowed to bring in duty free and your deductibles. It is at this point you may be told you need a customs broker, as described earlier.

You pay the amount of duty indicated on an invoice at a nearby bank, which may even be in the same building. After paying the duty you will still have to press the red light/green light. If you get the red light you will need to show the officials your invoice for the goods, which should then receive only a cursory inspection.

Theoretically you should always use the declaration lane with a *menaje de casa*, or even if you have more than $1,000 worth of goods total per car that you are importing in your vehicle. It is always safe to use the declaration lane if you are not sure. The law is on the books that your car and its contents could be seized if border agents decide you were trying to deceive them. What kind of a risk taker are you? In practice many expats always use the nothing to declare lane and take their chances on getting a green light.

It should be noted that Mexico has strict rules on bringing down used clothing and other items to donate to Mexican charities. If you are thinking of bringing down some old items to be donated to a local church or school in your new home, or an old computer to give to your housekeeper's kids, it may be better to make those items fall into your own personal use category and not mention that they are going to be donated.

Don't bother to think about bringing down unused medicines or prescription samples to donate to a clinic or agency in Mexico. You will need to hire a customs broker ahead of time to see if there is any way it can be done, and most likely it cannot. You will need a prescription from a doctor for medicines, to start with, and usually you will only be allowed to bring in three months' worth for your personal use. Any medicine with an expiration date that has passed will be tossed, even if somehow you did get a customs broker to negotiate such a border crossing for a donation to a Mexican charitable or health organization. If you have unused medicines you want to donate to someone, it will be easier to do so before you leave the US or Canada.

Now that we have gone into the mysteries of visas, *menajes de casas*, customs brokers, forbidden and limited items, passports, and border lanes, there is yet another morass of Mexican government regulations for new expats: bringing in your vehicle(s). You will take care of these permits about 12-20 miles farther south into Mexico at the next stop, the *Aduana*. This process will be explained in the next chapter. Remember, Rolly's sample *menaje de casa* is in the Appendix.

Chapter 10

Bringing in Your Car Legally

In this chapter: Only one vehicle is allowed in your name. 10-year permits for RV motor homes. What you need for the Temporary Vehicle Importation Permit. Baja has different rules. Article 106. Emissions testing. Crazy not to get liability insurance. Should you buy a Mexican-plated car when you arrive instead? Do you really need a car?

The following information applies only to mainland Mexico. The rules for Baja are different—vehicle permits are not required in Baja, and foreign license plates must be kept current in Baja.

Vehicle means car, pickup, motor home and trailer, and you can import only one vehicle in your name. If you have a spouse, or of-age children, each of them can register a car.

There is an exception to the one vehicle rule. If you are driving an RV motor home and towing a car, you will be allowed to register both in the same name; you no longer will need a second person to register the car. You can also get a 10-year permit for the motor home. This new rule does not apply to pickup campers.

A trailer does not count as a vehicle, but you will need ownership papers as though it were a car.

If you have motorcycles, ATVs, and other types of single-passenger vehicles being carried in your truck or being towed, these may be registered as part of the vehicle carrying/towing them.

There are restrictions: You can tow with your vehicle one to three motorcycles, beach cars, dune buggies, four-wheel motorcycles or ATVs, one each for up to three persons in your vehicle. You need to have proof of ownership for all the vehicles. All must be returned back over the border at the same time your vehicle leaves Mexico. Their importation is tied to the vehicle importation permit for the main vehicle. You will have to turn in that permit when you bring the sports equipment back across the border, and get a new vehicle importation permit for the vehicle alone when you reenter.

The permit that you will get is for the temporary importation of the vehicle. You must remove the vehicle when you leave permanently. You cannot sell it in Mexico. If you leave Mexico permanently, or when your FMT expires, be sure to stop at the car office at the border to turn in your permit and to allow them (not you!) to scrape the sticker off your windshield.

Be very sure to get a receipt showing that you turned in your permit. Keep that receipt, and bring it with you if you ever bring another car back to Mexico, because if their computer says you still have a car in Mexico, you will not be allowed to bring in another, and you will be in trouble for having a car in the country with an expired permit—especially if the car is not in the country. Show them the receipt if you have a problem.

If you really do have a car still in Mexico, you'll be in serious trouble. The Mexican government is very gung-ho on car rules. They state that imported car tracking is completely computerized across the country and connected to a central data base.

Getting your permit on the internet ahead of time

It is now possible to get your registration/permit papers and windshield sticker sent to you by express mail before you make your trip. This allows you to skip the car registration process at the border. You must allow at least 10 days for the material to be sent to you by UPS (hence a street address is required, no post office boxes). The cost will be about $49 USD instead of about $27 if you get it at the border crossing. Here is the Banjercito website with all of the information and application form to get your permit on the internet ahead of time: *www.banjercito.com.mx/site/imagenes/iitv/ instruccionesIITV_ing.html*

You can use the same link to download the application form ahead of time and have it filled out, to present to the Banjercito office at the border. Or you can obtain the form when you arrive at the office at the border and fill it out there.

The Mexican consulates in these cities may also issue the permits ahead of time: Albuquerque, Austin, Chicago, Dallas, Denver, Houston, Phoenix, Los Angeles, Sacramento, San Bernardino, San Francisco, and St. Paul. As always, check with the consulate to see if this possibility still applies at that consulate.

Here's what you'll need if you register at the border:

• Proof of ownership: The Mexican authorities want to be sure that you own the vehicle, so bring your title or registration papers. Carol and Norma were told they must have the title; registration papers alone were not enough. Others have needed only the registration—as usual, in Mexico it all depends.

If the vehicle is not paid for, you must have a notarized letter from your lien-holder (bank, finance company, etc.) granting you permission to bring the vehicle into Mexico. There should be a copy of the title, or the VIN number should be included in the letter. If the car is owned by someone else, or jointly owned by you and someone else, who is not with you, you will need a notarized letter from him/her granting you permission to bring the car into Mexico; include the VIN in the letter.

• Drivers license: must be valid and non-Mexican.

• A credit card or check/debit card: The card must be in the name of the person registering the car—read this sentence again to be sure you understand this iron-clad rule. Make sure the names match exactly—no nicknames or missing middle initials on one. There will be a charge of about $27 USD made to your card for the permit.

If you don't have a card, you can post a refundable cash bond of something like $400 USD—there is a sliding scale determined by the age of the vehicle. The myth persists that your credit card acts

as a bond that you will take your car out of Mexico, and that if you don't, your card will be charged. This is one of the many stories that circulate about all aspects of moving to Mexico.
- Your passport.
- Your FMT or FM3.
- You will need two photocopies of the ownership and driver's license as well as the picture pages of your passport and FM3 or FMT or of your entire FMT.
- Your permit is for temporary use of your car in Mexico. The permit is good as long as your FMT or FM3 is valid. That includes renewals of your FM3.

An FMT is good for a maximum of 180 days. After that time, you must return to the border to get a new one, but there is a small chance that you will not be allowed to bring a car back into the country for the next six months.

There is a largely ignored rule that on an FMT you can have a car in Mexico for only 180 days out of 365. If you have a spouse or someone else on the title who can get a new vehicle importation permit for the car for the next six months, you can continue to use your car in Mexico. It is not the car that is forbidden to return; it is you who cannot bring in a car for the next 180 days. Put this low on your worry list for now. But as more and more offices throughout Mexico become computerized and interconnect, this rule could be enforced more carefully in the future.

Changing from FMT to FM3 and notifying Customs

If you enter Mexico with an FMT and while in Mexico convert to an FM3, you will NOT be required to get a new car permit. Your original registration continues to be valid so long as your FM3 is valid. You will need to tell *aduana* (customs) of your changed status. Theoretically you can do that by mail, but do you trust that the letter will be received and the change recorded? Better to do the change at any of the 42 cities throughout Mexico that have an *aduana* office. There is no fee.

Here is the contact information for one of the *aduana* offices if you want to ask a question: Módulo de Importación Temporal de Automóviles, *aduana,* Nuevo Laredo, 867-712-2071.

Copy this law and carry it in your car

Here is the wording of Article 106, the actual law that says your registration permit is valid so long as your visa is valid, in Spanish and then in English. It also tells who can drive your car. (Your car insurance company may have additional requirements as to who may drive your car.)

Your vehicle importation permit is valid in Mexico so long as your FMT, FM3 or FM2 is valid. If you have changed from an FMT to an FM3 or FM2, your permit is valid, but you may be asked to stop at the *aduana* when you cross the border and update the permit so that your documents coincide.

Also, while you are allowed to drive in Mexico with expired license plates, if you enter Mexico with expired plates, you must use the car's title to get your car permit; you cannot use an expired registration card to get the permit.

For easy printing to keep in your car, go to *http://rollybrook. com/article_106.htm):*

Que se Entiende por Regimen de Importación Temporal
ARTICULO 106 LEY ADUANERA EN VIGOR (2004)

ARTICULO 106. Se entiende por regimen de importacion temporal, la entrada al pais de mercancias para permanecer en el por tiempo limitado y con una finalidad especifica, siempre que retornen al extranjero en el mismo estado, por los siguientes plazos.

FRACCION IV. Por el plazo que dure su calidad migratoria, incluyendo sus prorrogas, en los casos.

a) Las de vehículos propiedad de extranjeros que se internen al país con calidad de inmigrantes rentistas o de no inmigrantes, excepto tratándose de refugiados y asilados políticos, siempre que se trate de un solo vehículo.

Los vehículos podrán ser conducidos en territorio nacional por el importador, su cónyuge, sus ascendientes, descendientes o hermanos, aun cuando éstos no sean extranjeros, por un extranjero que tenga alguna de las calidades migratorias a que se refiere este inciso, o por un nacional, siempre que en este último caso, viaje a bordo del mismo cualquiera de las personas autorizadas para conducir el vehículo y podrán efectuar entradas y salidas múltiples.

Los vehículos a que se refiere este inciso, deberán cumplir con los requisitos que señale el Reglamento.

Rules for Temporary Importation
Article 106 Importation Law Effective (2004)
ARTiCLE 106. Temporary importation means the entry into the country of merchandise which will remain for a limited time and with a specific purpose, provided that it is returned to the exterior unaltered; for the following periods.

SECTION IV. For the period which coincides with the period granted for the immigration category of the owner, including any extensions.

The vehicles can be driven in Mexico by the importer, his or her spouse, their parents and grandparents, etc., their descendants, their brothers or sisters, even when those relatives are not foreigners, or by a foreigner who has the same immigration category as one of those herein referenced, or by a Mexican citizen, provided in this latter case, that a person authorized to drive the vehicle is within the vehicle. Such vehicle is authorized to make multiple exits and returns from and to Mexico.

Vehicles referred to in this section must meet the requirements pointed out in the regulations.

Other requirements

Note that the law ends with the admonition, "Vehicles referred to in this section must meet the requirements pointed out in the regulations." These requirements include, of course, having the vehicle properly registered with a hologram sticker on the windshield and a copy (not the original) of the registration paper in the vehicle.

Many expats take their cars to the nearest of the 42 Mexican *aduana* offices and get a yearly letter specifying their permit continues to be valid, though this shouldn't be necessary. Another gray area: does "same immigration category" mean any visa that allows you to import a car, or only another FM3 holder if the person who imported the car has an FM3? Can an FM3 holder let an FMT holder drive his or her car? Police who stop you or anyone else driving your car may not do nuances. You can ask *aduana* to confirm in writing who can legally drive your car, too.

Visitors to Sonora, south of the Nogales crossing, may be able to bring in their car under the "Sonora Only" program, with no credit card and no processing fee. The permits are good for 180 days and must be returned at the same *aduana*, Km. 21, Highway 15 south of Nogales. Call 1-800-4-SONORA if this option may work for you.

Emissions inspections

In many cities you are also going to need an emissions inspection every six months once you are living in Mexico, resulting in yet another car sticker, this one usually placed on your rear passenger window on the driver's side. The cost is about $11 USD. You may drive your whole life in Mexico and never get stopped at an inspection point for emissions testing, or you may live in an area like San Miguel de Allende where inspection points are frequent.

The major auto repair shops will have signs indicating they perform vehicle emissions testing. Those in some cities, such as Querétaro and Celaya, often have signs out front, *no multas hoy* (no fines today) if your certificate has expired. This testing is another part of Mexico's crackdown on pollution. However, the oldest smoke-belching Mexican-plated cars often have no stickers and don't seem to get stopped; it is expats in new vehicles who seem to be more likely to be stopped.

Crazy not to get liability insurance

Liability insurance is not required, but you'd be crazy to drive in Mexico without it. If you have an accident in Mexico without insurance, the damage to your car is likely to be the least of your problems as you sit in jail—no matter who was at fault—while the authorities sort out what happened, and until you and the other party come to an agreement on damages and injuries. This could take days. Get insurance! There is more on this subject in the next chapter in Part 4—Living in Mexico.

The Mexican government is very strict about the car rules. Don't expect to squeak by if you have not followed all the rules.

If you are not decided on what kind of car to buy for Mexico, and you are sure you want to live in Mexico the rest of your life, seriously consider buying a Mexican-plated car in Mexico. Use whatever you have or get down whatever way you choose, and then look around the town you have chosen and see what car dealers and repair stations there are. Mexican mechanics are notorious for being able to fix almost anything, even with wire coat hangers if needed, but if you want dealer-authorized replacement parts or have a less-common model with unusually-sized belts, tires, etc., it may be easier all around to buy a car in Mexico that already has Mexican plates.

If you buy a new car in Mexico, you will be paying a hefty tax on it based on sales price for the first ten years you own it when you renew your registration, the tax decreasing every year for ten years until it ends. The car itself probably will cost more than the same model if bought in the US or Canada, though sometimes some models are less, and there may be cheaper models available only in Mexico. Emissions and safety requirements may vary even within the same models depending on whether they were manufactured in the US, Canada or Mexico, a fact to be aware of if you hope to sell a Mexican-made car in the US or Canada. You will not be able to sell your US- or Canadian-plated car in Mexico or even give it away to anyone except Hacienda, the Mexican Treasury.

If you do decide to try to nationalize a US or Canadian-plated vehicle that meets the strict requirements, be aware that a vehicle can be nationalized only by a Mexican citizen; a foreigner cannot do it. If you want to nationalize a vehicle, you will need to sign the title to a Mexican that you trust. After the nationalization is completed, the new Mexican title can be signed over to you. There will be an additional fee for this transfer.

It is very difficult to nationalize a US or Canadian-plated car, and the rules and fees change frequently. Until recently, pickups over 10 years old that were made in another NAFTA country (the US and Canada) could qualify for Mexican plates the most easily. For other models until recently, they could be nationalized only in the year in which they became ten years old— except for occasional and unpublicized periods of looser nationalization rules.

The fees to nationalize a car doubled or tripled at the start of 2009 and could be $1,200-4,800 USD. (Some *aduana* officials will still say it is easy to nationalize a car and it only costs a few hundred dollars. As always in Mexico, you can find someone to tell you anything, and your experience will still differ when you go to follow that advice.) Is it worth the cost and hassle? Perhaps only if you really love the car and are going for *inmigrado* or Mexican citizen status, both of which do not allow you to have a US-plated car in Mexico in your name.

And depending on where you choose to live, you may also want to consider whether it is better to buy a beat-up used Mexican-plated car that you will not mind getting a few dings from parking on the street.

One consideration for sure is high road clearance, with the abundance of speed bumps, *topes*, in most of Mexico. They're cheaper than traffic lights in slowing down traffic. And you may find yourself on fairly rough roads if you leave the paved main highways.

Selling a US-plated car back in the US to a friend who wants to bring it back down into Mexico under his or her visa can be difficult. It sounds as if it should be simple: drive the car up and sell it to a lot, or drive up with a friend who wants to buy your car and have the paperwork done across the border.

Instead it took an entire day of red tape in McAllen, Texas, when Carol and Norma sold their car to another San Miguel expat. Texas required that the seller have current car insurance with 30 days validity remaining (though Carol and Norma were only going to own the car a few more hours) and that the buyer also have the auto insurance with at least 30 days remaining, plus a current Texas driver's license. (Their SMA friend had to give up her new California driver's license that had a good looking photo of her for a TX license with a photo she didn't like.) Carol, Norma, and the buyer found one of the small car insurance offices that are located all over McAllen, and both Norma and the buyer put both their names on the minimum 30-day policy.

All three took the car to a Suzuki dealer who could sign the papers that the car was in working condition with all necessary equipment like good tires, a horn, etc., and they waited three hours for someone to be free to do so. And then it started to rain and the mechanic said he couldn't do the inspection when it was raining!

They pointed out that the car was still sitting under a roof in the garage and had been for three hours and hadn't had a drop of rain fall on it. He signed. At one point in one waiting room, Carol whispered to Norma, "I feel like vandalizing something."

The three of them were exhausted and giddy when the transfer was complete. Mexican paperwork didn't look so unrealistic after that experience.

Do you need a car?

If you have chosen a city with abundant bus lines and taxis, consider seriously whether you even need a car in Mexico. Carol and Norma sold their Japanese-made small SUV when it was nine years old and, because it had a J on the VIN number indicating it was made in Japan, it could never be nationalized. They were hoping, and still hope, to get dual citizenship or *inmigrado* status, and knew they would have to give up the car then.

Norma wanted to sell the car when they arrived in Mexico in 2002, when it was worth about $14,000 USD. In Phoenix they drove it 30,000 miles a year. In San Miguel they drove 100 miles a month, usually one trip to Celaya or Querétaro for discount shopping. Counting everything, the car was costing them about $120 a month.

It was still a hard decision—the US puts much stock in car ownership, a car is part of who you are, and life is almost impossible without a car in most US cities.

But in San Miguel and in many Mexican cities, life without a car is very possible—though getting a car is one of the first things a Mexican family will do as soon as they can afford it, too.

What do Carol and Norma do about those shopping trips to Costco and the other discount stores in Celaya and Querétaro? A first class bus goes direct from the SMA bus terminal to either the Celaya or Querétaro bus stations for $2.50-$4.50 USD with their INAPAM discount cards. The Celaya one stops at the Home Depot where Carol and Norma do some shopping, then they take a $3 cab to the new Wal-Mart mall that has dozens of stores, 14 movie theatres, and a food court and Burger King. From there they take another $3 cab to the Costco and buy many big items there—the 36-roll packages of toilet paper, 40-pound buckets of kitty litter, etc. They bring along six or eight of the biggest plaid woven plastic shopping bags available in every Mexican market, and even the biggest items will fit in them. After check out Carol and Norma wheel their loaded shopping cart to the bus stop in front of Costco, where the direct first class bus goes back to San Miguel every hour.

A bus attendant will load their bags under the bus, and at the SMA bus depot another attendant will load them onto a luggage cart and wheel them to the taxi stand area, where a cab driver will load the packages into his taxi and take them home. Usually the driver will bring the heavy items upstairs for them for another couple of dollars tip.

It takes a bit more planning, and they can't go exploring the way they once did unless they hire a driver for the day. But it is very possible to do almost everything they did when they had a car by using buses and taxis. The $120 a month their car was costing them pays for a whole lot of bus and cab fares.

Not having a car is a freeing experience, and it gives you bragging rights in discussions on ecological issues. These are points to consider if you are doing long-range planning about your life in

Mexico, and, for most of us, car purchases are something to start saving for long in advance.

And now on to Part Four, Living in Mexico, starting with more on car insurance and other aspects of driving in Mexico, and then moving on to finding a rental, buying a home, remodeling or building a home, learning Spanish, choosing schools for your kids, hiring employees, possibly working yourself, and, finally, handling the idiosyncrasies of daily life in your new country.

Part Four

Living in Mexico

Chapter 11

Keeping a Car in Mexico

In this chapter: Driving is different in Mexico. "A Day without a Car" policy in Mexico City. Car insurance. What to do in a car accident. Some insurance companies. Motorcycles and RVs. Rental cars.

In the first three parts, we discussed the issues potential expats have about moving to Mexico, regions and lifestyles they might choose in Mexico, and the processes of making the move, including importing a car. **Part Four** is about living in Mexico, and this chapter gives more information on keeping a car in Mexico.

First, here are a few driving tips, some very different from the US and Canada. Once you cross the border in your car you will notice road signs may not be as abundant and clear as you are used to, besides being in Spanish. Carol and Norma kept checking Spanish dictionaries as they drove down the first time and verb tenses in particular just weren't in the books. *No tire basura*, don't throw trash, had them looking for what words might go with tires.

Mexican map books often have sections on road signs and differences in driving here, as do some insurance companies. Be very careful about speeding, especially around Monclava and Monterrey where many stops for bribes have been reported. Reread chapter 6 for suggestions on handling such stops.

Note the warnings not to drive after dark because of livestock on the road, poorly marked construction zones, and cars and rocks left on the road. Broken down vehicles will often have rocks placed in the road instead of road flares, and the rocks are not always re-moved after the vehicle is gone.

Turning left is different in Mexico. On highways, pull over onto the right shoulder to let traffic clear before turning. The left hand turn signal has two often-confused uses. Within cities drivers may use the left hand signal to indicate they are going to turn or change lanes. But in open areas more often a driver will use a left hand turn signal to indicate to you that it is safe (in that driver's opinion) for you to pass. You may not know which the driver intends.

Sometimes there are clearly marked left turn lanes, safe to use even when there is traffic. The traffic lights for making turns may seem confusing, the horizontal line of green and red arrows not al-ways clearly indicating which arrow goes with which lane.

In general, when there are two or more lanes in your direction, stay out of the left lanes unless you are going to pass a vehicle ahead of you in the right lane. High speed drivers will come up very fast and ride the bumper of those driving the speed limit in the left lane.

You will come across speed bumps, *topes*, often without warn-ing. If your car has low road clearance, you may want to approach the *tope* on an angle, as many cars do.

Take toll roads whenever possible. They can be costly, maybe $50 USD from the border to mid-Mexico. They will be well main-tained and have frequent Pemex stations with decent restrooms (usually three pesos) and convenience items. In mid-2009 Pemex froze the price of unleaded 87-octane gasoline to about $2.25 USD a gallon (liters converted to gallons, pesos to dollars 13:1). Here is a site to help you determine your best driving routes within Mexico and estimated tolls and gasoline costs: *http://aplicaciones4.sct.gob. mx/sibuac_internet/ControllerUI?action=cmdEscogeRuta*

Non-toll roads are generally narrower than in the US and Can-ada, often with no shoulders. The drop at the pavement edge may be enough to roll your vehicle if you slip off at high speed. You can round a curve to find a teetering truck overloaded with hay. Cars may pass both of you with no thought for oncoming traffic. Defen-sive driving is your best approach.

Using seat belts is required; police are cracking down in many areas. Trash receptacles will be along most highways, at Pemex stations and toll booths. If you get lost in a city you can hail a cab and follow the driver to the address you want but settle on a price first.

Less expensive than electric traffic lights at intersections are *glorietas*, or roundabouts. *Glorietas* are also used in historic Centro districts where traffic lights are forbidden for historical authenticity. If you watch other vehicles approach a *glorieta*, they usually won't stop unless they are going to hit someone, even if there is a stop sign. Vehicles within a *glorieta* have right of way. Rolly has much more on the rules of the road on his website at *http://rollybrook.com/living_in_mexico.htm#Car*

Hoy No Circula, "A Day without a Car"

If you are going to drive in Mexico City or the rest of the State of Mexico, you need to know about *Hoy No Circula*, a program to cut air pollution. It allows cars with license plates ending in a certain number to drive only on certain days of the week. It is tied to the vehicle-emissions testing program that determines from your license plate which days you cannot drive in Mexico City. The color of the hologram sticker on a car's rear driver's side window shows the days the car cannot drive. At least one day a week and one Saturday a month each car cannot be driven in Mexico City, except for newer (and antique) cars that may apply for exceptions. Violators will be heavily fined and their cars confiscated. Foreign-plated vehicles also may not drive in Mexico City Monday-Friday 5-11 am. Details of the program are in the Appendix.

Getting a Mexican drivers license

Your US or Canadian drivers license is perfectly acceptable in Mexico. When it is due to expire you need to check on the current renewal regulations in your home state if you wish to renew there. Sometimes renewals can be done by mail, sometimes they require a trip back to your home state which may require proof that you are an actual state resident.

Or it may be time for you to switch to a Mexican drivers license, which we recommend. Licensing is a state matter in Mexico as in the US, and the requirements vary among the states. Sometimes they vary from office to office within a state. Efforts are being made to standardize the requirements, but for now you need to inquire at your local office to know its requirements.

In general you will be asked to take a vision exam, usually administered in the office. You will probably be sent elsewhere for a physical exam to be sure you do not have an impairment that interferes with driving. You will almost certainly be asked to take a blood-type test, and the result appears on your license. Some offices send you to a specific clinic or hospital for the tests. Other offices leave it up to you to make arrangements for the tests.

If your foreign license is still valid, you may be exempt from taking the driving and written tests. If you are required to take the written test and your Spanish is weak, you might be allowed to bring a translator. Some offices will take your foreign license; in other places you are allowed to keep it.

Some offices issue a license for as long as five years, but three years is more common. In a few places, the license expires when your visa expires. This means you must renew the license each year when you renew your visa. You can expect to pay more for the license than in the USA or Canada, sometimes much more. (Carol and Norma paid about $50 USD for their five-year licenses. They used an attorney who charged an additional $50 to be certain they did not have to take the written and road tests.) This high cost is the reason many Mexican drivers don't have a license. Of course, without a license, you cannot get insurance.

Two states, Coahuila and Durango, won't issue a drivers license to a foreigner. They only license Mexican citizens, so if you live in either of these states, you must keep your foreign license valid. Three states, Guerrero, Morelos, and Puebla, will license an FMT holder. All the other states and the Federal District require an FM3 or FM2.

Mexican automobile insurance

Mexican automobile insurance and the way accidents are processed are different from the US and Canada. Traffic laws and accident procedures are local matters and may not be the same everywhere. But these are some guidelines.

You need to have Mexican automobile insurance. US or Canadian liability insurance is not valid in Mexico; you must purchase insurance that is authorized but it is not guaranteed by the Mexican government.

Regular Mexican insurance is not available to foreign-plated cars, but several Mexican insurers will write policies for automobiles brought into Mexico on tourist policies. These policies may require that you have an address in the USA.

Rolly has his pickup insured for full value less $500 USD with $50,000 USD liability and $15,000 USD medical. The liability and medical are standard amounts. Because Mexican law does not allow damages for pain and suffering and related possibilities, there is no need for huge liability coverage. But it is very important that the policy cover legal expenses and bail bonds.

Reasons for having insurance are the same in Mexico as in the US and Canada, but the ways accidents are investigated and responsibility is assigned are very different.

If you have an accident, three possible scenarios may follow.

Hit and run: Rolly's Mexican friends have said repeatedly the rule for dealing with accidents where you are at fault is that if your car will still run, drive away. If there is an injury, drive away faster. Rolly has experienced this when he was rear-ended; the hitter sped away before Rolly could get out of his truck.

Obviously this approach is both morally and legally unacceptable. It is also likely to be futile for an expat in a foreign-plated car: you are too easy to trace. When you get caught, you'll be in big trouble with the police, and your insurance company won't pay the claim and will drop you.

Private settlement: If it is a simple fender bender with no injuries and no cops around, the usual procedure is for the two parties to settle the matter on the spot with the hitter paying a cash settlement. The disadvantage to this arrangement is that you may not be able to get your insurance company to fix your car without a police report. But the repair may cost less than the deductible anyway. The advantage is the police are not involved. Twice Rolly has clipped a guy's fender while parking. Both times he settled with the driver for 200 pesos—no hard feelings or hassles with the police.

Police and insurance: If the police see the accident, or if there is major damage or an injury, they will be involved.

Immediately call your insurance company's emergency 800 number so that an adjuster can be dispatched to the scene as quickly as possible. The fact that you have insurance, even with your original policy in hand, means nothing to the police. Only the adjuster can invoke the benefits of your policy. Until he or she gets there, you are, effectively, uninsured.

If you have not bought the legal and bail bond rider for your policy, the adjuster cannot keep you from being arrested if the police decide they want to do that, which they surely will if there is an injury or major damage. You do not want to experience Mexican jails.

If you are uninsured, or if your adjuster does not arrive on the scene before the police complete their on-scene investigation, you and, perhaps, your passengers will be detained at police headquarters until fault and financial agreements can be worked out. If you have no insurance adjuster working on your behalf and the police decide you are at fault, you'll be hanging around until the other party is satisfied with the financial arrangements and says the police can let you go.

Many expats expect they will automatically be judged to be at fault in any accident requiring the police. Rolly leaves it up to his insurance company to fight it out if he ever is in such an accident. Norma and Carol never had any kind of accident or ticket the six years they owned a car in San Miguel. A friend had a car stolen, however, and it took six months and repeated pressure and stress until she was reimbursed for the car. If you do receive an auto insurance settlement for a stolen car it will probably be taxed heavily, one way the government tries to prevent false reporting of car thefts.

It is likely that the adjuster who comes to your aid is not an employee of the insurance company; rather, he or she is probably an on-call contractor. As such, the adjuster will need proof from you that you do indeed have the insurance you claim. Talk to your agent on whether you should carry the original or a copy of your policy in your car. Also keep in your car a couple of copies of your usual important papers: passport, visa, car title, registration, vehicle importation permit, anything the police may want to see.

If alcohol or drugs are involved, your insurance will not save you. A DUI will cause you major problems and your insurance will be cancelled.

Insurance considerations

When you are moving to Mexico, you may want to buy short-term trip insurance prior to crossing the border to cover you for the few days you're on the road to your new home town, and then find a local insurance agent for long-term coverage.

Although any insurance company can send an adjuster to the accident scene, it's helpful, sometimes vital, to have an insurance agent close at hand to help with the follow-up. Rolly uses AXA, which recently bought out the Mexican operations of ING Commercial America, despite knowing that he could get much cheaper insurance online. He chose AXA because the agent is a personal friend who will make sure Rolly is well cared for if he has a problem. He would not feel comfortable with a company that did not have a local representative he knew and trusted.

If you expect to travel around the country, be sure before you sign that your insurance company has a network of claims adjusters who can quickly respond to your needs anywhere in Mexico.

In almost all Mexican insurance policies, theft coverage is listed as total theft. Don't be misled: that total means you have coverage only when the total car is stolen and not recovered. If part of the car is stolen, say the wheels, you are not covered. If the car is stolen and stripped with only the chassis recovered, you will not get any compensation. Some companies offer a rider for partial theft.

Be very careful about buying Mexican insurance online. There are several good, honest companies, but there are also shady characters whose prices look good but the coverage is not what you need. They may want you to buy the insurance before you have a chance to read the policy, which could result in your getting less than you thought you were buying.

For example, a friend bought from an online company believing that her insurance coverage was comprehensive. After she signed up and paid, the policy was faxed to her. Then she discovered it was third-party liability only. The company was willing to change it, but the price for comprehensive was astronomical. Always read the policy before you pay.

Article 106, cited in full in Chapter 10, spells out who may drive your car, but your insurance probably will impose other restrictions. Ask your agent for a clear explanation of these provisions in detail. If a non-listed person is driving your car, you may not be covered in case of an accident. What is allowed under Article 106 has no bearing on what is allowed by your insurance company. Rolly has a file folder full of sad stories from people who did not understand their insurance companies' requirements.

If you buy an annual policy, be sure that it actually covers you for the full year in Mexico. Rolly examined a policy that was good for 365 days but said in the fine print there could be only 30 days of actual exposure in Mexico. Be sure that the policy does not require that you reside outside of Mexico for some period of time each year.

If you don't plan to keep your US (or other) registration current, be sure the policy doesn't require it. Most don't, but there are some that do require valid registration back in the US or Canada. Some even require that you keep up your US or Canadian car insurance. Be sure to ask before you buy.

If your insurance company requires US registration to be valid, consider using Clay County, South Dakota, which will let you handle the registration process online. Do not contact any other office in South Dakota, just the Clay County Treasurer: 211 W. Main St. Suite 201, Vermillion, SD 57069, phone 605-677-7123, FAX 605-677-7104, *treasurer@claycountysd.org*. It is best to call first. That office will direct you to the online forms: Application for Motor Vehicle Title and Registration, Tax Payment Verification Form, Damage Disclosure Form, Your State's Certificate of Title, Copy of Social Security Cards for the owner(s) of the vehicle. You mail them your original documents and a check for the indicated amounts for mailing charges and the registration cost, which varies by vehicle. No car insurance or vehicle inspection is necessary. You will receive your new South Dakota license plates in the mail at your mailing service or address. You can also renew each year the same way. Many expats and RVers use Clay County for this registration. Another reason to keep your car registered in the US is if you plan on driving back to the US with the car.

Insurance policies in Mexico are governed by the Spanish version of the policy. If a mistake was made in the translation into English, the Spanish will apply.

Here are a few car insurance companies

The following is a partial list of insurance companies or agents who write auto insurance for foreign-plated cars in Mexico. No recommendations—as with everything else in Mexico, everyone's experience is different. Rolly uses AXA, Carol and Norma used Lewis and Lewis when they owned a car. As with everything else, laws change, requirements change, companies change. Verbal promises are not binding. Make sure your areas of concern are spelled out in the policy.

Again, these questions are key: Is there adequate legal representation available 24/7 wherever in Mexico you will be traveling? What are the requirements for having your car registered or inspected? Who can drive your car besides you? Do you have to live in the US part of the year? What exactly is covered by theft and other provisions?

Some companies allow online ordering. You may prefer, as Rolly does, to go through a recommended local insurance agent, who may represent one or more of these companies, because of the personalized service, even if it is more expensive than buying a policy online.

The best known because of its detailed mile-by-mile guides for the route you tell them you're taking is Sanborn's Mexico Insurance, *www.sanbornsinsurance.com*, P.O. Box 52840, 2009 S. 10th, McAllen, TX (tel. 956/686-3601; fax 800/222-0158 or 956/686-0732). The company has offices at all US border crossings.

Other companies include:

Lewis & Lewis, *www.mexicanautoinsurance.com/*

AAA Auto Club, *www.aaa.com*

Oscar Padilla Mexican Insurance Services, Inc., *www.mexicaninsurance.com/*

Insurance for Baja, *www.insuranceforbaja.com/*

Drivemex.com, *www.drivemex.com/*

Mexpro, *www.mexpro.com/index.php*

Mexico Insurance Services, *www.mexinsure.com/*

Grupo Nacional Provincial, *www.mexicanautoins.com/*

Genworth Seguros Mexico Insurance Company, a subsidiary of GE Capital Assurance, *www.mexbound.com*

GMAC Travel, *www.gmacmexicotravel.com*

Adventure Mexican Insurance, *www.mexadventure.com*

San Carlos, Sonora, Mexican Auto Insurance, *www.sancarlosmexico.com/insure.html*. Also offers coverage for RVs.

Motorcycles

Few companies insure motorcycles in Mexico. It seems to be available only for foreign-plated motorcycles. Rolly has found no insurance available for bikes with Mexican plates. The website *www.cyclemex.com* contains useful information about motorcycle coverage.

Two brokers provide quotes from several insurance companies for cars, pickups RVs, motorcycles, boats and trailers: *www.insuranceforbaja.com* and *www.insurance4mexico.com/*.

Again, you may prefer to use a local insurance broker who can answer your questions personally and who will know the best companies to meet your needs, especially when you are new to Mexico.

Rental cars

Insurance coverage offered by rental companies in Mexico is typically expensive, often costing more than the car rental. It is, therefore, tempting to find a way to avoid these high costs. Some credit card companies provide collision coverage for rental cars in Mexico. By law, they cannot automatically provide liability coverage, which must be purchased from a Mexican company or from the car rental company.

One very important provision of all credit card plans: you will have to come up with the money out of pocket to pay for any damage to the rental car and then be reimbursed by your credit card company. Read the fine print of the car rental sections of your credit card contract and Mexican provisions.

American Express has a premium insurance program available for a small fee. They also offer a free program for selected credit cards. Both programs have a variety of restrictions, including the requirement that the user be a resident of the US. Visa and Master Card do not seem to have this restriction.

Ten-year tax on new Mexican cars

When you think of the long-range costs of owning a car in Mexico, one factor to remember is the *tenencia* vehicular tax on Mexican-plated vehicles, supposedly a temporary tax added to pay for the 1968 Olympics. Forty years later, it's still here, though President Calderón has vowed to end the tax before his term expires in 2012. The more than two billion pesos it brings in each year are now important to local governments, so it will be interesting to see if this tax actually disappears.

This is the hidden addition to the purchase price of new cars in Mexico. The first year the tax is about 10% of the car's cost, and it keeps going down each year to nothing after 10 years. Drivers can pay the tax at banks or online, by cash or credit card. Mexico City drivers in particular need to pay the tax as part of the verification process for a new car, so that they can get the hologram determining what days of the week they are allowed to drive in Mexico City.

Driving a car is different in Mexico. Ignorance of a law is never an excuse anywhere.

Chapter 12

Your New Home

*In this chapter: Some new terms—*fraccionamientos, ejidos, fideo-comisos, notario públicos. *How to find an inexpensive apartment. Buying, building and remodeling. Overseeing employees and the construction process.*

By now you realize the importance of doing your homework for your move to Mexico, including what kind of home you will choose. You will not automatically fall into your dream home, finding a cheap apartment right in the heart of town your first day, or automatically having an easy buying experience, or building or remodeling a home with no problems. This chapter will help you with that research.

Condos, gated communities, neighborhood associations, home-owner associations and similar concepts are the same in Mexico as in the US and Canada. One term that may be unfamiliar to you is *fraccionamiento*, which could mean a subdivision, development or neighborhood association. *Colonias* in a city are distinct neighbor-hoods, while *barrios* are informal neighborhoods. As in the US and Canada any new development may not yet be connected to water, sewers, trash pickup, street lighting or even police protection when you move in, and it may take awhile to get your title. Some devel-opments include many winter-only Canadian residents, summer-only Texans, or weekend owners from nearby big Mexico cities. The feeling of the community may change drastically depending on the time of week or year. Part-time residents may also be less likely to follow the rules.

The Mexican Constitution forbids foreign ownership of residential property within 100 kilometers (about 60 miles) of a land border and within 50 kilometers (about 30 miles) of the ocean, which are the **Restricted Zones**. But you can get a *fideicomiso*, a trust held by a bank, which will allow "ownership" of residential property in restricted zones. A *fideicomiso* is a trust held by a bank. You as the beneficiary of the trust have complete control of the property and can sell it or pass it on in a will. *Fideicomisos* usually run for 50 years and can be renewed more or less forever. A *fideicomiso* is usually restricted to a land area not exceeding 2,000 square meters (about 20,000 square feet). Larger areas require a special procedure which your attorney or *notario* can explain to you. It is also possible to form a Mexican corporation to own land; explore the pros and cons carefully with a good lawyer.

All land within 20 meters (about 66 feet) of any permanent body of water—oceans, lakes and rivers—is considered to be in the Federal Zone and cannot be owned by anyone, but you can get **conditional concessions** for limited use of this land. Anyone else can get a concession in that buffer land as well—a taco stand could go up on your beach, which is why many owners whose properties abut federal zones make sure to get conditional concessions. You'll need them if you want to add something like a boat pier, too. Federal Zones also occur along federal highways and under and next to high-voltage electrical distribution lines.

Another concept to understand is *ejidos*, communal lands redistributed by the government to groups of farmers and soldiers after the 1910 revolutionary war broke up the great haciendas that were like feudal serfdoms. Membership in an *ejido* is hereditary and members must get permission from, first, other *ejido* members, and then the local government before being allowed to sell their part of the *ejido*.

Real estate agents are totally unregulated in Mexico—no special training or licensing required. They have no obligation to tell you about defects or other problems with a property. The concept of a multiple listing service is rare. The only person you can rely on for accurate legal information is a *notario público*, a licensed attorney with advanced training in real estate law and other government regulations. The *notario público* prepares the title and legal documents for property transfers and determines the capital gains and other taxes and fees.

Finding an inexpensive rental

Before buying a home most people advise that you rent first until you know the neighborhoods in your chosen community. Those on tight budgets may never be able to buy a home, and some expats prefer to rent even if they have the choice. The same tactics apply for finding an inexpensive rental as in the US and Canada. Check local newspapers (including Spanish language ones, not just bilingual newspapers which are less likely to carry the cheapest apartment ads). Walk the streets reading every flyer and bulletin board notice. Look for the few long term rentals on *www.vrbo.com* and *www.craigslist.com*, though these tend to be more expensive. Tell everyone you meet that you are looking for an inexpensive apartment.

Be aware that unfurnished units in Mexico may lack stoves, refrigerators and even towel racks, toilet paper holders and light bulbs. Look past your initial impression of an unfurnished place and ask if you can paint and make other changes, such as a new sink or cupboards. Real estate agents usually won't handle lower-end apartments because of the lower commission, but check with them anyway. Landlords can legally raise the rent 10% a year; try to get a feel for whether the landlord you are considering renting from has a reputation for holding rents steady.

Many neighborhoods in Mexico do not receive continuous water delivery and so *tinacos* (storage tanks, usually on the roof) and/or cisterns below the ground are used to store water. Ask how often the water comes on. Is there a sufficiently large *tinaco* on the roof and/or cistern to make sure you have access to water all the time? Flush the toilet and run the tap to see if there is enough pressure.

First floor apartments have better water pressure from gravity than do upper story units. Be clear in initial interviews with the landlord what is included, both in terms of furniture and utilities. Check where the nearest bus line is, or parking arrangements, or any other details important to you. If your prospective landlord gives only a genial, vague wave, pinpoint how many blocks away that bus station or parking lot is.

Verify with the landlord ahead of time who will be responsible for repairs. Carol and Norma have found that it is easier to just do repairs promptly themselves, in the way they want the repairs done. Repair costs are far less expensive in Mexico.

But it is important to do all of this questioning in the Mexican way of doing business—not abrupt and rushed. Most Mexican landlords will use a standard lease available from a *papelería*, a stationery store. You'll probably have to pay a month's security deposit that often cannot be applied to the last month's rent. Don't expect to get it back promptly if at all.

Often the water, power, telephone and cable TV services will be in the name of the landlord, included in the rent or not. If the utilities were in the name of the last tenant who left an unpaid balance, you may have to pay their bill to get services. For a long-term rental, you may want to get the utilities in your name, though your landlord may not want to give up that control.

Buying a home

If and when you decide to buy a home, you can check to see if there have been complaints about a particular real estate agent or developer at PROFECO, the Mexican consumer complaint agency: *www.profeco.gob.mx/english.htm*. Expect zoning laws to be non-existent or unenforced. As always you have no guarantees that a wonderful view will stay for long. High value homes may be on the same block as hovels, muffler shops, or churches with loud services. Try to find a building inspector to check for major defects. Neither the seller nor the real estate agent has any obligation to tell you about defects. The property is sold "as is."

Consider title insurance

Making sure of clear title is even more important in Mexico, where lax paperwork and feuding relatives may gum up the limited title searches that *notario públicos* conduct.

Financing for real estate purchases is not widely available from Mexican banks, and if it is, interest rates and closing costs will be high. US banks and mortgage companies are starting to enter the Mexican market, however. Seller financing is sometimes available, but be sure to have a good attorney. If the seller is a private party rather than a business, you cannot rely on PROFECO in a dispute.

Make sure the names on all the papers exactly match your passport and visa, as described in Chapter Eight. The *notario* will keep the original signed deed and give you a certified summary, which he will probably report to the town registrar for you. Usually the *notario* will also first obtain permission for you to buy land in Mexico from the Secretario de Relaciones Exteriores (State Department), a formality.

The purchase price and appraised value (usually not the same) should be stated accurately. The seller may want to list a smaller sales price to reduce the tax liability, which is both illegal and not in your long-term interests. If you sell the property down the road you could be hit by the capital gains tax the previous owner escaped paying by getting you to sign off on a lower sales price. Be sure to keep all your utility and tax receipts for as long as you own the house so that you can prove you continuously lived in the house for that capital gains determination.

The *notario* is selected by you, not the seller, but the *notario* is not your representative. He or she represents the State and, by law, is a neutral party in the transaction. The government filings have fixed fees or fees based on the selling price, all non-negotiable, but you may be able to negotiate on the *notario's* fees. The maximum is set by law and may range from 0.2 to 2%. Closing costs may shock you; it is not unheard of for them to be 5-10% of the purchase price.

Any kind of real estate deal might involve a scam, such as bait and switch schemes where you pick out a property on a developer's schematic, pay the deposit, and then are told that property is not really available and you need to choose another, even though all other choices cost more money.

Mexican wills and when you need one

Be sure to update your will to include your newly acquired property. US and Canadian wills are completely valid in Mexico but for Mexican property it may simplify your estate to have a separate Mexican will on that property. This can be a simple "legacy will" on your assets in Mexico only to supplement your will in the US or Canada. Make sure that lawyers who prepare both wills are aware of the existence of both wills and that there is nothing in either will that could present a problem with the other will. Also give directives to whoever is likely to be involved in your final affairs on where to locate both wills.

It is best to include your beneficiaries on your deed when you buy property—but only parents, spouse or children are allowed to be listed as beneficiaries on a deed. (If any of your deeds was once a trust deed from a bank that you've transferred to a direct deed, you cannot go this route.)

If these beneficiaries are also listed as co-owners with full signing authority on all financial accounts you have in Mexico, you may not even need a Mexican will. Probate for a bank account can take months or years, but your beneficiaries will probably need access to your money immediately for your final expenses. If you have several properties, cars, and other assets in Mexico it will be easier to have a will made in Mexico. If your desired beneficiary is not a legal parent, spouse, or child you will need a regular will. A same-sex marriage certificate may or may not be recognized as legal proof for a beneficiary; to be safe, make a will.

Notario públicos are the only ones who can draw up wills, and the documents must be in Spanish. Translations into English must be done by a government-authorized translator, not by a friend.

Though many expats don't like to let any government official "know their business," it really is good to register with the US or

Canadian consulate or consular agent nearest to you. That is who will be called if you are in a serious accident or you die unexpectedly. It will be much easier if contact information for relatives or friends and the location of your will(s) are on record. To register online, US citizens start with *https://travelregistration.state.gov/ibrs/ui/* and Canadian citizens start with *https://www.voyage2.gc.ca/Registration_inscription/olrportal-eng.aspx?Page=Start_commencer.*

Time share agreements

Profeco, the Mexican consumer protection agency, has a page in English with valuable guidelines if you are considering purchasing a time share: *http://www.profeco.gob.mx/revista/publicaciones/otas_pub_06/timeshares_abr06.pdf*

Building or remodeling

One of the many differences in construction projects in Mexico: on May 3, Holy Cross Day, construction workers bring a blessed cross to the worksite that morning and the employer is expected to provide a meal—beer and tacos are usual. Many an expat has been caught by surprise.

Building and remodeling is such a complex topic that it deserves its own book, and Rolly's website with his personal experiences in building his own home and two other Mexican building projects has very thorough information on this subject: *www.rollybrook.com.* The general advice is that construction anywhere will always take longer and cost more than you expected, especially true in Mexico. Note especially the guidelines on registering construction employees with IMSS, the Mexican social security system, which Rolly describes as his biggest hassle in his two construction projects in Durango. His website also has a Spanish-English dictionary of construction terms, including illustrations of common tools.

Chapter 13

Employee Law

In this chapter: Hiring a housekeeper, gardener, or other employees. Work permits for yourself. Renting out property. Starting a business. Teaching English.

This complex section was compiled largely by Rolly and his friend David Bodwell who operates an English language book store in Mazatlán. Rolly has a lengthy summary of labor law at *www.rollybrook.com/labor_law.htm*. Nothing in this section should be considered legal advice, and you should rely upon a lawyer or accountant for the final word on these employee issues. Consider this information a guide only, and remember that the Mexican Constitution and legal system are heavily weighted on behalf of the employee.

A question that is particularly troublesome for many expats is which employees should you register with IMSS and pay for their social security benefits. Definitely a full-time employee should be registered by you. Definitely an independent contractor who comes in occasionally for specific jobs like plumbing leaks does not need to be registered by you. A housekeeper who works for many families a few hours a week each would probably not be registered by any of them. Artisans, craftsmen, non-salaried workers paid by the job, and domestic help are considered not covered.

But if you are a housekeeper's primary employer for at least half time, she still should be given the option to be covered by IMSS

243

paid for by you. She may choose to opt out—she may already be covered through her husband, for example. But where there could be a question if the employment did not end amiably, it would be better to have her decision in writing.

An unhappy worker can always go to the Labor Board or an attorney, and the employee will almost always win. Too many complaints against you with the Labor Board and you could fined or even be deported as undesirable, though we have never heard of this part of the law being enforced.

Payday

Employees are to be paid weekly in cash. Payday is the last day worked each week. Payment must be made in cash, not by check or by commodities. If a worker is hired to work by the week, the daily rate is the weekly amount divided by 7. If s/he is hired by the month, the daily rate is the monthly amount divided by 30.

The law requires that the following items be paid whether or not the worker is registered with the IMSS:

Aguinaldo (Christmas bonus)

The *aguinaldo* must be paid in cash on or before the 20th of December. Gifts, Christmas baskets, and other presents may be in addition to the *aguinaldo*, which must equal 15 days of salary. The simple way to figure an *aguinaldo* is to take two weeks' wages and add an extra day's wages to that amount.

For the exact way to calculate the amount for a part-time employee, divide the number of days worked during the year past by 365. Multiply that figure by 15 x the daily salary to determine the amount of the *aguinaldo*.

Examples:

If you have an employee who works only a very short time one day a week for 50 pesos: 52/365 x 15 x 50 = 106.85 pesos

If the worker is paid by the week and has worked a full year, use a multiplier of 2.14 to make the math easier. If the worker is paid 500 pesos per week, then it is: $500 x 2 .14 = 1,070 pesos

If the weekly worker has not worked a full year, divide the number of weeks worked by 52.14 X 15 X the daily salary (weekly salary divided by 7) to determine the amount of the *aguinaldo.*

Vacación (Vacation)

The *vacación* must be paid in cash, either before the vacation or before the end of the year if no vacation has been taken.

Vacación pay must equal six days of salary plus an additional 25% of the six-day amount. To calculate the amount, divide the number of days worked during the year past by 365. Multiply that figure by 7.5 to determine the amount of the *vacación* pay due. As you can see this is exactly 1/2 of the *aguinaldo.*

Examples:

If you have an employee who works one day a week for 50 pesos: 52/365 x 7.5 x 50 = 53.42 pesos.

If the worker is paid 500 pesos per week: 500 x 1.07 = 535 pesos.

Note: The 6-day minimum vacation is only for the first year worked. The base increases by 2 days each year through the 4th year. The 5th year it increases 3 days to 15 days. Thereafter, the time increases by 3 days each 5th year.

Year 1 — 6 days

Year 2 — 6 + 2 = 8 days

Year 3 — 8 + 2 = 10 days

Year 4 — 10 + 2 = 12 days

Year 5 — 12 + 3 = 15 days

Year 10 — 15 + 3 = 18 days

Year 15 — 18 + 3 = 21 days

The simple estimate for vacation pay each year is the employee's wages for the number of days according to the above schedule, plus another 25% of that amount. Use the formula above to be exact.

Holidays

If your worker works on any of the Mexican legal holidays, the law says you are to pay double time plus the regular pay; i.e., triple time. If the worker is paid for the holiday, but doesn't work, you cannot deduct the day from the "days worked" in the preceding computations for *aguinaldo* or *vacación.*

If your worker works on any Sunday, the law says you are to pay an additional 25% of the daily wage. For weekly workers, you divide the salary by 7, then add 25% to the daily amount for the Sunday pay. This assumes that you have given the employee some other day off during the week. If the employee worked the full 7 days that week you also owe overtime pay. That gets much more complicated. Talk with your accountant.

The Mexican legal holidays are:
- Jan 1, New Year's Day
- 1st Monday in Feb, Constitution Day
- 3rd Monday in March, Benito Juarez's Birthday
- May 1, Labor Day
- Sep 16, Independence Day
- 3rd Monday in Nov, Revolution Day
- Dec 25, Christmas

There are several other commonly accepted holidays such as Dec. 12, Feast of the Virgin of Guadalupe, and Good Friday (the banks may even be closed), but these seven are the only legal holidays.

Maternity Leave

A woman is entitled to six weeks before and six weeks after delivery with full pay. If she is unable to return to work after that leave, she's entitled to a period not to exceed 60 days at half pay.

Termination Pay

Mexican labor laws are very pro worker. Even if you have employed someone part-time for only a short time, that employee is now considered permanent and entitled to three months' severance pay and other benefits, unless:

1. The employment was for a specified period of time, such as while building a house, or for temporary house sitting. Have the time stipulation in writing.

2. The termination is for just cause. You will definitely need the help of a labor lawyer if the employee appeals to the labor review board. What constitutes just cause is spelled out in detail in the law.

Stealing and being drunk on the job are among the just causes, but they can be very hard to prove.

Termination pay shall include 3 months salary plus 20 days for each year worked plus prorated vacation and Christmas pay. If this termination package cannot be paid at the time of termination, regular salary shall continue until the termination is paid in full.

If the employee quits voluntarily, termination pay is not required. But you may still be sued later if the voluntary quit is not in writing. It becomes your word against the employee's, and you will lose the suit. A common tactic to avoid termination pay is to induce the employee to quit, but the law specifies what an employer cannot do to harass a worker and his family.

In the US and Canada business owners know they can terminate or lay off employees during down times to help even out business expenses. But in Mexico, you will still have to keep paying wages and benefits during a layoff.

When in doubt, check with a Mexican labor attorney before a problem can arise or if you have any questions that require a current, locally valid answer.

Working yourself

Most of this information was also compiled by Rolly's friend David Bodwell. First, some basic ground rules:

To work legally in Mexico you must have an FM3 or FM2 visa which must be endorsed authorizing you to work at a specific job for a specific employer. (After five years in Mexico on an FM2 you may apply for *inmigrado* status that will allow you to work at any job without any further work papers, or you may apply to become a Mexican citizen also with no employment restrictions—read Chapter 8 on visas for details.)

You cannot change jobs or employers legally without getting a new endorsement. If you are caught working without a permit, you can be deported. More likely you will be given a large fine and you will still have to pay to get working papers—the government probably will prefer to get the money.

It is very possible you could get caught: somebody will turn you in to immigration, either a competitor you can undercut in price because you are not paying taxes, or a disgruntled customer, or someone who is jealous or nasty. It happens every day. (Many expats are working illegally in Mexico.)

Second, the rate of unemployment is very high in Mexico, so the government will not grant a work permit to a foreigner if it is for a job that a Mexican can do. Usually an artist or writer can get a permit because each artist's and writer's work is unique.

Third, every year some people come to Mexico expecting to enjoy a working vacation, without permits.. Hotel, bar and restaurant pay is so low that you would have a hard time paying basic expenses with nothing left for your vacation—assuming you don't get caught and deported.

Fourth, the law says that you must provide proof of your ability to do the job for which you are requesting a work permit. The proof will vary depending on the job and the requirements of your INM office. In general, proof includes college degrees (diplomas), professional certificates (TEFL/TESL, Teaching English as a Foreign/Second Language, certificates for teachers), etc. These will need to be notarized and have an *apostille* attached, a letter of verification from the issuing state that the document comes from the agency or institution it claims. (See Chapter 8 on visas for complete information on the *apostille* process.) These documents may need to be translated into Spanish.

The two main kinds of work permits are for a job you are already being offered by an employer, and for self-employment in one particular field.

Getting legal if you have a job offer

Even if your prospective employer handles the process, you may still want to hire an assistant, or Mexican attorney, to assist you in getting your work permit the first time—especially if your employer-to-be doesn't seem to be handling it smoothly. You are going to need all the documents and photos you ordinarily use to apply for either an FM3 or FM2 visa, whether you have them already or not (again, read Chapter 8).

You will also need a letter in Spanish and a copy from your prospective employer, on his or her letterhead, stating why you are needed as an employee, what your job title will be, your expected earnings, the employer's RFC number (or if you're being hired by a legal foreigner, his or her visa number and work permit), and the request that you be issued an FM3 or FM2 visa with the correct work endorsement.

You have 30 days after receiving your work permit to register with Hacienda to have your taxes paid and then return to Immigration with that documentation.

Most employers take care of this process for you. If you have to do it yourself, you will need the help of a local registered accountant, who may charge $20-35 USD a month. And, you are going to need a CURP, the Mexican national identification number, similar to the US Social Security number. Immigration will tell you where to get yours. Here is a chart that shows what the 18 digits stand for in a CURP: *http://curp.troyaestrategias.com/.*

Getting legal if you are self-employed

If you are not hired by an employer and want to work self-employed as an artist, writer, photographer, etc., it is recommended that you hire someone to help you who knows what kind of documentation the local immigration office requires to issue a general work permit.

It can only be for one occupation—no hyphenated writer/photographer/artist/massage therapist. Once you have your work permit you can apply to have additional job categories added on, at additional cost and documentation.

Though it is unlikely anyone will ever report you to Immigration for working on your computer out of your home in Mexico, with clients or employers based in the US or Canada, be aware that the law states that if the work is being performed physically in Mexico, you are still supposed to have a work permit. If you're in the public eye or have enemies or jealous competitors, you might want to get legal, even if not a cent of your income is coming from Mexico.

Some volunteers may need work permits even to volunteer

Mexican law does say that all foreigners should obtain work permits even if they are doing volunteer work. Immigration is supposed to keep track of not only what and where foreigners are in Mexico but what they are doing. In reality, if you are an officer or on the board of directors of a large volunteer organization and especially if you have any say over where money is spent, employees hired, or contracts awarded or you are speaking to the media representing your group, your organization should arrange for work permits for its major volunteers.

Even if you serve unpaid on the board of your homeowners association, which is making similar decisions, you should probably contact a Mexican attorney to determine whether your board members should obtain work permits for their volunteer work. It is unlikely that anyone will ever crack down on you for socializing kittens and puppies at the local animal shelter a few hours a week.

It may seem unfair to have to get a work endorsement for what you consider minor or occasional work. Admittedly many people work under the table in Mexico—as also happens in the US and Canada to avoid taxes. Lost taxes from the underground or informal economy is a major part of Mexico's economic problems. Consider the bureaucracy of getting a green card for a Mexican wishing to work in the US. Also keep in mind expats' desires for Mexico to provide more and more services and get rid of corruption and favoritism, at the same time as many expats hide from paying taxes or following Mexican laws themselves.

Renting out your property

If you are earning money in Mexico you need to get a work permit and register with Hacienda and use a Mexican accountant to determine what taxes you need to pay—and that includes renting out a room in your house or any other rental arrangement where you are getting income from a tenant.

Getting the work endorsement on your FM3 or FM2 is the same as above. You will need an accountant. Within 30 days after receiving your work papers you must register at Hacienda as owning rental property and bring the paperwork proving you have registered back to Immigration. You will probably be registered as a *pequeno contribuyentes* or small business.

You file taxes monthly. The amount differs depending on whether you are renting out an apartment or house or whether you are providing services such as a bed and breakfast. Your accountant will help you determine the best category for you to file under and the percentage of taxes you are to pay, and then prepare your end of year declaration to report income and taxes. You don't pay taxes on the property if it is vacant and not earning money for you. You must also report the income to the IRS if you are a US citizen, but it is highly unlikely you will have to pay any taxes on it in the US because your Mexico taxes will offset any liability. Many expats hire a property management firm to handle all of the rental work and maintenance of their property for them. Hacienda workers are very capable of checking *www.vrbo.com, www.craigslist.com,* and any other online rental service and print ads to find rentals that are not paying taxes. If you are going to rent out your property be sure your lawyer and accountant register you with Hacienda and get your work permit in the category in which you will pay the least taxes. Be sure to understand from them the best visa category to have and utility records you may need when you are about to sell your property for tax purposes.

Many expats also rent out their properties without registering or paying taxes, but periodically many Hacienda offices do crack down. Carol and Norma were visited four separate times by Hacienda inspectors who had the wrong address for an unregistered B & B; each visit the inspectors peered into every closet of their apartment looking for that elusive B & B, until Hacienda figured out someone had made a typo.

When you sell a property that has been registered as a rental, you must report the sale to the IRS and pay any capital gains taxes required. You are now selling income-generating property and your taxes will be different in both the US and Mexico.

Starting a business

It is beyond the scope of this book to advise you on all the ins and outs of starting a business and making it succeed. Like in the US and Canada, most small businesses fail the first few years, mostly from undercapitalization. An attorney will help you figure out what permits and licenses you will need, regulations for possible business locations, zoning and employment laws, etc. For import/export businesses, contact the Commercial Service of the U.S. Department of Commerce (*www.buyusa.gov/mexico/en/*) for information. The Mexican counterpart is called ProMexico (*www. promexico.gob.mx*).

Business owners must also obtain work permits and register with Hacienda, Servicio de Administratión Tributaria (SAT), which has an English language site (*www.sat.gob.mx*) describing tax arrangements.

Very briefly, the most basic business structure is *Pequeño Contribuyente*, or Small Taxpayer, for companies with annual revenues up to two million pesos (about $153,800 USD). Above that your business is considered a *Grande Contribuyente*. Someone working independently as a sole proprieter, freelancer, consultant, etc., is called a *Personafisica con Actividad Empresarial*. Corporations are called *Sociodad Anónima*—you may have noticed SA after company names in legal documents. You might also want to form a simple limited partnership (*Sociodad en Comandita*, or SC), a limited liability company (*Sociodad de Responsibilidad Limitada*, or SDRL), among other choices. You will need a *notario público* to help you choose the best structure and how to get started.

Just in the US, a small business owner must be careful about mixing personal and business expenses, such as paying residential electrical rates and then claiming electricity as a business expense.

Cultural differences between doing business in Mexico and elsewhere are outlined in many books, most notably Boyé Lafayette de Mente's *Why Mexicans Think & Behave the Way They Do* (DBA Phoenix Books, 2005), and Ned Crouch's *Mexicans & Americans: Cracking the Cultural Code* (Nicholas Brealey Publishing, 2004).

Starting a business in Mexico is just like starting a business in the US or Canada—except for all the differences.

Teaching English in Mexico

This section is written from the experiences of friends who are experienced ESL (English as a second language) teachers. It is by no means a complete discussion but it does answer some of the basic questions. Carol and Norma have friends who have taught both on-line and in high schools and universities in San Miguel de Allende and have had excellent experiences, though this section warns you about some of the problems others have experienced.

A very helpful "teaching in Mexico" information resource is the Mexico Job Discussion Forum at Dave's ESL Cafe website, *www.eslemployment.com/daves-esl-cafe.htm*, where persons who are now, or who were in the past, teaching English provide up-to-date information and share experiences.

Documents necessary to apply for a teaching position

Since application requirements are inconsistent and not uniform in Mexico, over-prepare when you are still NoB. Bring your birth certificate, university/college transcripts and diploma, and letters of reference from persons in a professional field attesting to your good moral character. If you are married, divorced or widowed, you will need those certificates.

If you arrive unemployed, the letters of reference can be helpful when you interview for a job. These documents will probably have to be notarized and *apostilled* and translated into Spanish.

Finding work before you arrive isn't likely to happen. More likely you'll be investigating school, corporate and tutoring opportunities in the city where you have chosen to live once you arrive.

Most people from the US who teach in Mexico are working for a school (elementary, secondary, or university), for a company that provides language training classes to employees of client companies at the offices/plants of the client, or for one of the many (mostly franchised) language institutes.

Many who have taught in other countries say that teaching English in Mexico ranks at the bottom of the scale of TEFL/TESL (teaching English as a foreign/second language) jobs. Relatively few foreigners who come to Mexico hoping to teach English end up enjoying their time in Mexico, and most complain about the low pay and lack of hours.

Mexico City, Guadalajara and Monterrey are the cities where you'll find employers paying the best wages to Americans teaching English. Some state and private universities scattered around the country also pay satisfactorily depending on your frame of reference.

Working for a school

Of the three types of entities hiring English teachers, working for a school is considered by most as the best teaching job: the work is almost always under a minimum one-year contract, the salary and benefits are better, the employer is typically reputable and reliable and pays salaries on time, and the working conditions are better. Landing one of these good jobs usually requires a teaching degree and prior teaching experience—not just ESL experience, but experience teaching other courses in English.

Corporate teaching

Companies providing language training classes to employees of their clients will be found in most cities of any size and where there is an active commercial scene. Few of these companies require you to have prior teaching experience; being a "native speaker" of English (US-style English) is good enough for them.

No matter the experience level you bring with you from teaching jobs outside of Mexico, these companies typically start newcomers at the bottom of the pay and hours scales. Arriving with a TEFL/

TESL certificate may not even be a real advantage in securing a corporate teaching position. Some of the companies require teacher candidates to first complete their own proprietary corporate teaching course before being permitted to work for them even if they've successfully completed a TEFL/TESL course.

Some companies are not reputable, they frequently pay teachers less than promised, and sometimes pay teachers two to four weeks later than promised. Many newcomers, anxious to begin work, accept one of the first jobs offered and later regret it. In larger cities, there are many companies in which to work, and the best ones are typically the ones for which it takes a little longer to find work. But it may be worth the wait. The problem is that a new applicant, other than using instinct, isn't likely to know which company is better than the rest.

It's not always easy to do, but you may ask for permission to speak with current teachers (foreigners) at the company, and to see a client list. The company probably has many applicants for the position you want and will hire someone more agreeable.

While teachers working for these companies operate more as an independent contractor than a company employee, it's wise to have the company put in letter form the hourly rate you'll receive, benefits (if any), and all working arrangements and conditions. You may choose not to work for any company unwilling to document your verbal arrangement.

Language institutes

The language institutes (Harmon Hall, Interlingua, English First, Quick Learning, etc.) are usually in search of native speakers to teach English classes because the turnover in those operations is high and there are so many offices to staff. Even if a teacher candidate has prior experience teaching English, many of the institutes require the teacher candidate to complete their own proprietary teaching course (and often at a cost to the candidate) because their methods are rigid and teachers are not permitted to stray from the institute's lesson plan.

Again, the higher hourly wages are paid in the larger cities. One of the advantages often cited by foreigners who teach in the institutes is that they're offered more hours than in the company classes, and they don't have to travel from location to location several times each day to get to their classes. At language institutes, too, there have been complaints about low pay, not being paid on time, etc.

There are also language schools that teach solely via the internet. If you are lucky enough to find such an employer, you may find yourself with a camera and microphone attached to your computer, teaching a student in Brazil in the morning and one in Hong Kong at night.

Private classes

Often talked about, but not often found, are situations teaching private lessons. Putting up flyers on telephone poles and on bulletin boards will not automatically lead to a full tutoring schedule. Many who want to learn English cannot afford to pay for lessons of any kind and will hope you will teach them for free or for a bartering arrangement, maybe helping you with your Spanish in return. (Many expats do teach neighbor kids for free, as a way of giving back and also of building good relationships with their neighbors.) Teaching privately will involve all the problems you might expect—no shows, clients who don't really want to learn but are going through the motions, difficulties getting paid, etc.

Many who give lessons on the side found their students as part of other teaching such as by teaching for companies. While tutoring can provide a small amount of additional income, it will not be all that much for most teachers. Tutoring does provide the opportunity to get into people's homes to see how they live and to make friends with them and their families, when it does work out.

Some teachers who have shared their experiences report that high salaries are promised to lure them to Mexico, but when they arrive, having paid their own transportation, salaries and hours are cut drastically. Sometimes they are shown apartments to rent that turn out to be overpriced income supplements for friends of the employer. Turnover is often high but there is an unending supply of eager, enthusiastic foreign teachers ready to replace anyone who quits or even complains.

Sometimes the employer cites laws that limit foreign teachers to less than full-time at any one institution, under 19 hours, so they cannot receive benefits. Your classroom preparation time usually is not considered in your salary. If you work 19 hours a week each at two schools, you still will not qualify for full benefits.

Your schedule may be split to teach before-work morning or late evening classes for adults and late afternoon classes for school-aged students, so you are busy all day long with no time to prepare or enjoy a life. Back-up money is a must if you are considering coming to Mexico to teach. You may find a wonderful teaching opportunity, or you may have to change your plans.

Hiring employees and working yourself in Mexico can be quite a different experience from what you expect from your US or Canadian background. Like everything else about Mexico, you will be making your own life, dealing with whatever circumstances arise for you, with no guarantees. For some people who hate ruts, that can be an enriching, challenging opportunity. For others, attempting to work in Mexico can be less than rewarding. You probably shouldn't count on being able to come to Mexico and find a good job easily. For many expats, that does happen, but not for all.

Remember, the minimum daily wage in Mexico City in 2009 was 54.8 pesos, or $4.22 USD, A DAY. If you get any job in Mexico, it probably won't be at that low of a salary, but it probably won't be what you might expect to earn in the US or Canada, even considering lower living costs.

Still, some expats do very well working or starting new businesses in Mexico. With careful planning and realistic expectations, you could be one of those who succeed. And the joys of living in a better climate, a more pleasant environment, at less cost and stress, with greater pleasure in your daily life, may far outweigh the financial rewards you might have had to give up working in the US.

Chapter 14

Fitting In

In this chapter: Learning Spanish. Banking and ATMs. Phones. Internet. Mexican cable and satellite TV. Educating your children. Dealing with poverty around you. Stray animals. Shopping. Cooking techniques and food substitutions. Staying out of politics. The peso mentality. INAPAM card. The Mexican bus system. Cultural jolts. Differences in holidays and celebrations. Getting married. A final love story to Mexico.

At this point it is hard to give any kind of universal advice because everyone's life in Mexico will be very different depending on where you choose to live, your age, income level, sex, marital status, health, etc. But here are some guidelines that may or may not apply to your situation.

Learning at least the basics in Spanish is #1

Learning Spanish is the number one priority if you want to take full advantage of all your new country has to offer, and also to live the most securely and economically. Many books on Mexico say that you don't have to know much Spanish, especially if you settle in a city with many expats. You can survive with a basic course on social pleasantries, the numbers and money, directions, food items, cooking terms, and so on. But you will always be aware that at some point you really might need to know enough Spanish to handle an emergency. And if you meet someone you really want to know you'll wish you could say more than *"Buenas tardes, ¿como está? ¿Le gusta tacos?"*

That said, Carol and Norma have had eight semesters equivalent of Spanish classes (actually the first year over and over again) and are barely intermediate. It isn't easy for most expats, especially seniors. Most studies say older people have a harder time learning a second language, but a few say that it is actually easier for adults because they are usually more highly motivated and they already have the mechanics of learning a first language. Many expats say that their greatest disappointment with living in Mexico is that they have not been able to become fluent. Class work alone won't make you fluent, you have to practice constantly, and that's a lot easier to do in a living situation with no other English speakers around.

Your individual learning style and weaknesses will determine which teaching method is best for you. Carol and Norma both have slight hearing problems that often come with aging and find it much harder to understand spoken Spanish than to read and write it. DVDs, movies, TV, a tutor, and listening in on conversations will help you to hear the differences between Spanish and English, beyond book exercises.

If you didn't understand English grammar lessons as a child, you probably won't know what a Spanish teacher is saying about adverbs, objects, and tenses. If you hated all class work as a child you will probably want to concentrate on conversational programs.

If possible take some introductory Spanish classes or listen to taped programs and study the many free Spanish classes on the internet before coming to Mexico. Here's a site with Spanish slang: *www.mexicoguru.com/mexican-slang.php*. Check out what Spanish classes are available where you move to, and enroll as soon as you can.

Use multiple approaches to learning—educators say it is better to learn the same material many ways, not just reading the information. Some teachers say that you have to hear a new word as many times as your age in years to fully learn it! Some say that only by total immersion where you are picking up the language intuitively rather than studying it will you learn. Everybody who has ever taught or studied Spanish has a theory.

Everyone does agree on the need to practice as much as you can. Often Carol and Norma are practicing their Spanish with a cab driver who wants to practice his English on them, so they say something in Spanish and he'll answer in English. Whatever works. One hint is to not worry about making mistakes. Just use the infinitive of a verb if you can't figure out the correct tense and add something to tell what time frame you are talking about. Your listener will figure it out.

Another hint: many average Mexicans speak sloppy Spanish themselves. Most will also be very patient and instruct you on the correct phrase if you at least make the effort to try. There's always *"Repete por favor, mas despacio."* (Please repeat, more slowly.) Most Mexicans will, though a few will hang up the phone or call for someone who speaks some English to deal with you if they're in a rush. Never in Mexico has anyone spat at Carol for making a mistake in Spanish as happened in Paris when she misspoke French.

Rolly, Carol and Norma wish there were a magic wand to instantly turn you bilingual—first they'd use it on themselves.

ATMs have revolutionized banking in Mexico

Banking will be a major concern for most people. Many people retiring to Mexico have found that ATMs meet their needs for accessing their money from their home bank in the USA or Canada. A few have found benefits in having a bank account in Mexico. Mexico is largely a cash society.

Your three authors, as most expats, have their Social Security checks deposited in their old US bank and draw funds as needed from ATMs. The SS payments also can be direct deposited into your Mexican bank account if you have one.

ATMs are found almost everywhere: outside of banks, in shopping centers and supermarkets, in convenience stores and airports—the same kinds of locations for ATMs in the US and Canada. Just like NoB, some ATMs are more likely to be tampered with than others. Places where no one is paying attention like a bus terminal make it easier for someone to insert a false card reader and a hidden camera to record your PIN as you enter it.

The daily withdrawal limit is set by your home bank, not the ATM, although the ATM may have a per transaction limit, usually 4,000 or 5,000 pesos. If an ATM shorts you, you will be told by the local bank to take it up with your home bank, and usually the money will be returned to your account in a few days. Rolly has had to call Bank of America twice because of ATM malfunctions. Each time the missing money was credited to his account immediately.

Charges for use of a foreign ATM and the exchange rate are set by your home bank, not by the bank owning the ATM. Some banks have hefty charges for using a foreign ATM. Some pay poor exchange rates. There are some banks and credit unions that don't have charges and pay good exchange rates. Check with your bank or credit union before moving to find out its rules. Rolly has his SS check direct deposited into his account with Bank of America because they do not charge for use at certain foreign ATMs, and they pay a very good exchange rate. BofA has an arrangement with two banks in Mexico, Scotiabank and Santander/Serfin, that allow a BofA card to be used without any fees being charged.

Rolly recently did a test ATM withdrawal of 3,000 pesos on the same day to compare rates, using Bank of America and Banamex/USA. Here are the differing exchange rates for that day followed by the dollar cost of withdrawing the 3,000 pesos:

13.21 > $227.10 BofA ATM

12.98 > $231.12 Banamex/USA ATM

12.80 > $234.38 Banamex/USA funds transfer

If you have a budget of 20,000 pesos per month, using these example numbers, Banamex/USA ATM withdrawals would cost $36 USD per month more than BofA. Expanded to a year, it would be $432 USD more at Banamex. Using the funds transfer to a local Banamex account would cost $588 USD more for the year. You may want to do a similar comparison between your local banking alternatives to find your best rates.

For almost all expats, there are only two reasons to have a Mexican bank account: because you have a local business, or because you are building or buying a home and need access to more funds than would be practical using an ATM.

Mexicans are often reluctant to give out change, *cambio.* Your life may often be a constant hunt for coins and 20-peso bills for taxis and tips, while banks and ATMs want to give you 500-peso bills. You'll learn to offer your biggest bills for payments in the biggest stores, though you'll probably have to wait while the cashier hunts change. Pemex stations always have change for 500s.

Torn or defaced peso notes are no longer legal tender. The law says they are not supposed to be spent, and you can refuse to take one. If you end up with such a bill, take it to a bank to exchange it for a good one. Some banks do the exchange promptly and easily, others can make the exchange a pain, same as banks everywhere.

One practice that may surprise you is paying a vendor by making a deposit to the company's bank account. Sometimes a contractor or small business owner will give you their invoice and their bank and account number. You bring the payment to their bank and the cashier deposits it to the vendor's account directly.

Besides banks, other financial institutions in Mexico will set up a savings account for you from which you can have a check written in an emergency. They also offer a variety of investment programs. These other kinds of financial institutions include:

Actinver Lloyd (not to be confused with Lloyd's of London), *www.bursamex.com.mx/herramientas/OperadoraEng/WhoOP/*;

Monex, *www.monex.com.mx/*; and

Intercam, *www.intercam.com.mx/*

Their investment opportunities and money market accounts can pay somewhat higher rates of return than US banks, depending on how much you can invest, how quickly you want to be able to withdraw the funds, and how much risk you are willing to take. Note that these institutions are not protected by anything like the FDIC in the US. Funds can be transferred over the phone or sometimes on the internet between savings and investments.

Bancomer, *www.bancomer.com.mx/,* is one banking chain that actively seeks expat customers. In areas with many expats it provides Preferred Customer Units with English-speaking personnel. Other major banks in Mexico include:

Banamex, *www.banamex.com/*

Santander, *www.santander.com.mx/index.htm* (affiliated with Bank of America, *www.bankofamerica.com.mx/)*

HSBC, *www.hsbc.com.mx/1/2/*

You may choose to set up a bank and/or brokerage account with a major international institution in the US or Canada before moving, one that won't give you problems living in another country.

Many businesses in Mexico won't accept credit cards, but if you know you are going to make a major purchase on a US credit card and your billing address for the card is your mailing service that has an address in the US, call the credit card company ahead of time and say that you are going to be making a purchase in Mexico. Otherwise the purchase may not be approved because of automated fraud protection that stops any purchase in a foreign country.

Read all fine print carefully if you apply for a credit card within Mexico. Some of the most well-known chains including Wal-Mart charge 40-60% a year interest on their credit cards, and many will not issue a credit card to anyone over age 65, no matter your income or credit history. Discrimination is widely accepted in Mexico.

Travelers' checks are seldom used in Mexico and are more hassle than the protection they might provide. American Express has offices in many cities and you can purchase them there if you really want. With ATMs, travelers' checks are not as convenient as they used to be. Some clerks will have no idea what one is.

Finding a good school for your children

This section may not apply to many readers, but for those considering moving to Mexico with school-age children, this may be the most important section of all.

A little background on the Mexican education system: First, 44% of the country's population is 20 or under. The best private schools are as excellent as any NoB, and often as expensive. The worst Mexican schools are as bad as the worst NoB. Mexican literacy is very high now, about 93% overall, 98% in the younger generation. But just as in the US and Canada, knowing fundamental reading and writing may not mean functional literacy for a complex occupation or even for competency as a voting citizen.

Mexican schools tend to stress rote memorization, not theoretical and critical thinking. US students don't fare well on international standardized tests but Mexican students do even worse. In many rural areas the indigenous population doesn't speak Spanish. The government provides free textbooks in a dozen indigenous languages, but textbooks overall are inadequate and obsolete. The overwhelmed schools often run on half days, which allows more than 3.3 million children between 6 and 14 to work in agriculture or for family businesses, even though it is illegal. Girls in rural schools often drop out at puberty because of inadequate school bathrooms and water. A million Mexican children attend school via satellite, the *telesecundaria* program.

Only 35% graduate from high school overall, though in college prep high schools, the graduation rate is 60%. For comparison, the US overall high school graduation rate is 75%, and 100% in college prep high schools. The percentage of adults in major Mexican cities with a high school diploma is 23%, compared to 88% in the US. Of Mexican adults over age 18, only 8% have a bachelor's degree. Of Mexican college graduates, some 85% are unemployed, underemployed, or work outside the field for which they were trained (though there are many excellent Mexican universities, particularly UNAM, the top-ranking Spanish language university in the world).

The teachers union (SNTE) has a very strong influence and has opposed reforms such as standardized testing for new education graduates. Teachers who retire have often sold their positions for about $5,000 USD, and the jobs have been for life. Educational reforms are underway but are by no means complete.

In short, unless your research finds that there is indeed an excellent public school near you, you will probably look for a bilingual private school for your children. And finding out about one will be difficult. Mexican businesses do not all have good websites. You will probably need to ask for school information on whatever expat internet forums you can find for the cities that interest you. Both Waldorf and Montessori preschools and elementary schools are available in many Mexican cities; research their educational philosophies and methods to see if they are a fit with your child.

When you check out potential places to live, of course ask to tour the schools and make the same inquiries you would when choosing any school, with additional questions on the English and Spanish instruction and whatever supplemental help may be available. English will probably be taught at a lower level than your child is already at, and you will need to continue to advance your child's English education as well as Spanish tutoring, especially vocabulary. Just as with adults, not all children pick up Spanish easily, and parents cannot assume their child will pick up Spanish via immersion.

In the lower grades in a bilingual school, classes may be taught both in English and Spanish, while in higher levels English is taught as a second language an hour or so a day, and all other classes will probably be taught in Spanish. If you want your child to compete well on SAT tests for top US universities, you need to provide additional reading and vocabulary tutoring.

While checking out a school, ask to see the textbooks, and see if you can purchase a set for your afterschool tutoring. After you see the textbooks you may not want to buy them, even if they are available.

Find out ahead of time what documentation to bring for registration: birth certificate, passport, certified grades and levels completed, possibly a letter of good conduct from former principals, vaccination records, etc. Possibly the school may require the records to be *apostilled*—see Chapter 8—and that is easier to accomplish while you are in the states.

Fees for private schools can be expensive. The fall registration fee could be $400-$700 USD, usually reduced if you have more than one child in the school. Then there's a monthly fee of perhaps $250-

500, plus you pay for uniforms, books, and school supplies. Before you enroll your child there may be an entrance exam with another fee, perhaps $30 USD. Some private high schools require a mandatory drug test that parents pay for.

You may choose home schooling, though it is generally not recognized in Mexico. Many home-schooled students do very well by many criteria in the US. Some internet educational organizations for parents who home school provide the structure and also some kinds of accreditation and official certification for your child's grade level. Internet learning programs can also help you supplement your child's education.

Some parents think that moving their children to Mexico, exposing them to a new culture, language, and school system, will be wonderful for their kids. In most cases, it will. But in reality some kids do not adjust as easily as others. As soon as you start thinking about moving to Mexico, involve your kids in the process. Get them into some sort of Spanish instruction program, even if it's DVDs, computer lessons, cartoons in Spanish, or *Plazo Sesamo* (*Sesame Street*) on TV.

If they're young, read them books about Mexico, including books featuring Mexican children their own age. If they're of reading age, introduce them to simple books and DVDs in Spanish with English subtitles, or vice versa, to get them used to hearing Spanish and seeing how words and phrases translate differently across the languages. Teach them about Mexico's history—while you're learning it yourself.

Talk to them about stereotypes and bigotry and all the issues they will hear from their friends when they announce they are moving to Mexico. They need to have answers ready when their friends repeat the anti-Mexican statements they may have heard from their own parents. Moving is hard for any child of any age, even across town to a new school, much less to a very different culture.

Your children need to know about Mexican culture before they arrive and create good or bad lasting first impressions. The book *Why Mexicans Think and Behave as They Do* by Boyé DeMente has good sections on *machismo* and sexual expectations that may help you and your older child understand the new culture.

For both public and private schools, remember how cruel students can be to a newcomer who does not fit in or know the language, and provide all the additional support you can to make the transition go smoothly. Mexico is very much a class society where those from wealthy and older families may form exclusionary cliques, just as in US and Canadian schools.

One educator Carol knows says privately that to bring down an unwilling, unprepared English-speaking-only child to be placed in a grade above fourth in a Mexican school is a form of child abuse. But other parents have had no problems with their children adjusting almost instantly to Mexican schools and culture. How your child will do depends on your child, the school, and you, with infinite variables.

And your child will be changing constantly, too. Entering adolescence means major changes in any child's life; the complete integration you thought you'd both achieved one year may be topsy-turvy the next.

Helping your child learn to adjust to a new life in Mexico may be harder than for yourself. You will have to be involved. But this could be the best educational experience you could ever provide for your child—and yourself.

Beggars, street dogs, scams

The sight of beggars and street dogs may be a shock if you have not traveled in Mexico or other countries. Carol and Norma agonized for months over what to give beggars and finally came up with their own set of rules so that they don't have to think about it anymore. They put 15 pesos in small coins in a separate pocket and give three pesos each to the first five beggars they meet that day. After that it's "*Lo siento, no mas cambio hoy.*" (Sorry, no more change today.)

Their rule is no money for kids, only money to the frail aged or the handicapped. Make your own decisions ahead of time and then you won't be wondering constantly how "worthy" a certain beggar appears and how much you can afford to give that day.

Occasionally you will be hit by a hard luck story that you can't verify—the new gardener shows up late to tell you his wife was in a car accident and he needs 500 pesos for the hospital bill. If you give it to him, you may never see him again. Or he may promise to repay at 100 pesos a month from his paycheck—you may want to deduct it. Some stories are scams, same as in the US—begging with a twist.

When and what to tip

Tipping standards can vary from region to region, so ask other expats or neighbors what is standard for the area. In San Miguel, Carol and Norma find the average is to tip 15% in restaurants (20% for excellent service) unless you get really poor service or the person only brings you a beverage. Carol and Norma tip the guy delivering 40-pound water bottles up the stairs to their house at least two pesos a bottle. They didn't tip the guy who pumped their gas unless he also washed their windshield—then maybe three pesos. If he checked the air in their tires and refilled one or two, that was worth at least another five pesos. If there is an attendant in the bathroom, put three pesos in the tip bowl.

The woman or kid who puts your groceries into bags for you at the supermarket probably isn't being paid—Carol and Norma give at least a peso even for one bag, and up to five pesos depending on how full their grocery cart is. If you're wondering whether you should tip or not, do.

Easier to say no if you're giving back elsewhere

Every community has places to volunteer, and in cities with many expats there will be dozens, maybe hundreds, of organizations where you can find the perfect fit for your time and talents. Many expats work privately with their neighbors instead, teaching them English or mentoring their kids in one way or another. Sometimes it will seem as if a new expat would rather found and head a new charitable organization than join an existing team effort. The internecine infighting in a few expat organizations can make you laugh or cry.

Sometimes one of your employees will ask you to be a godfather or godmother to one of their kids. This is a great honor and great responsibility. You will be asked to provide many things for that child from then on, perhaps tuition for their schooling or the wedding dress or a case of liquor for their marriage. There may be other godfathers and godmothers for that child. It takes a village. Before saying yes automatically, try to find out exactly what will be expected from you in the future if you do.

When you're invited to a Mexican event, don't come on time. Carol and Norma and any other gringos invited to their landlord's parties are the only ones who do.

The poor street dogs and cats

Street dogs and cats are another source of disturbance for many expats newly arrived in Mexico. In many cities the situation is improving. Even in seven years, Carol and Norma have seen a great reduction in the number of feral dogs and cats in San Miguel. Many expats end up with one or many street animals themselves and feed and sterilize others. Mexican schools now often have educational programs to teach children about animal rights, so things are improving.

Growing awareness of ecological issues

Ecological issues are the same—a friend of Carol and Norma was considering buying rural property and asked the seller about trash collection. You throw your garbage down the arroyo, the owner shrugged. Ecology is now taught in many schools, there are workshops and conferences throughout Mexico on all of the ecological issues, and the building permit process is starting to take more seriously the ecological impact of a project.

Many expats are trying to find ways to leave a low footprint themselves and are installing solar panels as one big step toward reducing their energy usage. In many areas small perma communities are springing up that utilize as many environmental protections as possible. Just as in the US and Canada, ecological issues are a work in progress; Mexico is starting quite a few years behind.

Fine line on political involvement

It may be a temptation to try to influence local politics on some of these issues but be careful of the fine balance between welcome citizen participation and unconstitutional political involvement for which you can be deported. Volunteering on a committee that is investigating a problem and coming up with possible solutions is one thing; campaigning for a candidate who supports those solutions is another. Demonstrations can turn from a peaceful march on a generic issue like peace to a group being used by a political organization to influence the government.

Big chains versus neighborhood shops

The big discount stores and chain supermarkets are popular in the US and Canada for a reason, and as Mexicans earn more money and have more choices, they appreciate one-stop convenience and more choices, too. Working women around the world are turning to convenience foods.

Many expats love to learn the complex recipes and techniques of traditional Mexican cooking and prefer to shop in local *tianguis* for Mexican ingredients. They'll buy cookbooks by Rick Bayless and Diane Kennedy and learn more about the different kinds of chiles than they ever imagined.

Others seek to reproduce their favorite ethnic foods and learn to order gourmet spices and sauces over the internet or search for imported food shops in the larger cities, no matter the cost of file gumbo or garam masala. Rolly's website has an excellent Spanish-English dictionary of food items for those who want to cook themselves and need to know what the Spanish words are for their favorite ingredients. If there is an imported gourmet food shop nearby they can probably get cornmeal, Fritos and Bisquick at imported gourmet prices.

Cooks new to Mexico will find that oven temperatures are usually inconsistent and they'll need an oven thermometer for all sensitive dishes. Their oven may not even reach high temperatures when the propane gas tank on the roof is below a quarter full. They may find that high altitude cooking differences must be learned for all baking. Boiling an egg will take longer. A pot of beans left on for hours may still not be tender. (Google to find thousands of pages on high altitude cooking tips—here's one: *http://milehighkitchen.com/*). Learning to cook all over again, finding food substitutes, and trying new recipes and ingredients are part of the learning curve.

The internet is almost everywhere

No matter their age, many expats are thoroughly enmeshed in the internet age and have every electronic gadget that comes on the market. High-speed and wireless internet is available in all cities and many smaller areas. Many Mexicans use cell phones, sometimes for the cost and convenience of only having to buy occasional phone cards for as low as 50 pesos, sometimes because they cannot get phone service to their home, and sometimes for the same reasons as every teenager NoB has a cell phone—it's part of a new way of life. They have friends who have brought down ham radios, weather satellite stations, every kind of iPod, iPhone, and gadgets they don't know the names for themselves.

You may want to invest in a WiFi hot-spot locater so you don't have to turn on your laptop to determine if a particular café, park or town square has WiFi. Internet cafés are almost everywhere, for those families who cannot afford a computer and connection. Spanish keyboards have many keys in a different place—to get the @ for an email address hold down alt while you click 64 on the numeric key pad. If you have an English-language keyboard on a PC and want to get common Spanish accents, again hold down alt and use the numeric keyboard while you touch these numbers:

160 for á   130 for é   161 for í   162 for ó
163 for ú   164 for ñ   129 for ü
168 for ¿ (the upside down question mark that Spanish uses at

the start of questions as well as the regular question mark at the end of a question).

173 for ¡ (the upside down exclamation point that Spanish uses at the start of exclamations as well as the regular exclamation point at the end of an exclamatory sentence).

For Macs with English keyboards, press and hold down the option key while you also press the "e" key. Release both and then press the key you want accented. For example, press and hold down the option key and then add the "e" key, release, and press "a" to get the á. When you do this with "n" you'll get ñ. Option-1 gives you the ¡, and Shift option-? gives you ¿.

Many kids have flash drives attached to chains around their necks to carry their computer contents with them to school and to internet cafés. Charitable groups are doing their best to put computers in every school in the country.

Sometimes you'll find that you can't get through to a US business. The problem may be that the particular website you want does not allow connections from foreign countries. There are several paid and free software programs that you can use to hide your foreign internet address. (One is at *www.hidemyass.com*.) Click into one of these programs first and then type in the internet address that you want where the program tells you.

Making phone calls

Land lines are of course available almost everywhere in Mexico, and in most cities it no longer takes weeks or months to get a land line installed. You can get Vonage, Skype, Magic Jack and all the other alternatives to land lines using your computer. Sometimes you will still need a land line to make and receive local calls.

Long distance calls within Mexico

When making long-distance calls within Mexico, callers have to dial 01, the area code and the number.

Long distance calls from Mexico to other countries

When calling internationally from Mexico to Canada or the United States, you must dial 001, then the area code and the number. All other international calls from Mexico must be dialed with 00, followed by the country code.

Long distance calls within Mexico

For long-distance calls within Mexico the code is 01 plus the area code and phone number.

Long distance calls to Mexico from another country

When calling internationally to Mexico, the country code is 52. In other words, to call a Mexican land line number from the US or Canada, dial 01152 first, then the area code, then the seven-digit number.

Calling Mexican cell phones

To dial to Mexico cell phones from another country dial: 011 + 52 + 1 + area code + number .

If you're within the area code of the Mexican cell phone number you wish to call, you need to dial 044, then the area code, then the phone number.

Outside of the area code but within Mexico first dial 045 and then the area code and phone number

Mexican cell phones are under a plan called *el que llama paga*—the person who makes the call pays for it.

Calling USA 800 numbers

To dial a United States 800 number FROM Mexico, replace the 800 prefix with the prefix shown below:

800 numbers dial 001-880-then the number

866 numbers dial 001-883-then the number

877 numbers dial 001-882-then the number

888 numbers dial 001-881-then the number

Area Codes

In the three largest cities of Mexico (Mexico City, Guadalajara, and Monterrey), the area code is two digits and phone numbers are eight digits, whereas in the rest of the country area codes are three digits and phone numbers are seven digits. Since you're dialing the same number of digits in the end, you may not notice the difference, but it's there. Here are the area codes for the three cities:

Mexico City 55

Guadalajara 33

Monterrey 81

Though lagging behind the US and Canada, the phone systems and choices in Mexico keep improving. In July, 2009, Mexico's central bank issued rules that allowed the use of mobile phones for banking services for rural regions. Cell phone companies can now offer banking services that are linked to the phone account, a practice that is becoming common in other parts of the world.

Phone cards

Phone cards, *tarjetas telefonicas*, for use in pay phones can be bought many places such as grocery stores, newsstands and pharmacies in denominations of 30, 50, and 100 pesos. Pay phones no longer accept coins. If you need a phone card for pay phone use, ask for a *tarjeta LADA*, to distinguish from pre-paid cell phone cards. It will be cheaper to call from a pay phone. There are also businesses called *caseta telefonicas* that offer telephone and fax services to the public. Many internet cafes and occasionally other kinds of businesses have VOIP long distance phone service available to customers for a small fee.

Emergency phone numbers

You do not need a phone card to call 3-digit emergency numbers from a pay phone. Not every area has these same emergency numbers yet but there is an ongoing effort to make them standard throughout Mexico just as 911 is now accepted throughout the US:

Emergency 066

Red Cross 065

Police 060

Directory assistance 040

Tourist protection and information within Mexico: 01 800 903 9200 or 01 800 987 8224. Tourist help from the U.S. and Canada: 1 800 482 9232 or 1 800 401 3880.

If you haven't been able to find a free white and yellow pages for your city even at your Telmex office where you pay your landline bill, you can purchase one online for a hefty price from *www. mexicophonebooks.com/*

Satellite and cable television

When you are evaluating which kind of phone and internet service to use, take your television services into account as well. If you are going to be using the less expensive cable hookup for your television, you can probably get an inexpensive package for your internet as well, with choices of connection speed. Basic cable in Mexico will probably include many Spanish-language national and local programs plus perhaps International CNN in English and a few English language stations that show mostly old movies with Spanish subtitles. Getting US networks and HBO will be an additional cost. With Mexican cable you will probably not be able to get many US cable channels.

Recent US laws forbid a satellite TV provider from broadcasting outside of a certain area—advertisers want to know exactly who is receiving those programs for which they are paying with their ads. Satellite TV in Mexico is making inroads across the country. If you want to receive a US or Canadian satellite TV provider out of a US or Canadian city, discuss with other expats in the area in which you want to move, to see what they may have been able to arrange.

You can also get Netflix mailed to you and catch all the movies and past TV series you want, a little later than their first airing. And many TV shows are also aired on the internet.

Going to the movies

Most larger Mexican towns will have at least one movie theater, and major cities will usually have cinemas with as many as 16 screens showing different films. Cinépolis (more than 200 theaters in 65 cities) and MM Cinemas are two of the largest chains. For the MM Cinemas in San Miguel, Carol and Norma check each Friday on what's playing next week on the interactive website (*www.mmcinemas.com*). Some films will be labeled *doblada*, meaning they are dubbed into Spanish. Some are labeled *subtitulos*, meaning they are in the film's original language with Spanish subtitles. The information on each film will say whether the film was originally made in the US or another country. If the film is from France, for example, the film was probably filmed in French and will shown in French with Spanish subtitles.

Even if neither *doblada* or *subtitulos* is given, you can figure that a film made in the US will be presented in English with Spanish subtitles anyway. Call the cinema and ask to be sure, though if you are not fluent your question may not be understood and you may not understand the answer. Ask again when you buy your tickets.

One exception is children's movies and animated films—both will almost always be dubbed whether the website says so or not. The reason is that young kids cannot read subtitles, and all animated films are assumed to be for children.

Movies like the *Harry Potter* and *Lord of the Rings* series were shown dubbed only, in movies with only one or a few screens, because they were supposedly children's films, even though their greatest audience was adults. If a theater has many screens there is a better chance that a popular US movie that has both an adult and children audience base will be shown both dubbed and in the original English with Spanish subtitles. (Reading the Spanish subtitles as you hear the English is a great way to improve your Spanish, too. Many Mexicans go to the English language films to improve their English as well. Sometimes, however, there seems to be little resemblance between a pithy bit of dialogue in English and the lengthy Spanish subtitle for it, and swear words will be cleaned up.)

INAPAM/INSEN cards

The INAPAM is the Mexican senior discount card, available to any resident over 60, including expats with an FM3 visa or higher. One of the places you will probably use an INAPAM/INSEN card the most is at the movies. The second most likely place you will use this Mexican senior discount card is on Mexican buses.

Because of some recent transitions in the program, there is a lot of confusion about what the card is and how to get it. A few years ago only FM2 holders could get one, then for a few months those with FM3s could get the cards but only in some cities. Then the law was changed again to only allow FM2 holders to get one, and then the whole senior citizen discount card program was switched from the state level to a federal program and the name changed from INSEN to INAPAM, and FM3 holders over age 60 could again qualify.

You will sometimes run into someone who says you can't get one with an FM3, but here is the link to the official INAPAM federal government website that explains the new requirements: *www. inapam.gob.mx/index/index.php*

The name of the federal program is *Instituto Nacional de las Personas Adultas Mayores*. Often it will be administered by another government agency in a smaller town that does not have a separate social services program for seniors. Those who already had INSEN cards when the program was moved to the federal level were advised they should get INAPAM cards instead, even though there was no expiration date on INSEN cards, and there is none on the INAPAM cards. Technically you could continue to just use the INSEN card forever. Many people still call it INSEN and are puzzled when you say INAPAM.

But Carol and Norma decided to switch anyway, to avoid a possible future situation such as being in a line in a rush for a reduced bus fare and some young clerk who never heard there was once an INSEN card before the INAPAM card refuses to give the discount. You get half price on bus tickets, a big savings when you're taking a long bus trip within Mexico, and even on local buses.

A few times a bus driver has balked at seating expats holding INAPAM cards. One told Carol and Norma that it wasn't fair that wealthy *norteamericanos* should get a discount on his bus when he couldn't get a discount on US buses. They told him that in many US cities anyone over 60 or 65 can get a bus or subway discount, whether they are legal residents or not. He relented and let them on.

Sometimes only one discount per bus can be used, so if there are two of you, it is best to buy your ticket ahead of time and do it individually so that both of you qualify.

The INAPAM discounts are also good for Mexican airlines, Mexican museums, and discounts at many pharmacies on medicines. Some of the biggest pharmacy chains in Mexico, such as Farmacia

Guadalajara, already give as much as a 40% discount on most drugs and so do not offer the INAPAM discount, which is usually 15%.

Some restaurants give the INAPAM discount, including the Wal-Mart VIP and El Porton chains. Many big cultural events like the Guanajuato Cerventino international music festival and Mexico City Belles Artes concerts give INAPAM discounts on tickets. Some universities and private schools give tuition discounts. It never hurts to ask anyplace if they give INAPAM discounts, especially in Mexico City. Even some medical services in Mexico City give these discounts to seniors who hold the card. In Mexico City many stores and services have signs in their windows saying they give INAPAM discounts. In some cities homeowners can use the INAPAM card to get discounts on some utility bills.

To get an INAPAM card, you will have to ask locally where to apply. In San Miguel de Allende it is the DIF office on San Antonio Abad at Insurgentes, Mondays at 8-11 am. DIF stands for *Desarrollo Integrál de la Familia*, one of the major government social services agencies. As usual, each office's requirements can differ slightly, even though INAPAM is a federal program and the website above gives the documentation required.

In SMA you need the original and two copies of your FM3 or FT2 and passport, and proof of residency such as a copy of a utility bill. Again for those who rent and whose landlords pay their utilities, a letter from the landlord explaining that will usually do. You also need the name and phone number of a person to contact in case of an emergency. You need a photo ID; your passport should do, though your driver's license will also work.

You will need three copies of *infantil*-size color photos, which are smaller than passport size. You can get them at any photo studio in Mexico.

Most importantly you need proof that you are over 60. Carol and Norma had to present two copies of their birth certificates. Some offices want to see the original certified copy as well. Since your US or Canadian passport has your birth date on it, it should suffice but it doesn't always. But this is Mexico and each office, each desk, each person from before lunch to after lunch, may differ, so be prepared for a change in the requirements at any time.

Your INAPAM card may also serve as sufficient identification when you need to show picture ID within Mexico and you don't have a driver's license, passport, or visa on you. It's good to make a copy of your card for your files, to make it easier to get another if yours gets lost, and you should have the original laminated so that it will last. You'll probably be pulling it out a lot.

The ever-changing airline scene

All airlines are shifting service areas, routes, and prices in response to the economic downturn, so Google these companies to find out current schedules, destinations, and prices. Mexico is served by airlines from around the world including:

- Alaska
- American Airlines
- ATA Airlines
- British Airways
- Continental
- Delta
- Frontier Airlines
- Lufthansa UK
- US Airways (America West)

Mexican full-fare national and regional airlines

- Aero California
- Aeromexicana
- Mexicana

Low-cost Mexican airlines

- Alma de Mexico
- Volaris
- Avolar
- Click Mexicana
- Aviacsa
- Interjet
- Vivaaerobus

Unfortunately Mexico no longer has passenger train service except in Copper Canyon and a few tourist excursion lines.

The wonderful Mexican bus system

Carol and Norma both had terrible experiences on Greyhound and many local buses in the US. On an interstate Greyhound trip Norma had to make, she was striving for blotto unconsciousness by the end. The last time they were on a San Francisco bus the driver said, "Good luck" as they entered, and they found themselves among cursing, threatening teenagers who wouldn't give up the handicap seats, a religious proselytizer who kept asking if they had been saved, and a homeless man who had all his belongings laid out on the seats and was changing clothes. Thankfully, buses between cities and even within cities are much better overall in Mexico., though there are some pretty decrepit Mexican buses on the road.

For local buses, it will probably be difficult to get a bus schedule. But buses generally have signs in their front window listing the popular stops along their route. Ask people waiting at the bus stops or the driver if a particular bus goes where you want. Someone will probably tell you the right bus to take if that one doesn't.

You may want to avoid taking a local bus when school is letting out. Remember that many Mexican schools run on half days so that you might end up with 30 boisterous kids in the aisles on your bus around 1 pm and again at 6 pm, depending on local school schedules. Buses sometimes stop at a primary school to let mothers run out, grab their children, and get back on the bus, while you wait.

Often an entertainer or vendor will board a city bus at one stop and exit a few stops later, after singing a few songs, telling a few jokes, or selling a few ballpoints, hoping for a few pesos.

In some cities local bus service is supplemented by private shuttles and minivans.

Luxury bus seating nicer than many airlines

The top of the line luxury bus lines in Mexico (called *Ejecutivo* by the Estrella Blanca line, *Diamente* by the Estrella de Oro line, and *Lujo* by the Uno line) are nicer than most airlines' coach seating. Often they have only 24 seats to a bus, rows of two on one side of the aisle, single seats on the other. They offer more leg room, leg rests, chairs that recline almost horizontally, seatbelts, individual earphones for the movie soundtracks or music, and bathrooms similar to those on a plane. It is harder to maneuver inside the bathrooms on a moving bus, however. The movies may be in English with Spanish subtitles, or in Spanish, and may be of cable TV quality.

You can have your luggage placed in the luggage compartment of the bus and receive a ticket to claim it at your destination. Bring on board a sweater or something to keep you warm in case the air conditioning is too high. There is room overhead to stuff small packages above your seat, and the window curtains are thick enough to cut out all outside light. You can choose to make instant coffee or tea in the rear of the bus during your ride on many lines. You'll probably get a baggie with a sandwich (usually thin ham and processed cheese slices on white bread), soft drink, and a cookie or similar snack when you board. A few luxury lines even have servers to bring you meals on some routes.

First class buses (*primera clase*) are not as luxurious and generally do not provide food, though you can certainly buy sandwiches, snacks and drinks at the bus station stops. Second class *economico* (*segunda clase*) buses have a little less space per seat and you might find that more tickets have been sold than seats—on a bus ride Carol and Norma took between Mazatlán and Puerto Vallarta people were sitting two to a seat and in the aisles. They will probably stop at bus stands along the route as well as at bus stations, and sometimes stop anyplace they are hailed by a pedestrian. If there are movies they will probably be of the Jackie Chan action film variety, only in Spanish, with no headphones to drown them out if you choose. It's highly unlikely you'll be sharing your seat with chickens and livestock these days, perhaps only in rural areas. *Directo* buses have far fewer stops between destinations.

The *ejecutivo* buses go much less frequently, sometimes only once a day between less popular destinations. Rather than waiting, you will be fine on any first-class bus, and often Carol and Norma take *economico* buses at times that work out better for them, especially for shorter rides.

For any bus, keep your ticket—you may have to show it again a few cities later. Usually the seats up front have less bounce and sway. If you're prone to motion sickness, take Dramamine, Antivert or Bonadoxin (generic Meclizine) , before you feel any symptoms. If you sit in the rear, everyone who goes past you to the bathrooms will be grabbing hold of the back of your seat if the bus lurches, and you're more likely to be affected by bathroom smells. People who plan on a deep sleep the whole route usually plop in the rear seats. If you're riding by day think ahead which direction the bus will be headed most of the time, compared to the sun's route, and consider whether you want to be on the sunny or shady side. Those darkening curtains for night open wide for sightseeing by day.

Previously, to take the bus across the US border and beyond, you had to get off at a bus station before the border and perhaps catch a cab to the border inspection, then catch another cab across the border or walk to link with a Greyhound. Now several lines take you right across the border –but you still have to stop at the inspection station and get out of the bus with your luggage and carry ons while you and the bus are checked out. In many crossings a giant automatic wand like in a car wash passes around each bus while drug-sniffing dogs make their rounds.

Sometimes it pays to use a combination of buses and planes with a detour to a larger bus station to find the best deals and buses. Carol and Norma found it much cheaper, for a recent trip to a relative in Detroit, to take a bus from San Miguel to Querétaro, then a luxury Ave bus to San Antonio, where they flew Southwest Airlines on a bargain rate to Detroit. They were worried about the border crossing but as they got off the bus for the border inspections, they were met by someone from Autobus Americanos who knew their destination and transferred them seamlessly to another bus to San Antonio.

They have also taken Autobus Americanos, definitely not a luxury bus line, directly to San Antonio. Americanos continues on from the Mexican border into the US and Canada, via their affiliation with Greyhound and other bus lines. It can take about 12 hours to reach Nuevo Laredo from San Miguel de Allende, for example. (Fast private car drivers who don't stop long can make the drive in nine hours, for comparison.) The cost of about $100 one-way ($50 with an INAPAM card) is about the same as a private driver spends in tolls and gasoline.

From Guadalajara, Americanos runs to Laredo in about 14 hours; Houston, 21 hours; Kansas City, 37 hours; and Chicago, 44 hours, using Greyhound connections to serve much of the US.

The Autobus Americanos website is: *www.autobusesamericanos. com.mx/joomla/index.php*. Some of the buses may be more along the lines of an *economico* though they will say they are first class. There are bathrooms aboard. Be sure to be clear from the bus driver how many minutes each stop is for so that you don't get left behind.

Be as careful as you are in sizing up a street food stand when deciding what food to buy at the bus stations or from vendors who may come on board during the rest stops.

Most cities have a single bus station. They will usually go by the name Central de Autobuses, Terminal de Autobuses or Camionera Central (long distance buses are called *camiones*).

In larger cities there may be more than one bus terminal, and each terminal may have several modules, so be very clear exactly where your bus arrives if you are expecting to be met by someone. In Mexico City there are bus terminals in each of the four sides of that massive city, plus one adjoining the Benito Juarez International Airport, and it can be a hassle to go from one side of the city to the other by taxi if you get the terminal wrong. A list of the Mexico City terminals and the cities to which they link is in the Appendix.

The other major cities in Mexico also have extensive bus terminal systems. Guadalajara has two terminals, the old one downtown that still handles the buses to closer cities like the Ajijic/Chapala area, and the newer one that is actually in Tónala and has six modules in free-standing buildings. The third largest city in Mexico, Monterrey, has a bus terminal that can handle 60 bus arrivals at the same time. The Querétaro bus terminal is built like a horseshoe, many modules around the U. Make sure your taxi driver knows exactly which terminal and module you want.

When you depart your long distance bus it will probably be a bit of a walk to local bus lines, and if you have luggage you probably don't want the hassles of getting on a local bus anyway. But there are people available to help you for a tip. To get a cab from the larger bus stations you need to go to a kiosk while still inside and pay for a taxi ahead of time, and then take that receipt outside to the taxi lineup. You won't have to pay the taxi driver any more, and tipping is only suggested if you need help with luggage.

The luxury bus lines have their own private waiting rooms within the bus terminals with their own restrooms and perhaps food stands. Even in these private waiting rooms you will probably have to put three pesos in coins into the revolving metal bar doors to access the *baños*.

For an excellent chart of the major bus lines in Mexico, their websites and phone numbers, the areas they serve, and additional information such as the number of luxury buses, go to *www.mexicoguru.com/buses-in-mexico.php*.

Another good site for Mexican bus information is Larpman's Guide: *www.larpman.com/transportpages/buspages/bus.html*

ETN calls itself the most comfortable bus in Mexico and it is Carol and Norma's favorite. It takes credit cards and you can reserve ahead of time by phone. To choose the best bus for you it may be easiest to go to your departure bus terminal and walk from booth to booth, comparing routes, prices, and quality of buses, rather than trying to figure out comparisons from websites. Riding the buses in Mexico is fun, a great opportunity for people watching, and an inexpensive and reliable alternative to owning a car.

Those little cultural jolts

So much is different in Mexico, and there is no way to include every possible jolt you might get to your system when you encounter one of those differences.

Respect for lines? Not usually

You will probably find that Mexicans do not stand in lines the way US and Canadian residents do. Lines may be respected at a movie theater, but not at a convenience store where someone is likely to push ahead of you to pay. Be as forceful as you feel comfortable in doing in asserting your place, but go with the flow.

Mexicans' sense of personal space is quite different from NoB. Someone may stand right in your face on a bus even if there is more room. If you spread your towel on an empty beach, the Mexican family who arrives next may park their towels next to you, because it is the friendly thing to do, while you may prefer that they find a space at the other end of the beach.

Most places you don't flush the toilet paper

Another surprise: in most Mexican businesses and homes you do not flush the toilet paper down the toilet. In many areas with older sewage systems that have small pipes, you may need to put used toilet paper into a covered, lined, wastepaper container next to the toilet, or you will face continual blocked pipe plumbing bills. There are wastepaper containers, usually not covered, next to most toilets in Mexico. If there is no such container next to the toilet in a business or home, that is an indication that it is okay to flush the toilet paper; the house has new plumbing and/or an added water pressure system. Bathrooms on both sides of the US-Mexican border often have signs indicating whether TP should be flushed.

Of course Mexico doesn't celebrate July 4 or July 1

Some newbies are chagrined when they realize that Canada Day, July 1, US Independence Day, July 4, and the US and Canadian Thanksgiving Days are ordinary days in Mexico, and that *Cinco de Mayo*, a big deal in the US, is barely acknowledged in most of Mexico. (It is celebrated primarily in Puebla, the city where a small Mexican army was able to defeat a much larger French invasion, at least the first battle. The French came back with a larger army the next year and installed Maximilian on the throne of their newly conquered territory in 1864-7.)

When Carol and Norma were invited to a presentation ceremony for the three-year-old granddaughter of their housekeeper, they had to ask what that meant. Mexican tradition is that a child's baptism shortly after birth is not done with the child's awareness, and so there is a second similar ceremony at age three, without the pouring of water on the forehead. The three-year-old children of a parish enter the church in white dresses and suits. After a ceremony by the parish priest they are formally presented to God and the attendees as full-fledged church members. They kiss a statue of the baby Jesus as a sign of their commitment to the church.

Birthdays are not celebrated with the singing of the *Happy Birthday* song expats grew up with. Mexicans sing a far more beautiful and moving song, *Las Mañanitas* (little mornings) about awakening the birthday celebrant to see the beautiful morning to be shared, a special day just for the celebrant. For the lyrics in Spanish, a literal and a poetic translation in English, and the tune so that you can learn to sing along, go to: *www.musicalspanish.com/flashdemo3.htm*

At age 15 girls may have a *Quinceañera* celebration that is similar to a Sweet Sixteen party or a debutante ball in the US. The celebrations begin with a special mass at the church, and the party may be as grand as the family can afford, or borrow for. Expats who are friends or employers of the family may be asked to be *padrinos* and *madrinas* and pay for the girl's dress, the band, hall, liquor or cake. Some families today ask the girl whether she would rather have a big party, a car, a major trip, or college tuition. Richer families give all four. In some communities combined *quinceañeras* share the expenses among many families.

In Mexico, death and life are on the same continuum, and Nov. 1-2 are the days when it is believed that the barriers between the dead and the living are the thinnest and the deceased come back to visit their loved ones. Nov. 1 is dedicated to remembering deceased babies and children. Departed adults are commemorated on Nov. 2, *Diá de Los Muertos* (Day of the Dead). Families clean up cemetery plots and cover them with marigolds and other flowers. They bring the deceased's favorite foods, drinks, clothing, and items of special significance to the cemetery and spend the day in a family picnic. They may also erect altars in their homes.

Some areas have even more elaborate Day of the Dead celebrations,. All of the *Zócalo* in Mexico City turns into hundreds of altars, contests for *pan de muertos*, breads made in the shape of skeletons, city bus windows painted as if they are full of grinning skeletons. The usually-ceramic statues of skeletons, often females in elaborate dance hall costumes with one bony leg showing through a slit in the skirt, are called *catrinas*. Pátzcuaro is famed for its evening boat ride processions out to a ceremony on an island in Lake Pátzcuaro, fishermen reenacting the use of butterfly nets in a ballet against the night sky. Expats sometimes erect their own home or storefront altars to deceased family members to share in the Day of the Dead.

That night a Halloween-like public party may take place in the main square and children whose families have lived in the US often dress in Halloween costumes and say "Trick or Treat," hoping for candy from any passing gringo. Mexicans argue each year whether Halloween is taking over the religious and family importance of the traditional Day of the Dead.

Christmas Day itself is not celebrated as much as the *Posadas* of Dec. 16-23 in which groups reenact Joseph and the pregnant Mary on a burro going from inn to inn seeking shelter, only to be turned away. Traditional lyrics that vary from family to family, town to town, beg each of the inns to open up. The innkeepers reject the family night after night. The last night Joseph sings that his wife is the Queen of Heaven, Blessed Mary, and the last innkeeper responds, why didn't you say so? Come right in! At the party that follows, the traditional meal is *tamales, buñuelos* (fried dough dipped in cinnamon and sugar), *atole*, a corn meal-based punch reminiscent of hot chocolate, or *ponche*, a fruit punch similar to mulled cider. At the end of the *posada*, kids take turns swinging blindfolded at a suspended *piñata*, to break it into pieces releasing the candy inside.

Homes and businesses usually put up *El Nacimiento*, the nativity scene, but in Mexico the scene may also have Lucifer as a red devil or snake, and a complete landscape with mirror ponds, and every sort of animal and doll, no matter the duck is twice as big as the camel or Barbie. The empty crèche is not filled until Christmas Eve. Baby Jesus usually gets a new gown each year.

This is not to say that Christmas trees and Santas are not evident in December in Mexico. White-bearded gringos are often asked to fill in as Santa during the holiday. Some stores decorate for Christmas sales as early as October, same as in the US. And some critics decry the entrance of Santa and Christmas Eve gifting rather than the traditional January 6 Three Kings Day for presents. Lucky children get toys both days.

Other holidays are also celebrated differently in Mexico. Don't expect to find bunnies on Easter. Many towns reenact the Good Friday events in lavish and solemn processions. May 1 is Labor Day rather than in early September. Mothers Day is fixed, always May 10. Mexico's Independence Day is September 16, and at 11 pm the night before most cities celebrate *El Grito*, the cry, remembering Hidalgo's proclamation from the church steps in Dolores Hidalgo in 1810 launching the movement for independence from Spain.

December 12 is a major religious commemoration of the Virgin of Guadalupe, Mexico's own dark-skinned version of Mary who, it is believed by Mexican Catholics, appeared to a poor Indian peasant asking that a cathedral be built in her honor in Mexico City, and who gave him her image on his cloak and a bouquet of roses to help him prove his story to church fathers. December 28 is Holy Innocents Day, in Mexico similar to April Fools Day. If you loan somebody something that day you have given it to them.

There are so many elements to popular Mexican culture, you will constantly be learning more. This new way of looking at life will keep your mind and attitudes fresh.

Mexican marriages

In Mexico only the state marriage is legal; the church ceremony is optional. The Federal District (Mexico City) and the state of Coahuila already allow same-sex civil unions. Church-state separation is clear in Mexico when it comes to marriage.

Celebrations following the civil and possibly the church ceremony will be as varied as a couple's economic and familial resources. A burro decorated with a heart-shaped halo-like wire covered with flowers may accompany the couple's procession after the ceremony. Mariachis may be the band of choice for a party at home, or a family may hire a hall and have a grand party. Many Mexican poorer families never do have a legal or church ceremony. Traditionally it has been common for many wealthier Mexican married men to also have a mistress who is kept in a second house; everybody knows about the *casa chica* and pretends it doesn't exist.

So much cannot be covered in this book because each reader will lead a very different life, and not every possibility can be included. But for at least some of you, you may find yourself thinking about getting married here one day.

A Mexican civil marriage is legal anyplace, so long as it does not violate policy in another country. The marriage license bureau in any city or town is the Registro Civil. Two non-Mexican citizens who wish to marry fill out an application and present the originals and copies of their passports and visas (FMT, FM3, FM2, *inmigrado* card or other visa), medical tests done in Mexico, photo IDs, and *apostilled* copies of their birth certificates translated by an official translator. Two witnesses also must attend the marriage.

If either party is divorced, *apostilled* and translated copies of the divorce, or of the death certificate if either party is widowed, are also needed. Mexico requires a year's wait after final divorce papers before someone can remarry.

Applicants must be over 18 or, with parental consent, 16 for men, 14 for women. The couple may choose to be married under a joint or a separate property agreement, or "none of the above," perhaps because they have a prenuptial arrangement. The application fee is about $35 USD and there may be a waiting period of as much as a week. The couple can then have the civil ceremony at Registro Civil or have a judge marry them someplace else. The marriage certificate is called an *acta de matrimonio*—get several copies for the many future times it may be needed.

If one of the partners is a Mexican citizen, the foreign partner must first go to the Immigration office nearest to where the marriage will happen and apply for a *permiso para contraer marrimonio con un naciona* (permission to marry a Mexican citizen). The fee is about $130 USD and the waiting period could be two days to two weeks. You will need your US or Canadian passport to apply. As usual in Mexico, each Registro Civil and each Immigration office can differ in these rules.

You must apply at Immigration to adopt a child in Mexico or to divorce as well.

Bringing it all together in a love story

In case all of this detailed information has you overwhelmed, moving to Mexico is worth it. We'll end with a post by Ron Hoff from his website, *www.talkbaja.com/forum*, titled *How to Explain a Love Affair*. It ties this book all together—the reasons to move, how Ron fell in love with Mexico, and what it can be like to live here if you do decide Mexico is for you.

What made me move to Mexico?

The question is one I have answered countless times over the years since making the decision to set anchor here on the Baja California peninsula. I am sure that many like me who have made the move down here are often asked as well by friends and family north of the border. Some think I am crazy (and they are probably right) but they still keep asking me the question.

Living in Mexico is not for everyone but if I were to put a profile together of those who have made their life down here and still believe it was a good decision, it would look something like this:

- Baby Boomers
- Professionals
- Entrepreneurs
- Bohemians
- Adventurers
- Risk takers

- Easy going people
- Flexible people

I seem to find some mixture of those qualities in most of the expats who are generally happy with their lives down here. Living for years along the California coastline molded a large part of who I was and the lifestyle I worked so hard to achieve. Unfortunately, it was a lifestyle that was becoming more expensive than my cash flow.

Growing up in Southern California, I made frequent vacation trips down to the Baja peninsula, but living here would be a different experience, and each step a story. House hunting in Rosarito Beach involved finding a place big enough to accommodate all of my furniture plus Dakota, my big yellow Labrador. Moving all my stuff down and actually getting it across the border was a story in itself.

Some of the problems: figuring out how to get water from my *pila* (sink), and engineering a solution to a refrigerator that was too big for the space between my kitchen cabinets.

I can never forget meeting my neighbors, the local Señoras of the neighborhood, for the first time. They walked in unannounced through the open garage door bringing with them a welcome gift of a large tray of *pan dulce* (sweet rolls). They found me under the kitchen sink, cursing while attempting to hook up the ice maker, wearing only boxer shorts and a red face.

I remember how proud of myself I was that I had managed to score the best gardener deal ever, only to discover a month later that the gardener had not quoted me a rate in pesos but in dollars. Life was a daily adventure in those early months as I slowly learned to acclimate to the local culture and lifestyle. It wasn't always easy or straight forward, nor did it even make sense at times. Somehow I did get through it all, helped by so many people who expected nothing more in return than just a thank you and a smile.

Mexico is what it is and I learned that it was best to leave my American expectations and preconceived notions at the border. Driving down here you may find that the road is not always straight and there may even be a pothole or two along the way. This is not the US. This is not endless subdivisions of identical tract houses with strip malls at every stoplight designed by planning engineers who seem to have all graduated from the same school of architectural design. This is Mexico, and with all its troubles and faults, it remains a proud and independent country with a myriad of colors, flavors, designs, tastes, culture, opportunities and adventures. In all of my years here I don't recall two days ever being the same. When I am away for more than a couple of days I inevitably begin to long to come back home. Life anywhere else just seems plain and bland in comparison.

Life stories are written with memories ranging from the best to the very worst. Loss is a price we sometimes pay for risking to love and I remember an early morning phone call in April, 2004.

Olivia, my youngest daughter, had been found unconscious and was en route to the emergency room in Bakersfield. I remember countless friends and neighbors from Rosarito Beach, Tijuana and Ensenada calling me every day in Bakersfield as I stood vigil over my daughter, praying for a miracle. They were watching over my home, feeding and walking Dakota, watering the plants and even paid my electric bill when it arrived. They had all come to know Olivia on her frequent trips down to spend time with me and everyone was praying for her. They reminded me not to worry about anything back home as all would be taken care of.

Ten days later, on a very early spring morning I was a helpless bystander in that hospital room in intensive care. Watching as the breathing of my precious baby girl grew labored, I felt as though my own life slipped away with her as I held Olivia tightly in my arms. She took one last breath and everything in my mind and my life just seemed to go dark at that moment. I honestly don't remember much about the days that followed or how I even survived. One thing that I do remember and that will always stand out occurred days after the funeral, when I returned home to Mexico. The entire neighborhood came out to receive me as I got out of the taxicab. Right there in the middle of the street, in front of my home we hugged, cried, and grieved together. I don't even remember paying the driver his fare. I'm now sure that a neighbor must have taken care of that.

During the weeks that followed they cared for me as if I were a close family member, bringing meals, walking Dakota, spending time with me if only to listen and hold me up as I grieved. The strong sense of family here in Mexico is such an intricate element that makes up the very character of its culture and society. I never really experienced anything like that before in all my years but it felt as soothing as tired muscles slipping into a warm bath at day's end. Without even a word being spoken on the matter I was unconditionally incorporated into membership into each one of their families, into some as a brother and into others as a son.

The months passed and I learned to deal with the pain by immersing myself into my work more and more. I suppose that we all deal with loss in different ways and I did what seemed to come naturally to me. It was probably just self-preservation. My routine developed into what those close to me called "workaholic avoidance." At least that was the diagnosis of the *Señoras* of the neighborhood.

As stereotypical Latino culture dictates and in true democratic fashion a vote was taken. It was unanimous. This long single gringo was going to get a wife. He may not know it but he needs a wife, whether he likes it or not. The *Señoras* would see to that. A parade of dinner invitations soon followed.

Surprisingly there would always be a single female friend who they just "happened" to invite over. I always tried to act surprised. Not that I wasn't open to the idea, mind you. It was just that I had only chuckled at such scenarios in movies and sitcoms and never actually imagined myself playing the role of the "eligible bachelor."

What the *Señoras* didn't know was that their husbands sabotaged their plans each time with a preemptive strike, providing me with detailed reconnaissance of what awaited me that night in the dinner date rotation. I would get the complete profile including the woman's education, prior relationships, number of kids if any, her family, her job and income potential, medical history, natural hair color, what kind of car she drove, how much weight she had lost recently, status of her biological clock, and a few other details that I'm probably not allowed to print.

Oh, and they would always divulge her *real* age, because they were quite sure that I would never get an accurate count from the candidate or our matchmaker/dinner host that night.

The following morning the *Señora* who had hosted the last night's dinner would always find an excuse to stop by, bringing fresh cut flowers or homemade tortillas. What she really wanted was to get the complete report. Did I think she was nice? Did I think she was pretty? Did I ask her for her number? Did she give me her number? When was I going to call her?

It almost became a competition between the *Señoras* of the neighborhood as to who was going to be the winning matchmaker. I also think that some of the husbands were secretly running a pool on how long before the gringo was going down.

I started keeping my blinds closed and looked out the peephole before answering the front door. Life as a single gringo was becoming a bit dangerous.

As typically happens in life, love is a very difficult commodity to manipulate or manufacture, and in spite of the best efforts of those well meaning *Señoras* of the neighborhood, cupid was not to find his mark with this gringo at an arranged family dinner date. To their disappointment and my great surprise it would happen when least expected...in a cooking class in Tijuana.

A friend told me about a class given on Saturdays and I thought it would be fun to try something new. On the first day of class I was trying to duplicate the flair with which Master Chef Noe Cortez worked his knife on the vegetables laid out in front of us. Selecting an onion as a worthy opponent, I effortlessly diced it up in record time.

I looked at my work with great pride but before I could impress the rest of the class with my conquest I heard a sniffle come from across the counter top where I worked. All of my slicing and dicing had brought tears to a lovely young woman who had been overcome by the volatile sulfur released by the mutilated onion. Offering her my handkerchief, I knew little at the time that my life was to change forever that day. In the months that followed Cristina would become my constant companion and my wife.

Four years later, our family has grown to include two neurotic Siamese cats, and together we have moved into a larger home closer to the beach. Walking together on the sandy beach below, hand-in-hand with Cristina, I watch Dakota play in the surf. I am reminded what a rich, emotional and colorful experience my life on the Baja California peninsula has been. Cristina loves to remind me that I made her cry the first time we met.

Today we are beginning a new chapter as we build a place of our own down on a quiet beach outside San Quintin. As I look back on all my years here in Baja I have built up so many memories. Somehow and without warning I found myself blending into the fabric of the society, culture and lifestyle that this wonderful slice of Mexico has offered me.

I spent the majority of my life as a professional nomad of sorts, traveling and working abroad in many countries on different continents. Each destination had its own unique qualities and attraction but I always felt like an outsider in one way or another.

I probably came to Mexico with the same attitude, but my life and experiences here on the peninsula changed my course forever as I woke up to one day to discover that this stretch of peninsula had adopted this well-traveled gringo.

Here in Baja I have found love. I am learning to cope with the pain of loss. Cristina is now my life and Olivia will forever be in my heart. This is my home and where I hope to spend the rest of my days, God willing.

Open your heart and see if Mexico doesn't invite you, too.

Grocery Price Comparison between
Dallas, TX, and San Miguel de Allende

Here is a comparison of grocery prices at a Kroger's supermarket in Dallas, Texas, in March, 2009, and the same items at Mega supermarket in San Miguel de Allende the same month. All items are converted to equal the same size, i.e. a kilogram is 2.2 pounds, a pound is 453 grams. For example, a Mexican store brand peanut butter in a jar measured in grams and sold in pesos was converted to the same amount as a US peanut butter jar measured in ounces, and the peso price for that comparable amount was converted to dollars at 13:1. Whole chicken sold by the kilogram was converted to by the pound, etc. We weighed the produce so an average cucumber sold by the unit and not weight was about the same size in both stores, kilos converted to ounces, etc.

The Mexican prices include some representative items from among the 90 items imported from the US which were being charged 10-30% import duty mid-2009. These additional import duties were added after the Mexican government retaliated against the end of the pilot program to allow Mexican trucks into the US as NAFTA required to have happened by the year 2000.

We picked commonly used items that would be available in both areas. Even greater savings could come from frequenting outdoor markets and using more local produce and ingredients.

Overall these 28 items cost $65.47 USD at Kroger and $46.58 USD at Mega, a savings of $18.52 USD. Remember, all sizes have been converted to be equal, ounces changed to grams, etc., and pesos were converted to US dollars at 13:1. Where the Mega price was more, the amount in the savings column is marked by a + instead of a -. Sale items were not included. This is a one-day snapshot of prices at two similar chain supermarkets, not a guarantee that you will find the same prices at other stores other days.

GROCERY ITEM	KROGER	MEGA	SAVINGS
Iceberg lettuce, head	$1.59	$0.53	-$0.69
Plum tomatoes	$1.08	$0.80	-$0.28
Round tomatoes	$2.99	$0.63	-$2.36
Cucumber, average	$0.55	$0.65	+$0.10
White onions	$0.99	$0.69	-$0.30
Sweet green peppers	$0.55	$0.46	-$0.09

GROCERY ITEM	KROGER	MEGA	SAVINGS
Fresh green beans	$1.99	$0.61	-$1.38
Standard bananas	$0.54	$0.42	-$0.12
Pineapple, average	$2.99	$0.92	-$2.07
Gala apples	$0.99	$2.04	+$1.05
Cantaloupe, average	$0.99	$0.40	-$0.59
Whole chicken by pound	$1.19	$1.05	-$0.14
Store brand bacon	$5.49	$3.92	-$1.57
Butter	$2.50	$3.33	+$0.83
Pork loin	$2.99	$3.02	+$0.03
Hamburger	$1.98	$2.07	+$0.09
Cheddar cheese by block	$5.79	$3.29	-$2.50
Uncooked rice	$0.70	$0.52	-$0.18
Uncooked black beans	$0.99	$0.84	-$0.15
Uncooked white beans	$0.99	$1.21	+$0.22
Wonderbread/Bimbo	$2.49	$1.70	-$0.79
Orowheat multigrain	$3.99	$2.47	-$1.52
Smuckers strawberry jam	$3.18	$2.10	-$1.08
Peanut butter store brand	$1.52	$2.94	+$1.42
Vegetable cooking oil	$2.97	$2.31	-$0.66
Total cereal	$3.48	$1.98	-$1.45
Corn flakes store brand	$1.79	$1.48	-$0.31
Liquid laundry detergent	$8.23	$4.21	-$4.02
Total price	**$65.47**	**$46.58**	**-$18.52**

Mexican Consulates and Embassies —United States and Canada

Alaska
Anchorage
610 "C" Street Suite A-7,
Anchorage, Alaska 99501
Tel (907) 334-9573
Fax (907) 334-9673
consulmexalaska@hotmail.com

Arkansas
Little Rock
3500 South University Avenue,
Little Rock, AR, 72204
Tel: (501) 372-6933
Fax: (501) 372-6109
consulmexlir@comcast.net

Arizona
Douglas
1201 F Avenue, Douglas, AZ 85607
Tel: (520) 364-3142
Fax: (520) 364-1379

Nogales
571 N. Grand Ave.
Nogales, AZ 85621
Tel: (520) 287-2521
Fax: (520) 287-3175
consulmex2@mchsi.com

Phoenix
1990 W. Camelback, Suite 110,
Phoenix, AZ 85015
Tel: (602) 242-7398
Fax: 242-2957

Tucson
553 S. Stone Ave.,
Tucson, AZ 85701
Tel: (520) 882-5595
Fax: (520) 882-8959
contucmx@sre.gob.mx

Yuma
298 S. Main St., Yuma, AZ 85364
Tel: (928) 343-0066
Fax: (928) 343-0077
contucmx@sre.gob.mx

California
Calexico
408 Herber Ave., Calexico, CA 92231
Tel: (760) 357-4132
Fax: (760) 357-6284
informacion@concalexio.org

Fresno
2409 Merced St., Fresno, CA 93721
Tel: (559) 233-3065
Fax: (559) 233-6156
consulado@consulmexfresno.net

Los Angeles
2401 W. Sixth St.
Los Angeles, CA 90057
Tel: (213) 351-6800
Fax: (213) 351-2114
consulado@lapublico@sre.gob.mx

Oxnard
3151 West Fifth Street,
Oxnard, CA 93030
Tel: (805) 984-8738
Fax: (805) 984-8747
consul@consulmexoxnard.com

Sacramento
1010 8th St., Sacramento, CA 95814
Tel: (916) 441-3287
Fax: (916) 441-3146
sacramento@sre.gob.mx

San Bernardino
293 North "D" Street.
San Bernardino, CA 92401
Tel: (909) 889-9836
Fax: (909) 889-8285
conmexbe@hotmail.com

Yuma
298 S. Main St., Yuma, AZ 85364
Tel: (928) 343-0066
Fax: (928) 343-0077
contucmx@sre.gob.mx

California
Calexico
408 Herber Ave., Calexico, CA 92231
Tel: (760) 357-4132
Fax: (760) 357-6284
informacion@concalexio.org

Fresno
2409 Merced St., Fresno, CA 93721
Tel: (559) 233-3065
Fax: (559) 233-6156
consulado@consulmexfresno.net

Los Angeles
2401 W. Sixth St.
Los Angeles, CA 90057
Tel: (213) 351-6800
Fax: (213) 351-2114
consulado@lapublico@sre.gob.mx

Oxnard
3151 West Fifth Street,
Oxnard, CA 93030
Tel: (805) 984-8738
Fax: (805) 984-8747
consul@consulmexoxnard.com

Sacramento
1010 8th St., Sacramento, CA 95814
Tel: (916) 441-3287
Fax: (916) 441-3146
sacramento@sre.gob.mx

San Bernardino
293 North "D" Street.
San Bernardino, CA 92401
Tel: (909) 889-9836
Fax: (909) 889-8285
conmexbe@hotmail.com

San Diego
1549 India St., San Diego, CA 92101
Tel: (619) 231-8414
Fax: (619) 231-4802
info@consulmexsd.org

San Francisco
532 Folsom St.
San Francisco, CA 94105
Tel: (415) 354-1700
Fax: (415) 495-3971
confrancisco@sre.gob.mx

San Jose
540 North First St.
San Jose, CA 95112
Tel: (408) 294-3414
Fax: (408) 294-4506
consjose@sre.gob.mx

Santa Ana
828 N. Broadway St.
Santa Ana, CA 92701-3424
Tel: (714) 835-3069
Fax: (714) 835-3472
consana@sre.gob.mx

Colorado
Denver
5350 Leetsdale Drive. Suite 100
Denver, CO 80246
Tel: (303) 331-1110
Fax: (303) 331-1872
infodenver@sre.gob.mx

District of Columbia
Washington (Embassy of Mexico)
1911 Pennsylvania Ave., N.W.,
Washington, D.C., 20006
Tel: (202) 736-1000
Fax: (202) 234-4498
consulwas@aol.com

Florida
Miami
5975 S.W. 72nd. Street

Louisiana
New Orleans
901 Convection Center Boulevard,
Suite 119, New Orleans, LA 70130
Tel: (504) 528-3722 *
connorleans@sre.gob.mx

Massachusetts
Boston
20 Park Plaza, Suite 506
Boston, MA 02116
Tel: (617) 426-4181
Fax: (617) 695-1957
cmxboston@sre.gob.mx

Michigan
Detroit
645 Griswold Ave. Suite 1700,
Detroit, MI 48226
Tel: (313) 964-4515
Fax: (313) 964-4522
detroit@sre.gob.mx

Minnesota
Saint Paul
797 East 7th Street
Saint Paul, MN 55106
Tel: (651) 771-5494
Fax. (651) 772-4419
contacto@consulmexstpaul.com

Missouri
Kansas City
1600 Baltimore, Suite 100, Kansas
City, MO 64108
Tel: (816) 556-0800
Fax: (816) 556-0900
conkansas@sre.gob

Nebraska
Omaha
3552 Dodge St.
Omaha, NE 68131
Tel: (402) 595-1841-44
Fax: (402) 595-1845

Louisiana
New Orleans
901 Convection Center Boulevard,
Suite 119, New Orleans, LA 70130
Tel: (504) 528-3722 *
connorleans@sre.gob.mx

Massachusetts
Boston
20 Park Plaza, Suite 506
Boston, MA 02116
Tel: (617) 426-4181
Fax: (617) 695-1957
cmxboston@sre.gob.mx

Michigan
Detroit
645 Griswold Ave. Suite 1700,
Detroit, MI 48226
Tel: (313) 964-4515
Fax: (313) 964-4522
detroit@sre.gob.mx

Minnesota
Saint Paul
797 East 7th Street
Saint Paul, MN 55106
Tel: (651) 771-5494
Fax: (651) 772-4419
contacto@consulmexstpaul.com

Missouri
Kansas City
1600 Baltimore, Suite 100, Kansas
City, MO 64108
Tel: (816) 556-0800
Fax: (816) 556-0900
conkansas@sre.gob

Nebraska
Omaha
3552 Dodge St.
Omaha, NE 68131
Tel: (402) 595-1841-44
Fax: (402) 595-1845

Nevada
Las Vegas
330 S. 4th St.
Las Vegas, Nevada 89101
Tel: (702) 383-0623
Fax: (702) 383-0683
conlvegas@sre.gob.mx

New Mexico
Albuquerque
1610 4th Street NW
Albuquerque, NM 87102
Tel: (505) 247-4177
Fax: (505) 842-9490
consulmexalb@qwestoffice.net

New York
New York
27 East 39th St.
New York, NY 10016
Tel: (212) 217-6400
Fax: (212) 217-6493
titularny@sre.gob.mx

North Carolina
Charlotte
P.O. Box 19627
Charlotte, NC 28219
Tel: (704) 394-2190

Raleigh
336 E. Six Forks Rd
Raleigh, NC 27609
Tel: (919) 754-0046
Fax: (919) 754-1729
conraleigh@sre.gob.mx

Oregon
Portland
1234 S.W. Morrison
Portland, OR 97205
Tel: (503) 274-1450
Fax: (503) 274-1540
portland@sre.gob.mx

Pennsylvania
Philadelphia
111 S. Independence
Mall E, Suite 310, Bourse Building,
Philadelphia, PA 19106
Tel: (215) 922-4262/3834
Fax: (215) 923-7281
buzon@consulmexphila

Texas
Austin
200 E. Sixth St., Suite 200
Austin, TX 78701
Tel: (512) 478-2866
Fax: (512) 478-8008
austin@sre.gob.mx

Brownsville
724 E. Elizabeth St.
Brownsville, TX 78520
Tel: (956) 542-4431
Fax: (956) 542-7267
conbrownsville@sre.gob.mx

Corpus Christi
800 N. Shoreline Blvd.
Suite 410, North Tower
Corpus Christi, TX 78401
Tel: (512) 882-3375
Fax: (512) 882-9324

Dallas
8855 N Stemmons Freeway
Dallas, TX 75247
Tel: (214) 252-9250 ext. 123
Fax: (214) 630-3511
info@consulmexdallas.com

Del Rio
2398 Spur 239
Del Rio, TX., 78840
Tel: (830) 775-2352
Fax: (830) 774-6497
consulmexdel.titular@wcsonline.net

Eagle Pass
2252 E. Garrison Street
Eagle Pass, TX 78852
Tel: (830) 773-9255
Fax: (830) 773-9397
consulmxeag@sbcglobal.net

El Paso
910 E. San Antonio St.
El Paso, TX 79901
Tel: (915) 533-3644
Fax: (915) 532-7163
consulmexepa@elp.rr.com

Houston
4507 San Jacinto St.
Houston, TX 77004
Tel: (713) 271-6800 ext 1400
Fax: (713) 271-3201
conhouston@wt.net

Laredo
1612 Farragut St., Laredo, TX 78040
Tel: (956) 723-6369
Fax: (956) 723-1741
consul@srelaredo.org

McAllen
600 S. Broadway Ave.
McAllen, TX 78501
Tel: (956) 686-0243
Fax: (956) 686-4901
consumexmc@aol.com

Presidio
Juarez Ave.Y 21 de Marzo St.
Presidio, TX 79845
Tel: (423) 229-2788
Fax: (423) 229-2792
conpresidio@bigbend.net

San Antonio
127 Navarro St.
San Antonio, TX 78205
Tel: (210) 271-9728
Fax: (210) 227-7518

Utah
Salt Lake City
155 South 300 West, 3rd floor
Salt Lake City, UT 84101
Tel: (801) 521-8503
Fax: (801) 521-0534
consuladoslc@consulmexslc.org

Washington, D.C.
District of Columbia
2827 16th. Street N.W.
Washington D.C., 20009-4260
Tel: (202) 736-1000
Fax: (202) 2344498
consultas@aol.com

Washington
Seattle
2132 Third Ave.
Seattle, WA 98121
Tel: (206) 448-3526
Fax: (206) 448-4771
conseattle@sre.gob.mx

Mexican Consulates in Canada

Alberta
Calgary
Suite 1100, 833 4th Avenue SW
Calgary, Alberta, Canada T2P 3T5
Tel: (403) 264-4819
Fax: (403) 264-1527
concalgary.@sre.gob.mx

British Columbia
Vancouver
Suite 411
1177 West Hastings St. Piso 4,
Vancouver, B.C. V6E 2K3
Tel: (604) 684-1859
Fax: (604) 684-2485
mexico@consulmexvan.com

Ontario
Ottawa (Embassy of Mexico)
45 O'Connor Suite 1500

Ottawa, Ont. K1P 1A4
Tel: (613) 233 8988
Fax: (613) 235 9123
info@embamexcan.com

Toronto
199 Bay St., Suite 4440
Commerce Court West
Toronto, Ont. M5L 1E9
Tel: (416) 368-1847
Fax: (416) 368-8141
cgmtoronto@consulmex.com

Québec
Montreal
2055 rue Peel, Suite 1000 Montreal,
Québec, H3A 1V4 Canadá
Tel: (514) 288 2502 y (514) 288 2707 *
Fax: (514) 288 8287
E-mail: comexmt@consulmex.qc.ca

United States Embassy Consulates and Consular Agents in Mexico

United States Embassy in Mexico
Embassy of the United States
Paseo de la Reforma 305
Colonia Cuauhtemoc
Mexico, D.F. 06500
Phone: (55) 5080-2000
Fax: (55) 5525-5040
ccs@usembassy.net.mx

US Consulates in Mexico

United States Consulate General
in Ciudad Juaréz
Av. Lopez Mateos 924 Nte.
Ciudad Juaréz, Mexico
Phone: (656) 611-3000

United States Consulate General
in Guadalajara
Progreso 175, Colonia Juarez
Guadalajara, Jalisco

Phone: 3268-2100
Fax: 3826-6549

United States Consulate General
in Monterrey
Constitucion Poniente 411
Monterrey,
Nuevo León. México 64000
Phone: (81) 8345-2120

United States Consulate General
in Tijuana
Ave. Tapachula # 96
Colonia Hipodromo, 22420
Tijuana, Mexico

US Consular Agencies in Mexico (Affiliated embassy or consulate in parentheses)

Acapulco (Emb. Mex. City)
Hotel Continental Emporio
Costera M. Aleman 121-Local 14
Acapulco, Gro., 39670
Telephone: (01-744) 469-0556
Fax: (01-744) 484-0300
consular@prodigy.net.mx

Cabo San Lucas (Tij)
Blvd. Marina Local C-4
Plaza Nautica
Col. Centro
Cabo San Lucas, B.C.S. 23410
Telephone: (01-624) 143-3566,
Fax: (01-624) 143-6750
consulcabo@yahoo.com

Cancún
Plaza Caracol Dos
Segundo Nivel No. 320-323
Blvd. Kukulkan
Zona Hotelera
Cancún, Q.R. 77500
Telephone: (01-998) 883-0272,
Fax: (01-998) 883-1373

Duty Cell: (01-998) 845-4364
uscons@prodigy.net.mx

Ciudad Acuña/Del Rio
(Nuevo Laredo)
Morelos y Ocampo # 305
Col. Centro
Ciudad Acuña, Coahuila, CP 26200
Telephone: (01-877) 772-8661
Fax: (01-877) 772-8179

Cozumel
U.S.Consular Agency
(Office hrs. Mo-Fri 12:00-14:00)
Plaza Villa Mar en El Centro
Plaza Principal
Parque Juarez entre Melgary 5a. Ave.,
2° Piso, Locales 8 y 9.
Cozumel, QR. 77600
Telephone: (01-987) 872-4574
Fax: (01-987) 872-2339
usgov@cozumel.net

Ixtapa
Local 9 Plaza Ambiente
Ixtapa, Zihuatanejo
Telephone: (01-755) 553-2100
Fax: (01-755) 554-6276
Mailing Address. Pasco de los Hujes
236, Col. el Hujal
Zihuatanejo, Gro.40880
consularixtapa@prodigy.net.mx

Mazatlán
Hotel Playa Mazatlán
Playa Gaviotas No. 202
Zona Dorada 82110
Mazatlán, Sinaloa
Phone & Fax: (01-669) 916-5889
mazagent@mzt.megared.net.mx

Oaxaca
Macedonio Alcala No. 407
Interior 20
68000 Oaxaca, Oax.

Telephone: (01-951) 514-3054
Fax: (01-951) 516-2701
conagent@prodigy.net.mx

Piedras Negras (Nuevo Laredo)
Prol. General Cepeda No. 1900
Fraccionamiento Privada Blanca
Piedras Negras, Coahuila, C.P. 26700
Telephone: (01-878)795-1986, 795-
1987, 795-1988
Fax: (01-878)795-1989
Official Cell: (01-878) 788-0343
usconsularagencypn@hotmail.com

Puerto Vallarta
Zaragoza #160, Col. Centro
Edificio Vallarta Plaza, Int. 18
Puerto Vallarta, Jalisco 48300
Telephone: (01-322) 222-0069)
Fax: (01-322) 223-0074
consulagentpvr@prodigy.net.mx

Reynosa (Matamoros)
Calle Monterrey #390 esq. Sinaloa
Col. Rodriguez, Reynosa
Tamps. 88630
Telephone: (01-899)923-9331
Fax: (01-899)923-9245
usconsularagent@hotmail.com

San Luis Potosí
Edificio Las Terrazas
Av. Venustiano Carranza 2076-41
Col. Polanco
San Luis Potosí, S.L.P. 78220
Telephone: (01-444)811-7802
Fax: (01 444) 811-7803
usconsulslp@yahoo.com

San Miguel de Allende
(Emb. Mex. City)
Dr. Hernandez Macias 72
S. M.de Allende, Gto. 37700
Telephone: (01-415) 152-2357

Fax: (01-415) 152-1588
Cell: (01-415) 113-9574
consuladosma@unisono.net.mx
Mailing Address: Apdo. Postal 328
San Miguel de Allende, GTO.

Canada's Embassy and Consulates in Mexico

Embassy of Canada in Mexico City
Embassy of Canada
Consular section
Schiller 529, Col. Bosque de
Chapultepec (Polanco)
Del. Miguel Hidalgo
11580 Mexico City, D.F., Mexico
Telephone: (55) 5724-7900
Fax: (55) 5724-7943
Fax (Passport Section):
(55) 5387-9305
mxico@international.gc.ca

Consulate General of Canada in
Monterrey
Jurisdiction: State of Nuevo León
Edificio Kalos
Piso C-1, Local 108-A
Zaragoza 1300 Sur y Constitución
64000 Monterrey, Nuevo León,
Mexico
Telephone: (81) 8344-2753
Fax: (81) 8344-3048
mntry@international.gc.ca

Consulate of Canada in Guadalajara
Jurisdiction: State of Jalisco (except
the coast)
World Trade Center
Av. Mariano Otero 1249
Piso 8, Torre Pacífico
Col. Rinconada del Bosque
44530 Guadalajara, Jalisco, Mexico
Telephone: (33) 3671-4740
Fax: (33) 3671-4750
gjara@international.gc.ca

Consulate of Canada in Acapulco
Jurisdiction: States of Guerrero and
Michoacán
Centro Comercial Marbella, Local 23
Prolongación Farallón s/n, esq.
Miguel Alemán
39670 Acapulco, Guerrero, Mexico
Telephone: (744) 484-1305/
Fax: (744) 484-1306
acapulco@Canada.org.mx

Consulate of Canada in Cancún
Jurisdiction: States of Campeche,
Quintana Roo and Yucatán
Plaza Caracol II, 3rd. Floor, Local 330
Blvd. Kukulkán km. 8.5
Zona Hotelera, 77500 Cancún,
Quintana Roo, Mexico
Telephone: (998) 883-3360
Fax: (998) 883-3232
cancun@Canada.org.mx

Consulate of Canada in Mazatlán
Jurisdiction: State of Sinaloa
Avenida Playa Gaviotas 202, Local 9
Zona Dorada
82110 Mazatlán, Sinaloa, Mexico
Telephone: (669) 913-7320
Fax: (669) 914-6655
mazatlan@Canada.org.mx

Consulate of Canada in Oaxaca
Jurisdiction: States of Chiapas
and Oaxaca
Pino Suárez 700, Local 11B
Multiplaza Brena, Col. Centro
68000 Oaxaca, Oaxaca, Mexico
Telephone: (951) 513-3777
Fax: (951) 515-2147
oaxaca@Canada.org.mx

Consulate of Canada in Puerto
Vallarta
Jurisdiction: Coast of Jalisco and

States of Colima and Nayarit
Edificio Obelisco, Local 108
Avenida Francisco Medina
Ascencio 1951
Zona Hotelera Las Glorias
48300 Puerto Vallarta, Jalisco, Mexico
Telephone: (322) 293-0098
Fax: (322) 293-2894
vallarta@Canada.org.mx

Consulate of Canada in
San José del Cabo
Jurisdiction: State of Baja
California Sur
Plaza José Green, Local 9
Blvd. Mijares s/n, Col. Centro
23400 San José del Cabo

Baja California Sur, Mexico
Telephone: (624) 142-4333
Fax: (624) 142-4262
loscabos@Canada.org.mx

Consulate of Canada in Tijuana
Jurisdiction: States of Baja California
Norte and Sonora
Germán Gedovius 10411-101
Condominio del Parque, Zona Río
22320 Tijuana
Baja California Norte, Mexico
Telephone: (664) 684-0461
Fax: (664) 684-0301
tijuana@Canada.org.mx

Mexico's World Heritage Sites

Here are the areas in Mexico, in order approved, which have received UNESCO **World Heritage Site** designations. They are protected from development that does not retain the site's historical, cultural, and/or ecological importance.

- Historic Center of Mexico City and Xochimilco
- Historic Center of Oaxaca and Archaeological Site of Monte Albán
- Historic Center of Puebla
- Pre-Hispanic City and National Park of Palenque
- Pre-Hispanic City of Teotihuacan
- Sian Ka'an
- Historic Town of Guanajuato and Adjacent Mines
- Pre-Hispanic City of Chichén-Itzá
- Historic Centrer of Morelia
- El Tajin, Pre-Hispanic City
- Historic Center of Zacatecas
- Rock Paintings of the Sierra de San Francisco
- Whale Sanctuary of El Vizcaino
- Earliest 16th-Century Monasteries on the Slopes of Popocatepetl
- Historic Monuments Zone of Querétaro
- Pre-Hispanic Town of Uxmal
- Hospicio Cabañas, Guadalajara
- Archeological Zone of Paquimé, Casas Grandes
- Historic Monuments Zone of Tlacotalpan
- Archaeological Monuments Zone of Xochicalco
- Historic Fortified Town of Campeche
- Ancient Maya City of Calakmul, Campeche
- Franciscan Missions in the Sierra Gorda of Querétaro
- Luis Barragán House and Studio
- Islands and Protected Areas of the Gulf of California
- Agave Landscape and Ancient Industrial Facilities of Tequila
- Central University City Campus of the Universidad Nacional Autónoma de México (UNAM)
- Monarch Butterfly Biosphere Reserve
- Protective town of San Miguel and the Sanctuary of Jesús Nazareno de Atotonilco

Pueblos Mágicos

Here are the cities within Mexico that the Tourism Department has declared
Pueblos Mágicos, or Magical Cities, receiving additional attention and funds:

- Mexcaltitán, Nayarit
- Huasca de Ocampo, Hidalgo
- Real de Catorce, San Luis Pótosí
- Tepoztlán, Morelos
- Taxco, Guerrero
- Tepotzotlán, Estado de Mexico
- Tapalpa, Jalisco
- Comala, Colima
- Pátzcuaro, Michoacán
- Dolores Hidalgo, Guanajuato
- San Miguel de Allende, Guanajuato
- Cuetzalan, Puebla
- Izamal, Yucatán
- Tequila, Jalisco
- San Cristóbal de las Casas, Chiapas
- Real del Monte, Hidalgo
- Parras de la Fuente, Coahuila
- Valle de Bravo, Estado de Mexico
- Mazamitla, Jalisco
- Álamos, Sonora
- Tlalpujahua, Michoacán
- Cosalá, Sinaloa
- Bernal, Querétaro
- Coatepec, Veracruz
- Papantla, Veracruz
- Real de Asientos, Aguascalientes
- Cuitzeo, Michoacán
- Santiago, Nuevo León
- Todos Santos, Baja California Sur
- Bacalar, Quintana Roo
- Jerez de García Salinas, Zacatecas
- Huamantla, Tlaxcala
- Mier, Tamaulipas

Hoy No Circula, Mexico City's Vehicle Pollution Control Policy

Mexico City and State have reciprocal vehicle emissions testing arrangements with the states of Hidalgo, Puebla, Querétaro, Morelos and Michoacán. Here are the days of the week you cannot drive a vehicle within Mexico City depending on the last digit of the vehicle's license plate:

Monday, plates ending in 5 or 6, yellow hologram
Tuesday, 7 or 8, pink
Wednesday, 3 or 4, red
Thursday, 1 or 2, green
Friday, 9 or 0 and those with letters only or temporary plates, blue

Here are the Saturdays of the month on which certain vehicles cannot drive and the restrictions:

First Saturday of the month, plates ending in 5 or 6, yellow
Second Saturday of the month, 7 or 8, pink
Third Saturday of the month, 3 or 4, red
Fourth Saturday of the month, 1 or 2, green
Fifth Saturday of the month (if it exists), 9 or 0
and those with letters only or temporary plates, blue

In addition, foreign-plated vehicles cannot drive in Mexico City between 5 and 11 am Monday-Friday. So if your car has Arizona plates ending with 6 and you do not have an 00 exemption, you cannot drive In Mexico City between 5 and 11 am Monday through Friday (because your car is foreign plated), or on any Monday, or on the first Saturday of the month.

If your car is less than eight years old, it may be eligible for a 00 rating. When you go for emissions testing you will be told if your car qualifies for 00 by age, mileage and amount of emissions, and you may be exempt. Also exempt are emergency vehicles, solar and electric powered vehicles, government and school buses, vehicles used by those who are disabled (even if their handicap plates are not from Mexico City or the state of Mexico), and diplomatic vehicles.

In environmental emergencies, the laws may be made stricter. On some holidays, the rules will be lifted.

Here's another exemption, the *Pase Turistico*, for those whose cars are not older than eight years and who are going to be driving in Mexico City for less than two weeks, from early December to early January. The pass is available at special tourist councils throughout Mexico, the list at *www.sma.df.gob.mx/pasetur/listado_canacos.php*. However, it does not apply to the rest of Mexico State and so you'd still need to follow the *Hoy No Circula* rules getting into the city. Antique cars can also get an exemption—for about $1,000 USD a year. For more information, see *www.sma.df.gob.mx/pasetur/*.

Mexico City's Four Hub Bus Stations

Terminal de Autobuses del Norte, Av. 100 Metros 4907, Colonia Magdalena de las Salinas, 5587 1552. Metro (subway) station stop "Autobuses del Norte" (Line 5, yellow). This is the largest bus station in Mexico and can handle 100 simultaneous bus arrivals, 24/7. This terminal serves most of the buses to and from the US border cities, and such destinations as Acapulco, Guadalajara, Guanajuato, San Miguel de Allende, Puerto Vallerta, Monterrey, Leon, Querétaro, Aguascalientes, San Luis Potosí, and Hermosillo.

Terminal de Autobuses del Poniente, also called *Observatorio*, Av. Sur 122, Colonia Real del Monte. Metro station *"Observatorio"* (Line 1, pink). Serves destinations to the west including Colima, Manzanillo, and Toluca.

Terminal de Autobuses del Sur, also called Taxqueña, Av. Taxqueña 1320, Colonia Campestre Churubusco, Metro station "Taxqueña"(Line 2, blue). This terminal serves southern destinations such as such as Acapulco, Ixtapa, Oaxaca, Tepoztlan, and Puebla.

Terminal de Autobuses del Oriente, also called "TAPO", Calzada Ignacio Zaragoza 200, Colonia 10 de Mayo. Metro Station "San Lazaro" (Line 1, pink). It serves the south and Gulf of Mexico including Campeche, Cancún, Mérida, Villahermosa, Veracruz, and Jalapa.

Rolly's Sample *Menaje de Casa*

Household Items		*Menaje de Casa*	
Box #	Item	*Caja #*	*Articulo*
1 - 11	books	1 - 11	*libros*
12	books, papers	12	*libros y papeles*
13	plates, bowls	13	*platos, tazones*
14	cups, bowls	14	*tazas, tazones*
15	glasses	15	*vasos*
16	pots, frying pans, knives, forks, spoons, waste baskets, towels	16	*ollas, sartenes, tenedores, cucharas, cesto para papeles, toallas*
17	pots, frying pans, knives, forks, spoons, spatula, tongs, strainer	17	*ollas, sartenes, cuchillos, tenedores, cucharas, spatula, tenazas, coladera*
18 - 20	serving bowls, yard lamp globes	18 - 20	*platos hondos, gloabo para la lamparae de Jardin*
21	photographs and legal papers	21	*fotografias y legajos*
22	photographs and books	22	*fotografias y libros*
23 - 24	knick-knacks	23 - 24	*adornos, decoraciones*
25	cassettes, CDs, books	25	*cassetes, CDs, libros*
26	hanging lamp, small lamps, clocks	26	*lampara de techo, lampara pequeño, reloj*
27	hanging lamp, small loud speakers	27	*lampara de techo, altavez pequeño*
28 - 31	couchpillows, bed pillows, sheets, covers, pictures, glass shelves	28 -31	*ojins de sofa, almohadas de cama, sabanas, colchas, pintura, anaquel de vidrio*
32	clothes, shoes	32	*ropas, zapatos*
	rug		*alfombra*
	beds (3) and mattress (4)		*camas (3) y colchones (4)*
	chests of drawers (2)		*comodas (2)*
	sofas (2)		*sofas (2)*
	dining table and 2 benches		*mesa de comer y 2 bancos*
	chairs (6)		*illas (6)*
	rocking chairs (2)		*sillas mecedoras (2)*
	folding tables (5)		*mesas que doblas (5)*
	folding chairs (16)		*sillas de doblars (16)*
	book shelves (4)		*estante para libros (4)*
	dish cabinet (in two parts)		*aparador (en 2 partes)*
	kitchen cabinets (in 7 parts)		*cabinete de la cocina (en 7 partes)*
	cabinet with kitchen sink		*cabinete con fregadero*
	video tape cabinet with tapes		*cabinete para cassets con video cassetes*
	bathroom vanity cabinet & wash basin		*cabinete con lavabo para el bano*

fireplace (in 5 parts)	chimenea (in 5 partes)
computer table (in 5 parts)	mesa de computadora (en 5 partes)
large loudspeakers (2)	altavez (2)
small table	mesa pequeño
TV cabinet	mesa de televisor
mini blinds (7)	percianas (7)
painting	pintura
mosaic	mosaico

Electrical Items

Box #	Item	Make	Model	Serial #
33	crock pot	Rival	RD-4053	30313
33	can opener	Sunbeam	05321	none
33	mixer	Hamilton-Beach	54100	A2849
33	mixer	Sears	400.82810	none
33	mixer	Braun	4169	none
33	electric skillet	Presto	06821-3599	none
33	heater	Arvin	1320	none
33	heater	Patton	HF-50	94H50-021782
33	amplifier	Realistic	32-1200B	208239
34	microwave	Sharp	Carousel	183468
35	ceiling fan	Hunter	none	none
36	ceiling fan	Hunter	none	none
37	vacuum cleaner	Black&Decker	9330A	none
37	vacuum, hand	Eureka	3110	892356294
38	VCR	JVC	HR-S4600U	154E1618
38	television	Gold Star	CMT-4842N	60087044
39	VCR	Go-Video	GV-4600	542460090189
40	cassette recorder	Sanyo	RDW33	05129702
40	CD player	Sony	CDP-CX200	8866456
41	receiver	JVC	RX-815VTN	139C1730
42	television	Sharp	19C-MI00R	none
43	air filter	Kenmore	Hepa220	none
44	radio/CD	Sony	CFD-539	none
	television	NEC	CT-2700S	67409861
	washing machine	Frigidaire	Horizon 2000	XC34424881
	refrigerator	Amana	TRD18KW	811146523
	heater	HeatRite	none	none
	floor fan	Duracraft	none	none
	floor lamp	none	none	none
	air conditioner	Amana	Cool Zone	none
37	drill	Makita	6012HD 9307	none
37	battery charger	Makita	DC9700A	0793

37	battery charger	Schauer	CR612	none
37	drill	Skil	6340	none
37	circular saw	Skil	5150	none
37	jig saw	Black & Decker	7543	none
37	grinder	Chicago Electric	SKU1711	97057577
37	multi tool	Dremel	395	G4K01-01
39	scanner	Microtek	MRS-1220E6	S648106324
9	scanner	Microtek	PTS-195035T	S698301411
39	speakers	Altec	ASC400	600013963
39	computer	Altec	ASC250	MCW0010687
48	computer	Clone	Pentium III/500	693-686A
48	digitizer	Kurta	IS/One	90110650
49	printer	Alps	MD-1300	B48D0003M
49	printer	Alps	MD-5000	B19A0231H
50	computer screen	MAG	720V	MA58H10192

Articulos Electricos

Caja #	Articulo	Marca	Modelo	No. de Serial
33	olla de hervir	Rival	3526	0524
33	olla de hacer arroz	Hitachi	RD-4053	30313
33	abrelatas	Sunbeam	05321	nada
33	mexclador	Hamilton-Beach	54100	A2849
33	mexclador	Sears	400.82810	nada
33	mexclador	Braun	4169	nada
33	asador electrico	Presto	06821-3599	nada
33	calenton	Arvin	320	nada
33	calenton	Patton	HF-50	94H50-021782
33	amplificador	Realistic	32-1200B	208239
34	microonda	Sharp	Carousel	183468
35	ventilador de techo	Hunter	nada	nada
36	ventilador de techo	Hunter	nada	nada
37	aspirador de polvo	Black&Decker	9330A	nada
37	aspirador de polvo	Eureka	3110	892356294
38	video casetera	JVC	HR-S4600U	154E1618
38	televisor	Gold Star	CMT-4842N	60087044
39	video casetera	Go-Video	GV-4600	542460090189
40	grabadora	Sayno	RDW33	05129702
40	disco compacto	Sony	CDP-CX200	8866456
41	receptor	JVC	RX-815	VTN139C1730
42	televisor	Sharp19C	MI00R	nada
43	aire purificador	Kenmore	Hepa220	nada
44	radio/DC	Sony	CFD-539	nada
	televisor	NEC	CT-2700S	67409861

	lavadora	Frigidair	Horizon 2000	XC34424881
	refrigerador	Amana	TRD 18KW	8811146523
	calenton	HeatRite	*nada*	*nada*
	ventilador de piso	Duracraft	*nada*	*nada*
	lampara de piso	*nada*	*nada*	*nada*
	aire acondicionado	Amana	Cool Zone	*nada*
37	*taladro*	Makita	6012HD	9307
37	*cargador de bateria*	Makita	DC9700A	0793
37	*cargador de bateria*	Schauer	CR612	*nada*
37	*taladro*	Skil	6340	*nada*
37	*sierra circular*	Skil	5150	*nada*
37	*sierra pequeño*	Black & Decker	7543	*nada*
37	*pulidor*	Chicago Electric	SKU1711	97057577
37	*pulidor pequeño*	Dremel	395	G4K01-01
39	*escaner*	Microtek	MRS-1220E6	S648106324
39	*escaner*	Microtek	PTS-195035T	S698301411
39	*bocinas*	Altec	ASC400	600013963
39	*bocinas*	Altec	ASC250	MCW001068
48	*computadora*	Clone	Pentium III/500	693-686A
48	*digitizer*	Kurta	IS/One	90110650
49	*tipografo*	Alps	MD-1300	B48D0003M
49	*tipografo*	Alps	MD-5000	B19A0231H
50	*pantella*	MAG	720V	MA58H10192

Patio Items	Articulos de Patio
Box#	Item	Caja #	*Articulo*
44	wind chimes	44	*espanta espiritus*
45	water hose	45	*manguera*
	shovel (2)		*pala* (2)
	pick		*pico*
	pitchfork		*horca*
	ax		*hacha*
	sledge hammer		*marro*
	coffee table		*mesa de centro*
	chair (2)		*silla* (2)

About the Authors

Former newspaper and magazine writer and editor, **Carol Schmidt** was public relations director for the medical research programs at Harbor-UCLA Medical Center in LA. She published three mystery novels now out of print: Silverlake Heat, Sweet Cherry Wine, and Cabin Fever. Her writing is in seven anthologies, including the *Library of America's Reporting Civil Rights* (*www.reportingcivilrights.org*), where she appears alongside Langston Hughes, James Baldwin, Alice Walker, Tom Wolfe and other writers on civil rights issues. Her freelance articles have appeared in hundreds of publications, including the *Los Angeles Times, Long Beach Independent-Press Telegram*, and *National Catholic Reporter*. Born and raised in Detroit, she moved to LA in 1970. She met Norma in 1979 when both were on the state board of directors of California NOW. Carol and Norma RVed full-time for more than three years and then lived in retirement RV parks in Arizona and Washington. Carol and Norma moved to San Miguel de Allende, Guanajuato, Mexico, in May, 2002, and Carol began to write columns and moderate the San Miguel de Allende forum on *www.mexconnect.com*. These columns and other writings were included in *Falling…in Love with San Miguel: Retiring to Mexico on Social Security*, published by Salsa Verde Press in 2006. Future books will include *San Miguel de Allende on a Budget, Falling in Love with Mexico by Bus*, and *Ten Years in Love with San Miguel*. Carol's blog, 1,300 photos, and the forums on *www.fallinginlovewithsanmiguel.com*, which has had nearly a quarter million reader views, are valuable resources for those considering a move to Mexico.

Former corporate accountant and tax preparer **Norma Hair** was director of accounting for a major mortgage company. Born and raised in Pontiac, MI, she reared three children before going to college at 39, and has four grandchildren and four great-grandchildren. As treasurer of Sunset Junction Street Fair, a Silverlake community effort that soon grew to a quarter million attendees in LA each August, Norma also did volunteer accounting and tax work for several community service organizations. She was honored by such LA groups as El Centro del Pueblo, a social services organization that works with local street gangs, for her community contributions. When she and Carol owned a hobby ceramics store in rural Michigan, Norma ran two statewide trade shows of the Michigan Ceramic Dealers Association.

Rollins "Rolly" Brook began a career in broadcasting at the tender age of 16 as a Country-Western disk jockey on his home town radio station in Lampasas, TX. After he graduated from the University of Denver, he continued his career as a broadcast engineer with a two-year hiatus to serve as a Mormon missionary in the New England states. Later he joined the international firm of Bolt Beranek and Newman as a consulting engineer for sound and broadcast systems. In that time he published numerous technical papers and co-authored a book on sound engineering. He was honored by inclusion in *Who's Who in Entertainment*.

After leaving BBN, he established his own consulting engineering company in Los Angeles. During his 20+ years in Los Angeles, he made many friends in the Latino community and began making frequent visits to Mexico. He reported that after visiting all 50 states in the USA and many countries around the world, he found himself most at home in Mexico. So it was only natural that he would choose to retire in the land he loved. When he moved to Lerdo, Durango, in 2000, he began a website to document his new life, *www.rollybrook.com*, and to moderate a forum on *www.mexconnect.com*, Home, Garden & Construction in Mexico. The purpose of his website was to show the daily life in his town, not to be "My Mexican Vacation." The website proved to be enormously popular and is part of the basis of this book.